Gustave Droz

Babolain

A Novel

Gustave Droz

Babolain
A Novel

ISBN/EAN: 9783337029289

Printed in Europe, USA, Canada, Australia, Japan

Cover: Foto ©Thomas Meinert / pixelio.de

More available books at **www.hansebooks.com**

BABOLAIN

A NOVEL

TRANSLATED FROM THE FRENCH

OF

GUSTAVE DROZ

BY

MS.

NEW YORK

HOLT & WILLIAMS

1873

BABOLAIN.

I.

To live one's own life, however humble it may be, is a triumph. To have an instrument of one's own and play upon it with ease! And to think that so many people have merely had the trouble of breathing into this instrument to draw forth the most charming airs, while I have not even been able to find the mouth-piece.

Yet it is not because I am completely devoid of intelligence. I always had enough to grieve that I possessed no more, which is something. Moreover, being gifted to a certain extent with a critical judgment and a spirit of analysis, I have formed opinions regarding others and myself which were sometimes perfectly just, but unfortunately never came in time to shed light upon my path and save me from errors. I will venture to say that I never long ignored or lost sight of myself. Through fear of ridicule—this dread was a perpetual torment to me—I was always uneasy, eager to examine my character, to sound the depths of my nature; and almost the sole result of these observations was to reveal the presence of the most prodigious pride. It is incredible that a passion should have been able to penetrate so deeply into the very groundwork of a poor man's existence.

Besides this, there was nothing, and yet many

things. In my unlucky brain everything was disjointed, confused, and ready to fall. I have often examined my skull: it is irregular, ill-shaped, humpbacked—and I suppose there are hollows inside.

To sum up the whole, I was a pitiable and—I was going to say, a useless creature! The blade of grass that vegetates between two paving-stones has its reason for existence, its little mission. By the mere fact that I have lived, is it not clear, my God, that Thou hadst reserved for me a place which I have doubtless been unable to find, entrusted to me a part I have failed to understand? I do not complain. I have had my joys, my share of sunlight, but how many showers!

My mother died the day after I was born, and six years later, at the time of the great inundation of the Loire, my father, who was a professor in the college of Orleans, and from motives of economy occupied a little house in the suburbs, was drowned.

As we grow old we involuntarily turn towards the road already traversed ; one might say that the Past pulls us by the sleeve. I can see again, as if through a veil, my poor father, sickly and pale like myself, adjusting his spectacles, or smoothing his hair with his thin hand before confining it under his cap, which he slipped on with the greatest care ; or else bending his head with a faint, sad smile to the noisy authority of his younger brother, my uncle Babolain, who lived in the environs of Beaugency. Never were two persons, united by ties so close, more unlike each other. My uncle was as voluminous in mind and body as the space morally and physically occupied by the author of my days was small. Endowed with wonderful vigor, which his labors as the owner of a vineyard developed still more, self-confident, trusting in his own importance, rich, healthy, ruddy, spitting into his huge plaid handkerchief which he held spread out before him in his large hairy hands, crushing walnuts and hazelnuts by the mere pressure of his fingers, raising barrels, and stiffening the muscles of his arms, which in his good-natured moments he liked to have people' feel—he was a man on whom one could depend.

When he spoke or laughed, the hurricane that escaped from his huge chest made the windows shake and the ceiling tremble. Oh! my poor dear father, how little you resembled this hero, whose renown is not yet extinct for ten leagues around Beaugency! My uncle always seemed to me a wonderful and formidable person, who had a slight touch of the ogre in him.

After all, in spite of his roughness, uncle Babolain did all that he could for me. On leaving the cemetery where my father had just been interred, my uncle put over his dark green coat a large smock frock, embroidered upon the collar, and covered with a quantity of little buttons, arranged his handkerchief over the crape floating from his hat, for it was raining a little, and seizing me by the belt with one arm, deposited me in his cart, in the middle of the remnants of my father's effects which they had succeeded in saving. "To the left, on the bench, boy," he said, in his gruff voice. My emotion made me awkward, and my tears blinded me. He hastily got in himself, spite of the creaking of the vehicle, which seemed about to break, seized the reins, gave a peculiar whistle, and the nag started at a rapid trot, to stop a few minutes after at a harness-maker's shop. In spite of my grief I was very glad of it, for uncle Babolain had sat down upon my hand, and I felt a very sharp pain at every jolt. We stopped several times more before the shops, and at each place the cart was filled with all sorts of things, my uncle having taken advantage of the funeral, which brought him to Orleans, to make numerous purchases.

When his business was at last completed, he wrapped his huge limbs in an immense blanket, cracked his whip gayly, and we entered the lonely suburbs. The rain fell with redoubled violence ; the houses soon became more scattered, and we were in the open country, which was still covered with the large yellow pools left by the inundation. It seemed as if everything was crumbling around me ; the disasters that surrounded me mingled with my own misfortune, and through my sobs I bade farewell to the little houses, the bushes, the trees, that glided by—I would fain have clung to them.

But I dared not stir on account of my neighbor, of whom I was terribly afraid, and who glanced at me from time to time as we look at an ill-packed bundle we fear we may lose on the way. I pulled my cap, from which the rain was dripping, farther over my eyes, clasped my hands, and prayed to God with all my heart.

I was drenched to the skin and shivering from head to foot when, towards evening, we reached Closerie. The horse was led into the barn, the cart was unloaded, and my uncle ordered supper. My appearance was doubtless very pitiable, for when he saw me in the corner where I had taken refuge, his face assumed an expression of genuine compassion, and he sent me to bed at once.

I did not leave it for six weeks to a day, and then was scarcely recovered from an inflammation of the chest, which almost carried me off. I was, as may be supposed, paler and more feeble than ever, which increased my difficulties, for my uncle had an instinctive aversion to invalids. I knew that he had never been able to conceal from my father the contempt inspired by his delicate constitution, and I could not expect greater indulgence for myself. Yet I made great exertions, I will not say to get into his good graces, for I carefully avoided him, but not to shock the robust chubby beings by whom I was surrounded ; I tried to eat like the farm children, play their games bear their burdens—and I had attacks of indigestion, nearly broke my leg, and my natural awkwardness deprived me of all respect.

Then instead of making amends for my defects by qualities which I might perhaps have attained, I became jealous of all whose only crime was that of possessing a physical organization superior to my own, and my unhappy pride coming to my aid, I soon considered their advantages as so many inferiorities which increased my superiority all the more. I lived in retirement, shutting myself up in my infirmities as in a sanctuary inaccessible to the profane. In short, after a few weeks of this detestable life, when my uncle, who had had enough of his *rôle* of protector, told me that the college of Orleans had offered me a scholarship in recognition of my father's services, it seemed to me that this rehabilitation was really due to the exceptional merit of my despised intellect. I entered the college like a conqueror. I was at last going to live with my equals ! Poor dear father, why were you not near me with your gentle words and kindly glance !

Was it my dress, which certainly was a little peculiar, since no one had taken any care of it for a long time ; or was it my person ? I did not know, but one thing is certain, I instantly excited the merriment of my companions. When it was known that I was the son of that droll père Babolain, the merriment increased to mad laughter; the little scamps fairly went into convulsions. They sang couplets of which the dead man was the hero, declared that I looked like him, in fact was his very image ; little père Babolain certainly was not dead, he had only grown young again and become a pupil to atone for his past life as a professor.

My new comrades certainly did not suspect the deep sorrow they caused me ; people are cruel only through ignorance ; but at that time I had suffered too little to understand all this. At the evening recess, directly after supper, my resolution was formed: without the slightest hesitation I planted myself stiff and straight directly in front of one of the boys who had made most fun of me. He was one of the largest and strongest; I had chosen him on account of his height, so that he was at least a head taller. Yet every drop of blood in my body receded to my heart, and I really thought I was facing death.

"Monsieur," said I, stammering violently from emotion, "Monsieur, I won't have my family insulted, and you—you shall not do it."

I must have been very comical, for I instantly heard the abominable laugh which had welcomed me that morning, and pursued me, alas! so long.

"My little old man," said my adversary, merrily patting my cheek—the bystanders stamped with delight—"you will get thrashed if you don't behave yourself."

"You shall ask papa's pardon," I cried, rising on tiptoe and knocking my companion's hat a long distance off. Almost at the same instant I received a violent blow in the face, which made me lose all self-control; I rushed forward and struck furiously with both hands and feet, without seeing or hearing anything. I know not how long this contest lasted, for I did not recover my senses until I found myself in a bed in the infirmary, whither they had carried me. I was covered with compresses, the sheets were stained with blood, and when I tried to move I felt a terrible pain towards the end of my right arm.

"Ask God's pardon, my child," murmured the Sister of Charity who was standing near me with the doctor; "perform an act of contrition."

"The devil, the devil! pardon me Sister; the lunatic has dislocated his wrist," said the doctor gruffly.

"That's what people get when they fight with walls,
little savage."

It seems that in my fury, to the great delight of
the lookers-on, I had really attacked the wall and
bruised myself against the stones.

I remained in the infirmary a long time, and was
very dull, for the cause which had brought me there
was not one to arouse any sympathy for me. The
principal had not concealed the alarm which my per-
verse instinct inspired in him for the future, and
everybody undoubtedly considered me a most dangerous person. One evening when the Sister of Charity brought my porridge and leaned over me to shake
up my pillow, my heart suddenly swelled with such
gratitude that, throwing my sound arm around her, I
embraced her, bursting into tears. She hastily drew
back with sincere indignation, her face flushed deeply, and from that time I was nursed by a dirty
boy who had a very disagreeable smell. The desertion of the kind Sister caused me deep pain; another
punishment which I did not understand! I vaguely
imagined that she had felt an insuperable disgust
towards me, caused partly by my natural ugliness,
and partly perhaps by some infirmity with which I
was unconsciously afflicted. Still I never dared to
ask her how I had offended her; besides, I had no
time to do so, for two days after they sent me back
among my companions, still bruised and very weak,
but determined to bear everything from them.

There is a certain consoling joy in self-imposed
humility, it is the strength of the weak to bend
without complaining, to envelope themselves in indifference, take refuge in themselves and be able to
say: here I am master. It contains a triumph which
flatters vanity and lulls resentment to sleep, for the
human soul is so constituted that the feelings born in
it must balance each other; and the little victories
we obtain within make us forget the defeats sustain-

ed without: we have chains on our feet and laurels in our pockets.

I rushed into study as one throws himself into the water, from despair, and did so well that, after a few months labor, I was at the head of the class. Then the cruelties to which I had been compelled to submit gradually ceased, and they contented themselves with making fun of me. What a sensation of comfort I felt!

II.

One Sunday evening—I had as usual spent the holiday entirely alone—my next neighbor in the class, who was singing merrily, ran against me on the staircase leading to the dormitory. This young fellow's name was Timoléon, and he was numbered among the most influential personages in the division. Tall sturdy, skilful in every game, with thick fair hair surrounding a face as laughing and rosy as a girl's, his eyes beamed with an expression of such bewitching frankness and jollity that he was beloved by everybody, and although one of the wildest received the fewest punishments, yet no one dreamed of wondering at it. Moreover, this spoiled child was extremely idle; but he might have made even laziness attractive by the joyous grace with which he bore his ignorance.

"I have brought you something that will please you, little old man," said he, placing in my hands a package containing two brioches.

I was so unaccustomed to such proceedings that at first my embarrassment was extreme, and—I confess it with regret—I felt an emotion of distrust. Dogs which have been too much beaten run away when they are called.

"Why do you give me this?" I murmured.

"To please you, of course. You never go out, my poor little old man, nobody comes to see you, and you haven't a cent."

"I do not complain."

"I have been a long time in discovering what you really are—don't put your old spectacles on the end of your nose. Look here, Babolain,"—it was the first time that a fellow-student had called me by my name —"shall we be friends? Say, do you agree?"

I was touched to the very depths of my heart. I had never supposed that any one could address such sweet words to me, and murmured: "Then you are not afraid of bringing annoyances upon yourself by getting intimate with me?"

He drew himself up proudly like the brave, generous fellow he was.

"Annoyances! I should like to see any one find fault with what I do, or touch a hair on the head of him whom I call my friend. Give me your hand, is it agreed."

"Oh! yes, I will never forget this, Timoléon, no never."

"Good-night, little old man."

"Good-night, Timoléon."

I quickly got into my bed, and when I had lain down, slowly set about eating a whole brioche. I was hungry and happy.

Our intimacy, which never died out, for Timoléon has always played a part in my life, began in a way that greatly annoyed me; the third day after this famous Sunday he carelessly asked me to write his composition. He requested it as he would have begged me to lend him a ball, or pass him the carafe; I saw that he attached no importance to it, and I loved him too well, was too grateful to him, to refuse a service he valued so little, but it was very painful to me! I was timid, easily alarmed, a slave to discipline and my conscience told me plainly: "what you are do-

ing is dishonest and wrong." Yet I committed the
error, and regularly almost every week he made me
repeat it, without my daring to tell him, even once,
how much it troubled me. How heartily the great
child who never saw evil in anything would have
laughed if I had confessed my scruples. Dear Timoléon ! He always said : " Heavens ! how stupid you
are, little old man. Come, be quiet, or I will leave
you ! " I was always wrong—I loved him so much,
having no one but him.

We were afterwards separated when I entered the
normal school, but we did not lose sight of each other.
He even came to see me, although he was then very
much engrossed by the pleasures of the Quartier Lat-
in, with which he became a little too much intoxicated. Ah ! well, in spite of that he came to the infirmary of the school to see his little old man.

Such things are not forgotten. The sickness I
had on entering the normal school was caused by the
over-work I had imposed on myself during my last
years at the college. My mind was so slow, and I
had so many barriers to surmount before I could be
a professor ! Thank God, the prize I won in mathematics gained me protectors ; my uncle Babolain, who
came to see me crowned, slipped ten francs into my
hand, the mayor of the city embraced me, and publicly spoke of the future due to my talents. If he
had known by what terrible exertions I had obtained
that crown, he would have doubted my talents as
much as I did myself. However that may be, the
excellent man semi-officially promised me a pension
of three hundred francs, if the city, which was already
greatly involved in debt in consequence of the re-
pairs of its sewers, could undertake this new burden.

The good city never could ! However, I was authorized to remain at the college in the capacity of
usher, which enabled me to prepare for my examination without having recourse to any one's charity.

I had a charming little room, high up under the old roof. True, its temperature was torrid in summer, and freezing in winter, but through the little dormer window I could see the sky between two tall brick chimneys, the tossing branches of an old poplar tree —and at night what superb moonlight effects there were upon the old roofs! In this lodging I have experienced the purest and most perfect joys of my life. I had dazzling visions of happiness by the light of the little confessional lamp the almoner had given me, and whose wick I was obliged to raise with a nail, the machinery being broken. The goal seemed to be drawing near. I caught glimpses of the beloved diploma, a hundred times more desirable than the throne of France. Happiness is really desire and hope; the thing ardently wished for is only a coarse canvas which the man embroiders according to his fancy: the enjoyment is in the act of embroidering, the needle is of gold or steel, the threads of wool or silk, the tapestry may be large or small, insignificant or wonderful, what does it matter? The man has enjoyed the more the larger portion of himself he has put into his work, the greater the number of stitches in which he has left a fragment of his life.

Perhaps it would have been better if my efforts had been less passionate; I should not have fallen sick when I entered the normal school, and my successes being less rapid, I should not have been blinded by the foolish pride which took possession of me. I believed myself a remarkable person, and at the same time the wounds of former days re-opened with still greater pain than in the past; for in becoming a mathematician I had not changed either my manner or my face. The jeers of the normal school, though less brutal than those of the college, were no less cutting; on the contrary, they were directed with a surer hand, attacked more accurately and penetrated deeper.

I had now hád too unexceptionable proofs of
my intelligence—not to believe myself very witty,
and although it cost my timidity dear, I tried to defend myself and bring the laughers over to my side.
I was to be pitied. It must be confessed that my
face ill suited my subtle retorts: never was mirror of
the soul more intractable than mine. My unlucky
features were like the keys of an old worn-out harp-
sichord, from which Liszt himself could have drawn
nothing but discordant sounds only fit to make every
body run away.

Moreover, I had other vexations, having reached
that troublesome age when new horizons open before the mind, and the soul is assailed by an indefinable restlessness. The triumphant air of Timoléon,
whom I saw at rare intervals, the studied elegance of
his dress, the pleasures of his life, which he revealed with coquettish reticence, inspired me with mingled terror and jealousy. I knew very well that his
life could not be mine, but none the less did I divine
from it a world of emotions whose existence my innocence had never before imagined, and which attracted while terrifying me. The desire to conceal
my agitation augmented my shyness. On the few holidays my labor allowed me, having neither relatives nor
friends to visit, I wandered through the great city of
Paris, with dilated nostrils and sparkling eyes, ever
ready to shudder; it seemed as if my person would
attract every glance, that everybody would read in
me—where will pride hide itself—and in this crowd
where no one knew me, my constant care was to preserve my incognito.

Ah! well, in spite of all this, or perhaps because
of it, I was always attracted towards the most frequented places. Aristocratic elegance intoxicated
me with admiration. I watched it as a hunter lies in
wait for his game. At certain moments, I believe I
would have given my prize for mathematics and my

title as a student in the normal school, to be one of
the horsemen I saw riding down the avenue of the
Champs Elysées at a hand-gallop; to possess the
natural grace, the ease, the courtly bearing, no labor
can acquire; to mingle with the brilliant society I devoured with my eyes—from a great distance, as I
walked along the dark, damp avenue which borders
the terrace of the Tuileries. My heart bounded in
its ugly case, and all the women—yes all, seemed to
possess a superhuman beauty.

Sometimes the temptation to approach them was
so great that, buttoning my coat with a resolution I
thought heroic, I penetrated into the very centre of
the crowd. My situation then became intolerable.

I was like a man walking through fireworks with
a pack of hounds at his heels. I thought I heard
bursts of laughter falling in showers upon my head,
felt every eye fixed upon me, caught my legs in the
children's hoops, stepped upon dresses, jostled old ·
gentlemen, and abashed and flurried, fled back into
the dark avenue from whence I ought not to have
emerged.

It might be supposed that after this I should wish
for nothing but some lonely spot in which to hide
my shame; but this was not what I felt: scarcely had
I left these enchanting scenes when I once more
breathed freely, my step regained its assurance, and
I discovered treasures of audacity within my soul.
" Ah! next time I certainly will not be so foolish! "

I have spent my life in repeating this simple little
phrase.

When we have manipulated mathematical ab-
stractions a long time, the formula becomes the gold-
en key that unlocks all secret places, those of the
heart as well as others, and we always have this gold-
en key hung around our necks. Quietly and logically we make ourselves infallible, and then go forth
into the world with our caps on our heads, and a piece

of chalk in our hands, ready to make a positive inventory and note down the emotions.

Although too hesitating and timid to give way to this eccentricity entirely, I was not wholly a stranger to it ; once in the school again, I regained my former place, the air I breathed possessed an indefinable power to strengthen me ; I saw things from a higher stand-point ; was no longer suffocated by feeling, but conquered it ; and the impressions I had received from without seemed like physiological accounts, like the different terms of an equation to be solved. The realization of my mad aspirations was nothing more than a problem, like any other, which could not long perplex an intellect, trained as mine had been, to the processes of an infallible logic, and I said to myself ; " To be also a man of the world and take my share in these tempting delights, what is the sum total of all I need ?   A new hat, and a pair of gloves, nothing more."

Thank God, I was delivered from this absurd preoccupation of mind by my examination, which I passed very creditably, and immediately after which, I was appointed professor of mathematics at Carcassonne.

The emotion I felt in the diligence which conveyed me to my own new post can be understood only by conquerors.   It is impossible to be more vainglorious than I was then.   Of course the whole city was expecting me, and people were saying to each other: " Is he tall or short, handsome or ugly ? "

I decided beforehand upon my manner and the phrases I would use when I entered the principal's study, and practised the intonations of my voice amid the rattling of the carriage which served as an accompaniment.   It was all lost trouble : my arrival at Carcassone was as far from being a triumphal one as possible.   In a pouring rain, which somewhat damped my enthusiasm and drenched my clothes through and through, I followed the porter who had taken possession of my little trunk. Without the slightest hesitation he conducted me to a second-rate inn, where, on the strength of my appearance, they instantly gave me a room in the garret, although I had been unable to resist the pleasure of writing on my trunk: Monsieur Babolain, professor in the college of Carcassonne!

The series of disenchantments to which I was forced to submit were not sufficient to wholly dispel my intoxication; in vain did my pupils receive me with most indecorous hilarity; in vain did the principal, a man of superb physique, measure me from head to foot for three good minutes without concealing the surprise excited by my personal appearance—in spite of all this I remained a conqueror; I resolutely grasped my sceptre, and began my course of lectures; I wished to have it surpass all expectations.

These occupations and the prodigious inflation of my pride, which prevented me from distrusting my powers, momentarily delivered me from my worldly dreams; and it was only towards the close of the first year of my professorship that the moral restlessness, from which I had suffered at school, again manifested itself: my career had henceforth no farther obstacles for me; in spite of the want of discipline among my pupils; my course of lectures was highly esteemed, I was established in life, I had a title, a situation, my glance was steady, my judgment infallible, I already possessed a pre-arranged system in regard to human passions—in short, I had gloves! Had not the moment come for me to penetrate into the ideal of life, to loose the reins of my heart, which was still bounding unsubdued, unhappy heart! and take my share of the pleasures of this world?

Yes, the moment had indeed come. At the slightest wish I might manifest for them, the invitations which, until now, I had not dared to accept, would certainly be renewed ; the families of my pupils would eagerly receive me ; the principal, the mayor, and many others would stand upon their thresholds with smiling lips to welcome me ; I felt assured that I had only to present myself.

My sentimental walks began anew, but were disturbed by very different causes from those of former days, for I was now well known in the city—my personal appearance was not one of those which can pass unobserved—notoriety overwhelmed me.

This provincial city with its meannesses, certainly is not the theatre which is suited to me, I thought to myself, and regretted Paris, where I should have been less noticed, more master of myself, less laughed at in case of failure. On that vast stage I might have been able to work my way into the crowd, and enter society without attracting too much attention—my diffidence was returning. Providence was pleased by it, for one morning I received a huge letter stamped with the seal of the ministry, and containing my appointment as titulary professor in the college of Saint Louis.

While strapping my valise to return to the capital, I said to myself: "If only fate does not have too heavy a hand, and pledge the future by the excess of its present favors." I was terrified. How much more so should I have been if I could have known what was reserved for me in the immediate future ! I still shudder when I think of the violence of the blow by which I was overwhelmed.

I had been in Paris two or three months, and taken possession of my new professorship, when suddenly, without any one's having the least anticipation of it, my uncle Babolain, the vine-dresser of Beaugency, stumbled and glided into the tomb, leaving me, very involuntarily, an income of at least twenty-five thousand livres. I was the only relative of the deceased, and he had made no will.

Stronger heads than mine might have been shaken ; at first I was thunder-struck, then like a snail that has been startled, began to feel my way, while a pleasant warmth pervaded my frame from head to foot, and I seemed to myself like a man who, stunned without being wounded, on regaining his senses stretches himself in a nice soft bed. Poor uncle Babolain !

After the delicious calm that followed the first shock, the intoxication of such wealth suddenly burst forth ; I had not previously understood that the doors of a brilliant future were thrown wide open before me. Henceforth I was tall, I was handsome, I was strong, did I know exactly what I was now? I seized my cane, pulled my hat over my eyes without any of the caution habitual to me, and went out to breathe the fresh air. Paris no longer wore the same aspect, I possessed it all, how many surprises and delights I was going to enjoy.

Yet the devilish critical judgment, the gift of exact analysis that would never lie dormant in my brain, made me perceive that I was entering a ridiculous path, but it was in a manner so confused that it did not wound me ; it seemed as if to a certain extent my critical intellect bore a grudge against all humanity, so that while looking at apple-green cravats and Russia leather dressing cases in the shop windows, I was humming: " Man is, really, nothing but a box of follies, really, really."

When, after taking a great many steps, I again found myself in my humble little room seated before a large bag of crowns I had brought from the bank myself—at that time gold did not run about the streets—I thrust my hands into my pockets and began to philosophize. I would no longer be the dupe of my emotions like any ordinary parvenu ; I intended to be ignorant of no portion of my character, to keep the reins and whip in my own hands, and not let

2

my horses mount into the driver's seat. What have
I done, I said to myself, to deserve this wealth, which
perhaps might have turned my head if I had not been
a man of science and sound reasoning faculties;
what have I done to deserve these dangerous favors?
On the whole, I have been no more unfortunate than
others; or at least many others have been more unfortunate than I. Well, well, let us analyze (I always distrusted my first impulse), let us analyze;
thanks to my nature, which is good at bottom, very
good, I have always known how to find the best side
of things, avoid useless complaints, and content myself with almost nothing. How many people in my
place would have cursed their fate! I must acknowledge that my childhood was a little—hard—terribly
hard—what horrible years I had been forced to endure! Have I ever had in my life any pleasures
worthy of the name? No, never. You have never enjoyed yourself, my poor Babolain, and my past moved
rapidly before my mind. I remembered the long
damp galleries of the college and the school, the
gloomy walls, the grated windows, the toiling like a
galley slave, my obstinate struggles, and the cruel isola-
tion during the holidays while my companions were
happy with their relatives. Had I forgotten the jeers,
the abuse, my poverty, my perplexities? Must I not
have possessed a certain nobility of nature, must not
my heart have been incapable of rancor or jealousy
to have the proximity of all these people, who were
so much happier than myself, disturb me no more; to
enable me to remain the friend of Timoléon, for in
stance, who was such a privileged character? He
was tall, strong, and handsome; I was short, puny, and
ill-formed. He was rich, flattered, petted; I roughly
used. I was poor; he made game of me, and yet
for years I wrote his translations and exercises, and
solved his problems. Did he even thank me? Great

God, how many troubles! To be frank, Providence really owes me some compensation.

I opened my bag, took out a handful of coins, filled all my pockets with them, and went out to get my breakfast at a famous restaurant.

I had not reached the end of the street when I stopped short and said to myself: "Can I, by chance, have a base soul, is it possible that I am already contaminated! I, who wish to read the hearts of others, what is taking place in my own? I have been a rich man only a week, and already I am making a pedestal of imaginary woes to prove to myself that this fortune is a reparation which is owed me." I was shocked. "Well, wretch," I added, striking myself on the chest, "you shall breakfast on a roll this morning."

I turned abruptly to the right and entered a baker's shop.

A thin pale woman, accompanied by two children, was in the shop standing with downcast eyes before the baker's wife, who was saying in a very loud tone: "I'm sorry, but you've already got round me too often. What does Monsieur want?"

"I thought my husband would get about sooner," replied the poor woman; "when he is able to work again, we'll pay you for everything."

"Oh! yes, you've no lack of good reasons, I know that very well, but if I hadn't been ridiculously tender hearted I shouldn't have opened an account with you, and you wouldn't have run in debt to me. I ought to refuse for your own good. It is really for your good; it is for their good, Monsieur."

"Does she owe you much money?" I asked.

"For her, yes Monsieur; she owes me twenty-five or thirty francs. How can these people pay thirty francs?"

"Here they are," said I, placing the six crowns I had put into my pocket, on the counter, and hastily making my escape, for my position was very embar-

rassing: might it not be supposed that I had done
this merely from pride, and to make a parade of my
money, when it was only from indignation against
myself? I walked on, murmuring: " Have you ever
wanted bread, fool, wretch, scoundrel, parvenu ?"

The pale woman who had followed me, cried:
" My good gentleman, my good gentleman, pray let
me thank you."

I stopped short and said in a stern tone : " I am
not a good gentleman."

" Oh ! God will reward you."

Hastily and angrily I put all the money I had left
into her hand, and then fled to find some secluded
spot where I could analyze the sensations I had just
experienced.

On the whole, prosperity was a long time in re-
storing calmness to my mind ; it even seemed to me
that I had never been more agitated by these alternations of confidence and terror, in which my life was
wasting away.

The more ardent my desires became, the less possible seemed their practical realization. My critical
judgment clearly proved to me that in the lofty position in which I now found myself, my ridiculous inexperience was a more formidable obstacle than ever:
I was no longer permitted to be a simpleton and excite
laughter ; it was too late to run the risk of a first appearance ; precisely because I had solid theories concerning the play of human passions, I dreaded the
consequences of my smallest actions the more. I
would fain have meddled with these questions of the
heart, in which I was longing to show myself, but I
feared lest I should be awkward, compromise myself, and cover myself with shame. In that case
should I not have been like a commander-in-chief
who dishonored his epaulettes by obstinately making
the attack at the wrong time. The few timid attempts I
made to come out of my shell had no other result than

to lead me to re-enter as fast as possible the accursed prison where I was beginning to devour myself.

In the first hours of my delight I had hired on the Quai Voltaire a large suite of apartments in accordance with my position, but before taking possession, when in imagination I saw myself with my small figure and insignificant air, wandering through the great drawing room; when I heard the sneering laughter of my valet and my cook; when I thought of all the ridiculous things that would be rendered conspicuous by this magnificent frame, I instantly took a sheet of blank paper, and gave notice that I should not want the rooms after the end of the quarter.

It was the same with everything else.

Even my dress occasioned me unheard-of perplexities. I had a quantity of new clothes in which I had never ventured to go out, and whatever care I might take in arranging every detail of my toilet, it was very seldom that on perceiving me, kind-hearted Timoléon, whom I had met again more brilliant than ever, did not say, shouting with laughter : "Have you got yourself up for a scarecrow, my little old man ?" The words were harsh, but perfectly excusable from his lips : he had such exquisite taste in dress. What a charming cavalier ! How bewitching he was with his follies, his ease, and his mirth! I do not mean to say that I was jealous, but he always left me a little more thoughtful than before. About this time he often borrowed small sums of me. I was always troubled about it, I grieved that he should have to ask me for these trifles; it did not seem to be in the natural order of things that he should be under obligations to me. He dazzled me, I was always timid in his presence. Doubtless that is why I never dared to confess my sorrows and sufferings to him. Yet I think he guessed them, for he once said to me: "How foolish you are, not to be happy, my little old man."

"But I am happy, my dear fellow, very happy."

"You! Can't one read perturbation, anxiety, constraint in your whole person, your words, your movements, your face, which is wrinkled like an apple, nay even in your outlandish costume. Comical fellow!" He looked at me steadily a few seconds, and then continued: "You are clumsy and bold, simple and complicated, artless and assuming, intelligent and very stupid. You won't bear me a grudge, I am going to run away."

Bear him a grudge! He must have really loved me to have taken the trouble to watch me so closely.

III.

A short time before the year 1830 the garden of Luxembourg was an immense park, with cool dark avenues, separated from the nursery, still called the Close of the Carthusian friars, by a small low wall upon which I liked to rest my elbows. From this point one could overlook the whole enclosure. A pleasant odor pervaded the air and came to you in whiffs; the pear and apple trees groaned under the weight of their fruit; the clematis and bind weed climbed over the hawthorn; and the vegetables grew wonderfully. Under the roof of the well, a philosophic horse, with bandaged eyes and pensive mien, turned a crank, the water flowed into distant trenches, and you could see a fine rain issue from the red copper watering pots and fall upon the cabbage leaves with a noise that resembled the distant roll of a drum.

After sunset, when the bluish tints of evening began to envelope all nature, this Close, which the Carthusians seemed to have left only the evening before, had an irresistible charm. Moreover, nothing checked the vagrancy of the imagination: the coaches and miserable one-horse chaises of Fontenay-aux-Roses,

whose stand was in the old Rue d'Enfer, had ceased
their rattling—it seemed as if one was a hundred
leagues from Paris. The Rue de l'Ouest then resembled a road laid out through the open country; the
houses on it were very much scattered, small, and
buried in foliage; everything was calm, quiet, restful.
What a peaceful life the good Carthusians must have
led!

Sometimes I fancied I could see them and their
monastery: yonder was the mill upon its little emi-
nence overlooking the corn-fields, there the cemetery
where the priests came to meditate, the empurpled
vineyard, the huge trellises, and large cool cellars covered with tiles and thatched, and among all these
things the friars with their long beards and shaven
crowns, raking the hay, or devoutly tying up the salad.

This dream was dispelled by the murmurs of the
violins at the *Grande-Chaumière*, from whence the
sound of joyous rigadoons was borne by the west
wind. Meantime the cows, indifferent to these gaye-
ties, slowly approached the little wall, and their driver
ascending the steps of the staircase in his large
wooden shoes, took through the grating the bowls the
lovers of good milk eagerly held out to him.

On this evening I perceived among the group of
milk drinkers a tall, broad-shouldered young gentleman, whom I recognized immediately. His delicate
moustache was boldly twisted, his fair curling locks
fell upon the velvet collar of his closely fitting overcoat, which buttoned very high in the neck, his tight
light-colored pants extended in the shape of a gaiter
over a very pointed boot; a huge silk handkerchief
fluttered around his neck, and a large black felt hat
with slightly rolling brim gave this handsome young
fellow the air of a cavalier of the time of Louis
XIII., who had accidentally stepped from his frame.

Before and very near him, for the gentleman was
gaining ground every instant, stood a young girl with

a retroussée nose and sparkling eyes. She had placed her work basket on the top of the wall, and with up-raised arms and head thrown back was drinking some milk. Nothing could be prettier than the blooming cheek and saucy little nose half lost in the snowy contents of the cup. Unperceived by any one, I watched all that passed.

The Louis XIII. cavalier was apparently murmur-ing some very interesting and amusing things into her ear, for the young girl, between two mouthfuls, sud-denly burst into a fit of laughter which revealed her white teeth and scarlet lips, to which the little drops of milk were still clinging. When the nectar was all imbibed, the nape of her neck bent so prettily, and her arms curved with so much grace, that the young man, becoming more enterprising, said to her in a louder voice, looking at her caressingly, with his handsome blue eyes :

"Pâque Dieu! what a charming ear to kiss! Elvire, my beauty, do you hear the violins and flutes? Let us forget our sorrows, and dance. Afterwards we'll sup on some root and weep for love, will you, fair lady?"

As the grisette held her empty bowl in her hand, the gentleman twirled his moustache, and turning to-wards the man in the wooden shoes, cried :

"Holloa! Master Orsini, devil's innkeeper! hol-loa I my rude shepherd, take this lady's cup instantly."

While the milk drinkers murmured indignantly, the young girl said with great dignity :

"But Monsieur, I do not know you; leave me, Monsieur, leave me."

"You don't know me, Elvire? Ah! cruel girl!"

"My name is not Elvire. Come, come, I have had enough of your tomfoolery. I never saw you before in my life, you take me for somebody else. I am Mad-emoiselle Julie of the Passage Dauphine, and you shall know that my character is stainless, Monsieur."

So saying, she took up the basket she had placed on the wall, and went away with a rapid step, full of modesty and seductive grace.

The gentleman was undoubtedly going to rush forward in pursuit, when he felt some one pull him by the sleeve, and turning angrily, suddenly burst into a laugh.

"Well! What do you want of me, you confounded little old man?" said he. "Do you happen to be my rival?"

"I? Ah! Timoléon! come this way, I entreat you, in the name of our old friendship—resist the eagerness of passion for a moment; I implore you —my dear friend—at your age—this conduct—"

I was very much agitated, for people were looking at us, and at the same time, the unheard-of follies to which Timoléon had just delivered himself up, grieved me deeply. Perhaps he was going to allow himself to be dragged down one of those fatal slopes whose full danger I had measured in my dreams.

He suffered himself to be led into the Avenue de l' Observatoire, and when we had taken a few steps, suddenly placed his hand on mine, and said:

"Why are you eating your cane?"

I really was in the habit of raising the head of my walking stick to my lips when embarrassed. Without saying a word, I put it under my arm.

"Good," he continued, "and now you are fidgeting with your spectacles. Do you want to devour them too? Calm yourself, Babolain, and explain your scandalous conduct."

"You know how I love you, my dear Timoléon. Well—I thought it was my duty to interrupt you—being assured that you would be grateful to me afterwards—People were looking at you—I wanted to save —in a word, your dignity; therefore—"

It was with difficulty that I found words to express myself when in Timoléon's presence, but I was utterly confounded when he said in a grave, stern tone, which I had never heard from his lips:

" Monsieur, you have dealt my heart one of those wounds which between gentlemen—"

" Upon my honor, Timoléon, I did not intend to wound you."

" Good Heavens, how silly you are, little old man ! Don't you see I'm joking. I begged you not to eat your cane."

" If I had offended you, I should be the first to apologize, you may be assured, for—"

" You are an angel of frankness ; I love you ; say no more about it. Do you know what will cause me a perpetual sorrow? The dryness of your heart."

Without asking myself if this was also a jest, I was deeply moved by the accusation. It was false, utterly false, but appearances were against me. He pitilessly continued :

" You are astonished because at my age I have preserved that freshness of feeling, that thirst for tenderness, that facility of emotion, which are the most precious treasures of the human soul. You are astonished because the velvety neck of the Elvire from whom you have just snatched me thrilled my heart ; you are amazed at all this, you ugly little pro-fessor, wasting your life in galloping around the nar-row circle of practical realities ! And suppose, in my turn, I am amazed at your icy indifference, oh ! profound logician, withered heart."

" But, my friend, I understand love," I murmur-ed earnestly.

" He understands love ! And he treats as mad-men those who drink at its vivifying spring. Don't you see, child, that in this holy youthful ardor, this worship of woman, there is something more than the pleasure of the senses ; it is the soaring of the soul towards that ideal which is a ray from God Him-self."

I did not understand very clearly, but I was enraptured by Timoléon's ardent poesy.

" Yes, I admit that passion," said I—I was trying to rise to his height—" passion is a necessary power in the moral mechanism. But just as a body drawn by two inverse attractions—"

"Spare me your scientific porridge, Babolain. I am not, thank Heaven, a scholar like yourself, capable of putting God into a formula, weighing my tears in a pair of scales, and measuring every pulsation of my heart. I am only a poor fellow, who is full of aims and weaknesses. I have not the self-control you possess, but I have faith in the Divine mercy, and I believe, like Père Enfantin, in the rehabilitation of the flesh ; like him, I believe that all morality is contained in the worship of woman, for in her eyes we shall see truth."

" Truth itself cannot dispense with demonstration, and reasoning seems to me—"

" I reason with my heart. I am one of those persons who seek their moral development, and, so to speak, the purification of their hearts, in the succession of the different love affairs Providence supplies."

" What, you have loved them all ! " I murmured in amazement, for I had a vague knowledge of the considerable number of his successes. He answered with perfect frankness :

" Why, of course I have loved them all; were it not for that I should be the most contemptible of rakes. I am one of that class of persons authorized by Père Enfantin to bind themselves only by a succession of momentary marriages ; I condemn exclusive alliances, which are the negation of love and the debasement of the race."

" But, Timoléon, these are strange theories which must be subjected to a severe analysis, for after all, it is—"

He stopped, clapped me roughly on the shoulder, and said:

"If you want to go in, you must go and get your ticket, little old man."

"What ticket, Timoléon?"

I raised my head, for I was absorbed in my reflections, and saw before me a grave policeman in whose helmet, as in a mirror, was reflected a whole panorama of orange trees and lanterns. I was standing upon the very threshold of the *Grande-Chaumière,* which had always inspired me with a secret terror. I shuddered from head to foot.

It must be confessed that often, in former days, before entering the normal school, and even after my return to Paris, I had followed the fast young men going to the scene of their pleasures with a troubled glance; and while wandering around this infernal Paradise, had seen above the wall the chariot from the Russian mountains noisily bearing away a pair of lovers clasped in each other's arms. I had gazed with an eager eye down the avenue, carpeted with yellow sand, and adorned with lilacs and orange trees, at one end of which fluttering skirts gleamed through a luminous cloud. I knew the policeman—perhaps the father of a family—who kept guard at the door; I had envied him, I had also pitied him with all my heart, while thinking of the numberless temptations consequent upon his office, but I swear upon my honor I had never approached him. My present situation was even more painful: I, titulary professor of the royal college of Saint-Louis, established in the world, possessed of a character that claimed respect, I at the threshold of this door!

"Well, do you mean to come in or not? You are stopping the way, and the policeman is getting angry."

I was going to answer as I ought, when two very

elegant ladies, accompanied by a gentleman, passed rapidly by on the other side of the boulevard. The gentleman looked at me for a moment with an expression of doubt, hesitated an instant, then turning with a discreet smile waved his hand in a friendly salute.

"Great Heavens! Timoléon, my friend, I have been recognized," I cried, pressing his arm violently.

"What's the matter, what is it, little old man?"

"You see those ladies, who—"

"Do you know them?"

"Who have just passed? no, I don't know them." I was choking.

"Well then?"

"I know the gentleman, it is Prudent de la Sarthe. Oh! my friend."

"Prudent who?"

"De la Sarthe. I am lost."

And I rushed after the two ladies and their attendant cavalier, to whom I wished to prove my innocence.

When I think over all this, it seems astonishing that the meeting should have so deeply disturbed me. Had I an instinctive premonition of the never ending consequences it would entail upon me?

IV.

It was at the Odéon, where I went very often, that I had made the acquaintance of Prudent de la Sarthe, a very accomplished man about fifty years of age, and a most brilliant conversationalist. People called him an artist, but to tell the truth, I never saw in his studio, to which he was so kind as to admit me, either brush or paints. His whole work consisted of little sketches, which were very remarkable it seems, but always appeared to me extremely confused. However,

my opinion is unimportant, for I was then totally ignorant of all questions relating to art.   He worked
upon papers of all colors, prepared with the utmost
care.   The tint of these papers, their grain, their
thickness, their stiffness, the quality of the pencils,
the composition of the liquids by whose aid he rendered his work permanent, were a constant care to
the skilful artist, of which he often spoke to me. He
even asked one day for special information upon the
subject of an unchangeable white, whose constituent
elements he had been seeking for twenty-five years.
This had not prevented him from inventing with the
greatest ease several very ingenious little machines:
pincers with springs, pegs for easels, self-shutting
pencil-cases, and many other things whose importance did not at first appear.   But when, as a professional man, he discussed the importance of these
wonders, he did it with so much learning and authority, knew so well how to call to his aid the memory
of the great masters and the future of French art,
that these questions suddenly increased to unprece-
dented proportions, and even the little sketches whose
execution had been the cause of so much research,
assumed a magisterial importance.   Moreover, Prudent de la Sarthe was thoroughly well educated, courteous, a man of the world, protesting by the simplicity of his dress against the extravagant eccentricities
of the romanticists, and priding himself very justly
on being a wit.

Having an inclination towards the analysis of
things, and being gifted, as I have already said, with
a critical judgment, I took great pleasure in this instructive and charming conversation, which opened
horizons of art hitherto unknown.

It was wonderful to see with what intellectual ease
he flitted from one subject to another, and whether
he entered into the study of the works of Corneille,
or gave me curious hints regarding the manufacture

of drawing paper in the time of Leo X., always showed himself to be a superior person.

True, at first my somewhat slow intelligence found it difficult to follow the rapid changes of his. He sometimes smiled at it.

The peculiar, and to a certain extent, respectful esteem in which I held Prudent de la Sarthe, explains the eagerness with which I rushed in pursuit of him at the time of our meeting before the *Grande-Chaumière.* But in spite of all my efforts it was impossible for me to find him : the boulevards were then very dimly lighted, my sight was poor, and doubtless there was also some fatality about it. I was compelled to return home very sad and anxious.

The following morning I went to his studio, but he was absent ; and it was not until the third day that I met him at the Odéon, occupying his usual seat : I took the place beside him. He instantly held out his hand in a cordial manner, which somewhat restored my confidence. I saw plainly that he did not despise me.

"Well, my young friend," he said smilingly with a bantering air that sent a shudder through my whole frame, "how have you been since the other evening ? —you terribly sad dog ! " he added confidentially, pressing my hand still more affectionately.

"I assure you upon my honor," said I, "that I was there by accident, entirely by accident. You must perceive that in my position—even if my principles—in my position, I was saying, I should not expose myself — certainly not, consequently, — Good Heavens, I looked for you for half an hour to exculpate myself in your eyes, to assure you that chance alone—"

"All this is a matter of no consequence, my dear friend. Besides, don't excuse yourself too much, for this apparent escapade has done you no harm, far from it, in the eyes of those two ladies."

"The two ladies who accompanied you?"

"Exactly." My friend's pink, smooth-shaven face fairly beamed.

"But then they actually believed I was going to enter that—"

The learned artist became very grave, and with that authority of tone which no one ever contested, murmured, "One of those ladies is Evelina Paline, the other is Esther Paline, her daughter."

I waited an instant, hoping that he would add a few explanations to this revelation which gave me no information whatever; but he remained silent, and I replied:

"Ah! indeed, ah! I did not know, I did not suspect that those ladies—were—My story is both very simple and very extraordinary. I met one of my friends in the Luxembourg, and while talking we followed the avenue—"

"The fact is, that to see them pass in their simple dress, one would not suspect that they are two of the most distinguished, the most remarkable women, not only on account of their beauty,"—he smiled meaningly and played with the bow of his cravat,—"but far more from their elevation of mind and heart, their appreciation of art, their— They spoke of you at least three or four times in the course of the evening. You have made a conquest of them, my dear fellow."

"A conquest of them. I can't believe it—you are certainly making fun of me." I felt that I was blushing.

"I have so little idea of joking that I have given my word to introduce you to these ladies some Monday evening. Their receptions are not formal, pretentious affairs, as you may imagine: it is a purely intellectual circle. Artists, literary men, people of taste and culture—a most charming set. They discuss painting, music, art, take a cup of tea, and that is all. Seriously, I have promised to take you there."

It really seemed to me that Prudent de la Sarthe was not making game of me. The adventure was marvellous. "Why," murmured my frightful pride, "why should not these very superior ladies have discovered the far from commonplace qualities of your mind? Do not your career, your title, your position, prove your moral worth? Why should this worth escape keen eyes? These are no frivolous, ignorant fashionable women, who judge a man by the cut of his coat. Besides, your dress is perfectly presentable. Come, Babolain, incorrigible trembler, lift up your head at last, the occasion is a solemn one; rise to the height of the circumstances."

Pride told me all this, so that I answered with surprising ease: "No one can be more sensible of your kindness than myself. The ladies' indulgence overwhelms me, and I do not know how to tell you—but—"

"Oh! no buts. I have given my word; you are expected, and in fact I came here this evening solely to look for you."

"What! to look for me? It is impossible. Oh! no, no—To look for me?"

"Of course. Isn't this Monday? Take your hat, the interval between the acts is nearly over."

How was it that resistance seemed impossible, that the impassable gulf which had always separated me from society was suddenly filled up, and having taken my hat, I obediently followed the artist.

Mme. Paline and her daughter occupied a very plain house on the Rue Saint Sulpice. On reaching the door, my companion took the lead and we ascended a narrow, ill-lighted staircase: I was agitated as if at the approach of a formidable examination; yet the staircase seemed like a good omen, it could only lead to patriarchal surroundings; what I dreaded

most in the world, was a huge drawing-room blazing
with lights, and a tall footman loudly shouting my
name; a scene I had often witnessed on the stage of
the Odéon.

My conduct is all marked out, I thought to myself, as I mounted the stairs: I must be very simple,
yet unaffected in my manners, a little distant, as be-
seems a learned man, but affable and courteous.

"The apartments occupied by these ladies are by
no means stately," said Prudent de la Sarthe, stopping before a large watered ribbon which hung beside
the door, and served as a bell-rope. "Among artists,
you know, one does not find the showy luxury with
which the upstarts of the Faubourg Saint Honoré
adorn themselves; but you are a man of sufficient
taste to appreciate all that."

A fat cook, with a very respectable air, opened the
door for us, and we entered the ante-chamber. It was
evident at once that this was no ordinary dwelling:
the window represented a glass painting in the style of
the middle ages. The walls were concealed under a
multitude of engravings, statuettes, and articles of
every description; and upon a narrow table, covered
with a piece of black velvet, whose edges, cut in regular indentations, hung down all around it, a rose-col-
ored candle was burning by the side of a pair of
snuffers in wrought copper, on which the sun of Louis
XIV. was represented. Above the table hung a Venetian guitar and a fragment of a cuirass, while over-
coats and umbrellas were piled in one corner.

I had never seen anything of the kind, except in
the curiosity shops in which I had happened to glance,
and could not restrain a gesture of surprise, which did
not escape my companion's notice. "These ladies
are passionately fond of archæological souvenirs,"
said he; "but let us go into the studio, they assemble
there because they can talk more freely."

The noise of conversation proved in fact that

people were speaking without restraint. This studio was distinguished from any ordinary room only by the profusion of different ornaments accumulated in it. Scattered in every direction were pictures without frames, and frames without pictures, plaster hands and feet suspended by strings, fragments of flowered stuffs of odd designs drooping like conquered pennons, flower-pots, a warming-pan one or two centuries old, rusty swords—all manner of things, and on the mantel-piece a large metal bust, shining like a stove funnel. Six or eight gentlemen, the majority of whom wore very long hair, were looking at a picture of tolerably large size, placed upon an easel.

Scarcely had the fat cook announced me, when Mme. Evelina Paline, approaching, held out her hand with the most gracious affability. I was embarrassed for a moment, for I had been unable to get on the thumb of my glove, and was hiding my right hand in the bottom of my hat; but I hastily decided to give her my left, and made a tolerably successful bow. "You are very welcome, Monsieur," said she; "presented by our dear Prudent de la Sarthe, you are already numbered among our friends," then turning towards the rest of the company, while I was seeking some appropriate words with which to answer her: "Gentlemen," said she, "Monsieur Babolain, one of our most distinguished chemists."

"No—Madame, pardon me—no."

"And modest too! oh! we shall see."

It was not modesty, but a very natural desire not to adorn myself with a title that did not belong to me.

"I have never made any special experiments in chemistry," I murmured, "never; consequently—"

"Art and science are sisters."

"Yes, but not being a chemist, I should not like— it would be very painful to me if people—"

"Hush, hush; we must not interrupt the meeting. The historical landscape my daughter intends

to send to the Exhibition this year is now being crit-
icised."

She placed a finger covered with rings upon her
lips, and condescended to bestow upon me a smile
whose charm I could not describe. This lady certainly realized the type of nobility and beauty. I do
not think I exaggerate in speaking thus. A considerable amount of flesh, beneath which any ordinary
woman would have been overwhelmed, was in her
only an advantage, an attraction the more. Covered
with lace, necklaces and jewels, she glided over the
floor with majestic ease, while the long train of her
dress respectfully followed her. Grace and elegance
were revealed in her slightest movements. At last I
was in established social relations with a woman of
the world; I was seated by her side; she showed
sympathy for me. Could Timoléon, such an excellent man in spite of his follies, say as much? The
somewhat fantastic apartments, which had at first surprised me, grew poetic. It seemed impossible that
the unfinished pictures by which I was surrounded
should not possess great artistic value; that the objects
of every description should not be extremely costly;
the absence of all luxury, the want of ceremony that
reigned in the drawing-room, gave it a character whose
value could only be appreciated by the fastidious, and
persons initiated into all the refinements of art.

As to Mlle. Esther Paline, who remained motionless among her judges, my poor sight prevented my
seeing her distinctly, and I dared not take out my
large eye-glass, but it seemed to me that she had her
mother's admirable profile. She was rather thin, as
well as one could judge under the immense dressing-
gown of nacarat velvet draped about her figure. Her
hair, carelessly twisted on the top of her head, was
fastened by a huge shell-comb put in awry.

While I was trying to see more, Mme. Paline bent
towards me and murmured:

"You will excuse us for receiving you in our studio costume, won't you? Among artists — my Esther has been working to-day until the very last moment. She changed all her first plans in two hours."

I dared not ask the meaning of these words, which I did not understand, and merely bowed. She continued :

"The poor darling was fairly worn out. I even think she had a slight feverish attack ; consider that she was obliged to stop to put it into the frame, and the abominable frame did not come. I leave you to imagine the state of mind she was in ! To-morrow will be the last day, as you know. Don't you think the dear child has grown excessively pale ?" she added, raising an exquisite little pair of gold eyeglasses.

As my spectacles did not enable me to form an opinion upon Mlle. Esther's pallor, I followed her example and drew my glasses from my pocket.

"You are apparently very near-sighted, like myself."

"Oh ! I can see very well now. Besides, at this distance I—"

"Exactly like me. My sight is so variable that it baffles all the oculists. That is what made me give up painting."

"Ah ! then you—paint ? "

"Yes, yes, oh ! a great deal ; without rising to my Esther's genius however, but I never felt the least shadow of jealousy of her, the dear, beautiful darling. Besides, as I told you, my career was destroyed by the freaks of my sight. Alas ! we poor women are exposed to so many trials in life. First the sorrows an ill-assorted marriage entails—"

A deep sigh, which was undoubtedly the echo of heavy griefs, escaped her lips.

"The incessant tortures which stifle and crush art

as well as science, demand the whole soul, my dear
Monsieur. And then," she added in a confidential
tone, "there are some nervous, delicate natures which
cannot bear the too frequent assaults of maternity; I
was fortunate not to pay with my life for trials beyond
my strength, and to get off with this weakness of the
eyes which compels me to wear glasses constantly.
Oh! I should be three-quarters dead if it were not for
my eye-glasses. Ah! well, in this world we need
philosophy."

I bowed respectfully. Meantime I had succeeded in seeing the young artist's face.

"Not knowing your daughter's usual complexion,"
said I, "it is difficult for me to—"

"She is the only one left to me of three children,
so what I feel for her is not affection, but idolatry.
It might be supposed that I am proud, that her talent,
her reputation—no, oh! no."

"Undoubtedly—I think she is really rather pale,
but it is impossible for me to know whether she is
more so than usual, having no standard of compari-
son."

Mme. Paline started, and putting her beautiful
hand upon my arm, exclaimed:

"Why do you talk of my Esther's pallor? Oh!
God! do you perceive any symptom of illness, any
alarming token? Oh! speak, I implore you! My
daughter is so beautiful, so good; her soul is so lofty!
Do not fear to tell me all. I am strong."

Poor mother; she was trembling.

"Yes, I am strong. You doctors foresee the
future."

"But, Madame, I am no doctor, I—"

"And it is my affair, Monsieur, it is my affair."

"I am grieved to be the involuntary cause of your
emotion, Madame; I was merely answering the question you did me the honor to ask a few moments
ago. 'Do you not think my daughter has grown some-

what pale from overwork?' you said. I was answering that."

"Ah! yes, pardon me; am I mad? I still shudder at that idea of sickness!—I asked you a ridiculous, senseless question—I don't know why I talk to
you as if you were a friend of twenty years' standing;
it seems as if I had always known you. It is very
wrong; pardon me."

"Pray believe, Madame, that the confidence with
which you honor me—"

It cannot be imagined how difficult it is to finish
a sentence that has been awkwardly begun. I was
touched by Mme. Paline's disclosures: how much
feeling and delicacy there was in this noble heart, so
quick to take the alarm! And the aristocratic inco-
herency of this ever-changing, brilliant, delightful conversation, the inimitable grace, the simplicity of this
drawing-room, where the most famous artists assembled! No, my dreams had not reached this ideal.

"But let us be quiet," murmured my companion'
"hush! Cirbec is going to give his opinion at last.
I am as nervous as a child; think of it, the famous
Cirbec! A wonderful genius, is he not? Hark!
hark!" In fact, for at least ten minutes the famous
Cirbec, with frowning brows and arms folded across
his chest, had been looking at the young girl's picture.
Suddenly he stretched out his arm and said in a deep
voice:

"Good, very good."

"Don't you think, dear master," said the young
artist, "that I shall do very well to accent the waving
light that plays upon the rock."

Cirbec took hold of his chin, frowned again, and
remained silent, while every one awaited the decision
of the oracle in the most perfect stillness.

"The waving light," he said at last in a hollow
tone, "yes—a good idea—I thought of it."

"Unless it would be better to leave out the light

and the rock," continued Esther, biting her little finger.

" Right—yes—oh! oh! perfect!"

Having said this, the great Cirbec took his hat, which he had placed upon the piano, and regretfully withdrew, walking sideways, and casting a lingering glance at the landscape.

" Won't you take a cup of tea or chocolate with us?" said Mme. Evelina Paline, moving away from me.

" No, I regret that I must decline. An appointment with Cavé on business—Monsieur Thiers wants to speak to me—I am very sorry."

He saluted the company with a slight inclination of the head and disappeared, accompanied by the two ladies.

During the absence of the hostesses I took advantage of the fact that Mlle. Esther's picture was left in solitude, to approach it, and raising my glasses, I examined it carefully. Contrary to my expectation, it was almost impossible for me to understand what it was that I had before me. Perhaps in my inexperience, and being embarrassed by my shortsightedness, I stood too near it, for at one moment my nose —I am ashamed of these details—struck against a thick layer of paint, and I experienced a strange sensation of dampness.

Yet the approval of the famous Cirbec, the admiration, the enthusiasm of the company did not permit me to have a doubt as to the value of the work. I was evidently standing before a very remarkable painting, but how was I to ascertain its indisputable merit? In vain I fixed my attention upon it. Where was the rock of which they had spoken? where was the waving light? The sense of my powerlessness made me suffer deeply. What! I had toiled doggedly from my early childhood, my mind was enriched with various knowledge, my judgment formed,

I possessed logic, a critical intellect, and yet I was ignorant of a whole world. Were the purest joys of the human mind denied me? Could I not even seize the trace of the artistic feeling, the admirable fire that all these people possessed?

I was thinking thus when I heard a sweet voice behind me, saying:

"You are looking at my picture as a connoisseur, Monsieur; you are trying, I see, to detect my method."

What reason could I have for trying to detect methods?

"Oh! no, Mademoiselle," I replied, dropping my glasses, and for want of something better to say, added, "Painting must be very difficult."

The young girl looked at me with an air of confidence and composure that made me cast down my eyes, then thrusting her hands into the tiny pockets of her dress, answered: "Difficult, oh! no. When people take to it, it is the simplest thing in the world. In the first place you need rabbits' hairs; that is indispensable. If you had no rabbits, or if you were in a country where rabbits had no hair, painting could not be thought of."

Not being accustomed to this sort of jesting, I listened with increasing attention.

"Then you spread these rabbits' hairs upon a very clean table, divide them into little bundles upon the end of a stick about as long as this—"

"Don't you mean brushes?" I asked in an embarrassed tone.

"So you know the technical terms. Then what remains for me to say is unimportant. You buy different colored pastes, dip your little brush into these various pastes with taste and care, and then sweep it along to suit your fancy over a canvas stretched in a frame. That's what painting is."

Everybody began to laugh.

There was nothing left for me to do but to join in
the general mirth, so I accomplished a woeful grimace, but I felt the veins in my forehead swell, and the
drops of perspiration roll down my temples.

"That reminds me of a little anecdote of which
Cadamour is the hero," said Prudent de la Sarthe. "You remember him? Cadamour, Girodet's
model."

"Perfectly. The insertions of his muscles were
admirable."

"Yes, Mademoiselle, exactly. Well, one day—"

I should have very much liked to hear this story,
which would doubtless have initiated me into some
details of this wonderful world, but Mme. Paline,
from an excess of politeness, undoubtedly, sat down
beside me, and suddenly asked:

"What do you think of Cirbec? He is very good
looking, isn't he?"

"Certainly. He has great talent, apparently."

"Yes, yes, he is an extremely severe critic, and
the praise he has just given us touches me all the
more because there are evident resemblances between
his genius and my Esther's, which might well inspire
him with a little—jealousy; but Cirbec is above these
meannesses, a rare thing in the arts, my dear Monsieur."

"Indeed!"

"Undoubtedly: extreme delicacy of mind naturally produces irritability. Artists have very sensitive skins; hence the sufferings whose cause the
public cannot appreciate, hence their indignation,
their rebellion against the mere contact with commonplace things—I know what it is: it is terrible. Not
that my husband had a bad disposition, but the mediocrity of his intellect, his lack of power to rise to
our ideal! What is the secret, you will say, of certain marriages which seem monstrous? How does it
happen that a young girl of noble birth finds herself

some fine day the wife, the slave of a notary, lost,
buried in the depths of a province? In a word, you
will ask me how I could—"

"I should never permit myself to commit such an
impertinence, Madame."

"Good heavens! the Marquise de Salvain was no
less astonished than you are. 'You have had a terrible downfall, my beautiful child,' she said the day
after my marriage; 'what a frightful hole you are in.'

"The Marquise was a de Plancel, and her first
husband was the cousin-german of my mother, who
was a Martignac, a Martignac - Corbon, the younger
branch. You perceive, do you not, what a heart-
rending effect my marriage must have produced upon
such a circle. Ah! what strange things occur in life,
what chance, what fatality!"

"Chance is not compatible with fatality, Madame,
for if on the one hand—"

"Gently, my dear Monsieur, you will make me
mad."

While my right ear was receiving the confidences
of my fair neighbor, my left was besieged by snatch-
es of the noisiest conversation. One very short
young man, in particular, with flashing eyes and energetic movements, was gesticulating furiously. "Yes,"
he cried in a voice distinguished by a strong Southern
accent, "yes indeed, I will dip my pen in gall to blast
these scandalous reputations."

"Hark ye, my dear Tambergeac," replied another, "I admire your eminent qualities as an art
critic, but I think you are hard upon Cirbec. Have
you seen my Galatea? Cirbec's genius! Ha! ha!
ha!—Gentlemen, let us hear!—if people study the
Venetians— It is a dogma with me, and if you had
seen my Galatea—yes, dipped in gall, for I repeat:
artistically Cirbec is a contemptible fellow— As if one
could separate the man from the artist! Cirbec has
never been anything but a blackguard."

"After all this you must understand what my life was, do you not?" murmured Mme. Paline, who had not ceased speaking. "Compelled to consider the sensibilities of the de Martignacs, and at the same time—"

"My Galatea was a solid piece, and—which did not prevent its being refused a place in the Exhibition—I know it as well as you; it was at the same time as Mademoiselle's two dead natures."

"Which were two gems," cried Mme. Paline, suddenly joining in the general conversation. "It was the most revolting injustice, the grestest effrontery. That day the Institute showed its characteristics in all their nakedness, incompetency and meanness!"

"But what could be the cause of such an infamous thing?" cried I in my turn.

The general excitement was extending to me, and in spite of myself I shared my noble companion's indignation.

"The cause! Alas, it is the general hatred of commonplace, inferior natures against everything original, powerful, young, and individual; the eternal struggle of triviality which revenges itself by treachery, and seeks to reduce everything to its own level."

"But, Madame, that is horrible," I cried earnestly.

"It would be atrocious, if one did not have the esteem of one's friends," said the young artist, holding out her hand to me.

"And the future, my daughter."

V.

I passed a night disturbed by troubled dreams; two or three times I was obliged to get up and drink a large glass of water. Towards morning, however, I fell into a sound sleep, and on awaking felt a delicious sensation of comfort: the rays of the sun filled my room, everything around me was sparkling, my heart overflowed with joy and courage—I was a man of the world. I know not what strange want led me to a hair-dresser's shop that morning. Seating myself in an immense chair I gave myself up to the young man. After having shaved me he went away and came back holding in his hand a pair of curling-tongs, which he turned rapidly round and round while looking for a piece of paper on which to try the heat of the instruments. For the first time in my life I was going to have my hair curled.

I must at any rate have a tolerably good appearance to have such fopperies occur to this hair-dresser as a matter of course, without consulting me. Yet I wanted to laugh.

"Does not Monsieur want some toilette soap? We have some excellent kinds — combs, eau de quinquina for roughness of the skin. Monsieur knows how many maladies the bulb is liable to have."

Wrapped in my huge white cloth, with my legs stretched out as far as possible, I listened to this music which fairly delighted me. People were troubling themselves about me, paying attention to me, trying to beautify me.

"We have also a complete assortment of English brushes, round or oval, which we sell by the set or separately. Only the English brushes are all one can wish."

"What is the price?" said I. The question escaped me unconsciously, so deeply rooted were my economical habits. I was vexed, but my attention was soon distracted, for I saw in the glass every one of my obstinate locks rolled around the tongs, while a light *pich pich* was heard, and a fragrant cloud floated into the air. Then the tongs being carefully withdrawn by successive little twitches, 1 saw a beautiful curl replace the long, flat, stiff lock nature had bestowed upon me. Was not this the image of the physical and moral metamorphosis that awaited me ?

" The prices vary," said the hair-dresser, " according to the mounting which is in wood, ebony or ivory."

" Ah ! you have them in ivory." Hesitation did not seem possible, circumstances demanded the ivory brush, henceforth I could not dispense with such a trinket. And then what a delight it was to dare to throw money out of the window at last.

Ten minutes after, I left the hair-dresser's shop, carrying in my overcoat pocket not only an incomparable brush, but a pretty vial containing a perfumed liquid and tied with a pink ribbon. I felt a very great satisfaction, whose cause, however, I did not wish to investigate lest I might find in it some unworthy weakness. Did not Mme. Paline follow me with her noble gentle glance, while her daughter bestowed upon me an approving smile. It was for their sakes, after all, that I wished to be less ugly.

By chance I raised my head and saw a clock which reminded me of the college. In the midst of these worldly thoughts, I had been on the point of forgetting the sacred duties of instruction. Pursued by the odor of jasmine with which my hair was scented, I began to walk quickly on ; my steps, though short, were very rapid.

At the sight of the day scholars, who whispered together as they looked at me, and scarcely concealed their amusement, I remembered the artificial elegance of my hair. The first moment was disagreeable, but it was not on the morning after a triumph that I could be intimidated by a handful of young rattle pates. I cast around me the glance of a touchy man who is ready to seek a quarrel on the first pretext ; then advancing to the blackboard, said with great firmness : " Gentlemen, let A B C D E be the base of a polyhedron ; and M and N the apices."

I took a piece of chalk, and after pushing up the

sleeve of my gown with a hasty gesture traced a few
lines.

Yes, certainly, it was for their sakes that I wished
to be less disagreeable. What a cordial welcome,
what softness in the smooth delicate hand whose,
pressure I still felt! I took more care than usual
with the figures I traced upon the blackboard, I even
noticed that I raised my little finger with a certain
grace. The evening spent in the society of artists
had roused an unusual regard for the graphic portion
of my demonstration. During all this time the ivory
brush was swinging to and fro in my coat pocket and
rubbing my left leg, while the pretty vial tied with
pink ribbon tapped against my right, so that I was
reminded every instant of the hair-dresser's little
room, and from there by an involuntary connection
of ideas, found myself seated between the two ladies.

The lesson was very troublesome to me, for the
farther I proceeded in my demonstration the more
I was overpowered by the charm of the sweetest of
dreams, and I pronounced the last words in a voice
trembling with tender emotion : " Then, gentlemen,
two similar polyhedrons have similar homologous
faces, and the solid homologous angles equal. That
is what must be demonstrated."

The difficulty was to return to Mme. Paline's
house ; I was longing to do so, but how was I to accomplish it ? It was absolutely necessary to allow a
few days to elapse before the second visit, which now
seemed as perilous as the success of the first had
been complete. Depending upon some fortunate
meeting to renew my intercourse with these ladies,
I walked up and down the Rue Saint Sulpice ; and
on reaching No. 14 was seized with a most unaccountable trembling in the knees. At the hour when
the inhabitants of that neighborhood went to the
Luxembourg to breathe the evening air, I wandered
among the crowd, but cautiously, for the agitation of

my heart might have been read in my countenance.
On the third day after the great event I had not gone
ten steps into the garden—such things only happen
to me—when I found myself face to face with the
person whose keen sight I most dreaded. I mean
my dear Timoléon. He was gayer, franker, more
like a cavalier of the days of Louis XIII. than ever.

"Why, here is the little old man," he cried. "I
haven't seen you for a long time. What hole have you
been hiding in, my dear fellow?" Then drawing back
a step, "And in what a rig do I find you? nut-col-
ored pants, apple-green cravat, and curled hair!"

In fact, I had been foolish enough to go to the
hair-dresser's again. I tried to smile, nibbled my
cane, and perceiving that I should be compelled to
descend to falsehood if I wished to turn aside his
suspicions, replied: "Good heavens, I am working
very hard just now, am busy, and don't go out much.
But what a beautiful evening. Oh! a lovely evening."

"Little old man, little old man, you are going to
be married," he said, bursting into a fit of laughter.

I do not know what other pleasantries he added;
I did not hear them, for at that very moment, at ten
paces from us, the two ladies swept down the avenue
in the most imposing and elegant toilettes. I shivered from head to foot, and raising my hat with a
trembling hand, made my best bow.

"Do you know those princesses?" said Timoléon.
"Pâque Dieu, you are an epicure, my gentleman.
The youngest of the two goddesses, the daughter no
doubt, has incomparable legs."

If any one had publicly dealt me a blow in the
face I should have felt no keener suffering; and it
was my most beloved friend who had thus wounded
my honor. I drew myself up indignantly, and seizing him by the arm exclaimed: "Silence, silence, I
cannot endure these insults, these scandalous insinu-

ations. The ladies who have just passed are worthy
of all respect, both by their birth and rare attain-
ments."

I must have had a frightful expression of countenance as I said this, for I was really capable of brav-
ing every danger. Yet Timoléon was not very much
intimidated.

"But zounds! little old man, when people are so
desperately in love they give others warning. Come,
calm yourself. The young girl, on the contrary, has
horrible legs, she even has a wooden one—there, are
you satisfied? Made of old wood."

"Timoléon, I beg of you—I assure you I shall not
be able to contain myself."

"What can I do better? I told you made of old
wood. If you want proof, go to the museum about
three o'clock, and before the Rubens paintings you
will see the unfortunate girl mounted on a sort of
ladder with broad steps, from which she is copying
the head of a mustached individual in a cuirass.
Wait till the artist comes down to speak to her mother, who reads Lord Byron's poetry below; go up to
them, my friend, put on all your glasses, and you will
see that beside the moral virtues, this young person
has a leg—such as I have told you."

"If you add another word I shall break with you
forever. In the name of our old friendship I entreat
you to listen to me."

Yet I had vowed to keep everything to myself; but
it was necessary to convince him, to prove how false
was the judgment which, in his incorrigible heedlessness, he had passed upon them. I did not wish to
leave the shadow of a doubt in Timoléon's mind in
regard to Mme. Paline's respectability; my honor,
my dignity, were concerned in the matter—and I
opened my whole soul to him. At midnight we were
still talking, and a treaty of peace was signed.

This conversation produced a great effect upon

4

me. It was like a revelation of my moral state. In fact as I related my impressions they became clearer, grew more exact, all the confused emotions I had experienced for several days clustered together, were linked into each other, and I was terrified by the seriousness of my situation.

"You are desperately in love," cried Timoléon. "Sound trumpets; the little old man is pining for love!"

I defended myself as if the idea was sacrilege; it was impossible. And yet if it was true, if these symptoms did not deceive. Could I have within my heart, great Heaven! the germ of a passion!

From that time I tried to give an exact account of myself, I analyzed all my thoughts, discussed their nature, plunged into the secret depths of my soul, and thereby so greatly irritated this tiny spot, at first so insignificant, that on the day I returned to the Rue Saint Sulpice I had an angry sore—I loved. Was it the mother or the daughter? In, deed I could not have told; and the uncertainty increased my fears, for if I loved both I was the victim of a dishonest passion that might not be confessed. Into what hell was I plunged?

The cordiality of the welcome I received calmed me greatly, and was of immense benefit. Mme. Paline's mere presence was like a caress, a consolation. On seeing me, she eagerly held out her hand and uttered a joyous sigh, which was a hundred times more eloquent than a long speech. One would have said that she was expecting me. After an instant she murmured :

"We were afraid you would not come to see us again, Monsieur Babolain—yes, we really were. Esther was talking about it again this morning. Oh! I was wrong to tell you that—if my daughter should hear me!"

"Not see you again! oh! Madame!"

"Certainly: the world of art does not please every one; especially learned men who have the immense advantage of not allowing themselves to be blinded for any length of time by the often deceitful vividness of first impressions. Can we suppose that a man who is accustomed to trust only to his calculations can take pleasure in these artistic discussions, which are all pervaded with an unforeseen and often indiscernible feeling? A learned man must necessarily consider us frivolous beings, nervous to excess, impressionable to absurdity; he must judge our absence of formality, our somewhat peculiar manners, very severely—unless he is himself the most acute of observers, and unconsciously the most fastidious of artists.

She adjusted her curls with her beautiful hand, and the gauze upon the waist of her dress rose and fell several times very rapidly. It was enough to make me perceive that she was agitated, and I saw clearly that her last words applied to me.

"I am perhaps less brilliant than you think, Madame, but if—"

"I suppose you are jesting. Don't you believe I have either tact or shrewdness to enable me to judge of people?"

"If you would guide me a little, I should undoubtedly do much better."

She gave me a charming smile, and I felt I possessed in her a devoted friend.

It was in this delightful manner that my relations with the Paline ladies were definitely settled. How could I have remained insensible to the affectionate consideration, the attentions of every kind they condescended to bestow upon me? I soon felt more at ease, hazarded a few remarks, and mingled as well as I was able in the conversations I sometimes thought I understood, and they almost always approved of my words, saying: "That is just, very well thought, very well said ; that sums up the question admirably." I knew they manifested great indulgence, but it was this very indulgence, so new to me, that did me good. And then they consulted me, they confided a thousand things to me with the charming freedom of a friendship of ten years' standing. They asked about my headaches ; gave me a remedy for sore-throats to which I was subject. It sometimes seemed to me as if all these little attentions and sweet words were addressed to some other person whose place I was usurping. The poverty of my past life, the ludicrous peculiarities of my personal appearance, returned to my mind for a passing moment. "They think me better than I really am," I said to myself. "Have I not deceived them ; have I not been unconsciously playing a part? If they should perceive their error, oh ! God." I am unworthy of all this happiness—and yet if some day it should cease—I know not what vague ideas of the future; a hearthstone, a family, mingled with my fears.

How many times, after returning home in the evening, on finding myself alone, I have buried my face in my hands and wept to think of what they were doing for me. There was evidently a great deal of charity in their conduct, they had no reason for being so kind, they were even ignorant of the affection I felt for them, for I was very cautious in that respect, lest I should displease them.

Soon, not content with the numerous visits I paid to the Rue Saint Sulpice, I fell into the habit of going to the museum where the ladies spent a portion of the day ; I gave as a pretext the necessity of commencing my artistic education in good earnest. I had purchased a small glass with a single tube, which I easily concealed in my hand, so that I could see them at a long distance down the gallery. They were always dressed with a care and elegance I shall never meet with among other women. But what torture it caused me to walk across the slippery floor of that interminable gallery. I knew I was observed; I was alone in the very centre of that waxed wilderness, and a single slip might cause a catastrophe, the mere thought of which made me shudder. Would one believe that through feminine delicacy, consideration for my awkwardness, they pretended not to see me until I was within three paces of them. Then I walked on tiptoe that I might not disturb Esther in her work, exchanged a smile and shake of the hand with Mme. Paline, and moved on some little distance to take my station before the picture whose secrets I wished to analyze. It was always a Rubens, my friends' favorite master. Once there, I was happy. I felt that I was near them, and if I happened to turn my head, I saw the young girl upon her step ladder gazing at her palette with an inspired eye. What a mysterious depth there is in an artist's glance! She told me one day that the harmony of colors produced a species of intoxication, and that when before some of Rubens' pictures she experienced an emotion she was unable to subdue.

By what means was I to understand the cause of these emotions? And first—I wished to proceed methodically—what mysterious bond exists between a feeling and the juxtaposition of certain colors, the vibrations of the optic nerve, and the pleasant or painful sensation which results from them. There, as in music, there were numerical laws one might perhaps succeed in detecting, and deferring the theoretical study until later, I wished to submit to an experimental test. I concentrated my whole attention upon a little corner of the great picture, and called forth the emotions of my heart. That pink hue, I said to myself, is not there by accident, its effect certainly combines with that of the other bluish shade beside it. Both are probably modified by each other's vicinity; there is a sort of reciprocal exchange,

a fusion ; for if I draw back, the two tints are completely blended. But is it absolutely certain that one
touch is pink and the other bluish ? Is it not an
optical illusion, can I be already under the spell ? I
mounted a stool to examine the picture more closely,
and soon imagined infinite complications in the slightest touch, my sight became less distinct, everything
grew confused, mingled together, and the figures in
the painting seemed to be upside down.

How much learning, what prodigious calculations,
what marvellous combinations there are in a work of
art ! I put my glass back into my pocket, and, threatened with a violent headache, rejoined the ladies. " It
is bewildering," said I.

" Is it not beautiful, perfectly beautiful," the
young girl sometimes answered. Often also she slightly shrugged her shoulders, and said cavalierly : " Let
us alone, you don't know anything about it."

Decidedly it was impossible for me to explain
Mlle. Esther's character clearly. The love of art must
really have taken a very powerful hold upon her
mind : sometimes gay, careless, affectionate, she threw
herself into an arm chair, laughed continually, and
addressed a thousand jests to me ; sometimes she became grave and her large eyes remained fixed upon
vacancy. If any one spoke to her, she did not seem
to understand, moved impatiently, and turned her
head away, or else burst out laughing.

These oddities, whose effect Mme. Paline tried to
soften by her own unvarying kindness plunged me
into alternations of joy and anxiety ; but the more
difficult I found it to fathom this character, the more
eager I was to sound its depths. I summoned all
my critical faculties to my aid, studied the capricious
countenance of the young girl, her look, her gestures ;
I noted in my memory the minutest details of her
personal appearance—and each instant discovered
new attractions which enchanted me.

One day Mme. Paline, drawing me towards the window, said with her usual nobility of feeling and ease of manner :

" Come here, my dear friend, I see you are troubled ; what is the matter ? Confide in me, please push that footstool a little nearer, I will wager that Esther has been indulging in some freak—"

I would have sacrificed my little finger rather than confess the supreme importance I attached to the young artist's caprices, so I contented myself with an embarrassed smile.

" Ah ! well," said she, " I will open my heart to you ; I too need counsel. The affection and esteem I have for you can alone induce me to use such entire frankness—the subject is a very serious one."

" Good heavens ! what is it ? speak Madame. You do not doubt my devotion ? "

Her sole reply was to hold out her hand, then with a smile that agitated me greatly, she replied :

" A poor widow finds herself very much alone, especially when she suddenly perceives that the health, the life of her child are perhaps endangered."

My face doubtless expressed the anguish I felt, for the poor mother started in her turn as she looked at me :

" You have noticed it as well as I, have you not ?" she said. Do not deny it, oh ! do not deny it, you would not deceive me : I read your heart," and raising a handkerchief, even more richly embroidered than usual, to her beautiful eyes, she continued : " Oh ! God ! what hast Thou in store for us ? He too has seen that my Esther was drooping. My daughter, oh ! my beloved daughter, what will become of me without you ! Do you think her very ill ? "

" I have noticed nothing, I solemnly assure you, absolutely nothing."

" Be kind enough to treat me like a brave mother, my friend. The blow has fallen, what avails it to deceive me ? Let us speak lower, she is in the next room. Can I not perceive that her disposition has altered strangely during the last month or two, that the evil is increasing ? She vainly seeks to conceal her condition from me. You will tell me that she is an artist, that is, impressionable, sensitive to excess ; that the preoccupation of mind caused by her art must affect her temper ; that the refusal of the Exhibition to accept her great landscape must have exerted a great influence over her ; but she, who has always been so brave, would only have drawn fresh ardor from this rebuff; now you have seen that she has not touched a brush since, except to finish her superb copy of Rubens, and even that with how much effort ! How many times she has thrown herself into my arms, saying : 'Mother, I can do no more—I can do no more.' 'My love,' I replied, concealing my tears, 'you owe it to your own reputation to finish this copy.' You do not know, my friend, you cannot know, what treasures are concealed within the heart of that young creature of twenty. Alas ! alas ! she is too beautiful, too good for this world."

What infinite depths there are in maternal love ! How I understood the tears of my noble friend—how I sympathized with her sorrow ! Yet the first cause of this grief appeared to me to be somewhat ill-defined.

"Perhaps," said I with great caution, "perhaps you are alarming yourself unduly, dear Madame, the symptoms do not—"

"Do not go on, you would break my heart. Nothing can escape a loving mother. In spite of her efforts to conceal from me what she is suffering—for she seeks to conceal it from me, you understand, from me—do I not see her drooping, dying under the fatal action of some unknown mental torture ? She has lost her appetite, no longer takes pleasure in any-

thing, passes her best sketches with indifference.—
And her nights! Have I told you of her nights? I
really do not know, my head is so confused—her terrible nights! What is the cause of her nervous starts,
the incoherent words that escape her lips? And you
do not wish me to be terribly anxious? Ah! it is because you don't understand, or don't wish to understand."

"It is terrible. Good heavens! what is to be
done?" I cried.

"Ah! thanks, that is the right word. Yes, it is
terrible. I sometimes even ask myself whether I ought
to wish for her recovery." I shuddered at this mute
despair. "And undoubtedly for some too delicate,
too impressionable natures, it is a blessing to die
young. What man would know how to appreciate
her, where could I find a husband worthy of her?
Ah! surely it is better to die than to be exposed to
what I have suffered."

My eyes were full of tears, I longed to cry: "I
am the husband you seek; I am the man to devote
to her every hour of my life, to love, to adore her;
but besides not being sure that I was worthy of her,
I could find no appropriate words to express what I
felt, so I simply said:

"Do you fear any affection of the lungs?"

"I fear everything, my friend. At the present
time, the evil is mental I am sure. I know it by her
alternations of overwhelming sadness and wild gayety, by all the caprices which— Why, this very morning, I will tell you all, pardon me—this morning I entered her room to kiss her, and found her sitting in a
corner completely absorbed in reading a little book,
which was entirely unfamiliar to me. I went up to
her: 'What are you reading, my darling?' said I.
She held out the volume with the frank, graceful gesture you know—"

"Yes, yes."

"Where was I?   Oh, I looked at the book, it was a little treatise on arithmetic, she formerly used at boarding school.   I smiled and said. 'So you are beginning your old studies again, my dear.'   She threw herself into my arms and embracing me passionately, exclaimed: 'Science is so glorious, mother, so glorious.'"

It seemed as if every drop of blood flowed back to my heart, and I really do not know what incoherent words I summoned up strength to stammer. Mme. Paline had seized my hand and was searching my face with her anxious glance: "What is to be done, my friend, what is to be done?   How are we to apply a remedy to a disease of whose nature we are ignorant?   But hush! I hear a step, she is coming. And my eyes are red!   Be cautious and prudent, do not utter a word that could—"

I hastily rose and rushed towards the door; "it is impossible for me to stay," I cried.   "Excuse me— my class—impossible."   I crossed the dining-room and ante-chamber like a hurricane.

Mme. Paline followed me, saying:

"But what is the matter? You will come back to-morrow, this evening, will you not?"

When I reached the street I paused an instant, for my heart was beating so violently that I could not breathe, then took my course hap-hazard straight on, like a criminal pursued by remorse.

"I am the sport of a dream," I thought; I fancied I saw in Mme. Paline's terrible confidence a meaning which does not exist; I am wild, agitated by feverish dreams, mad with pride, and I cursed the fatal gift of analysis that murmured in my ear; "This young girl loves you, Babolain; do not refuse the evidence, consider the logical sequence of these details, whose result is perfectly clear."   And the poor

mother, who in her grief, sees nothing, perceives no
danger, does not suspect that she is betraying her
child's heart to me,—to me who adores her!

I took off my hat, my head was burning.

I struggled as well as I could against the intoxication which was gaining upon me, saying to myself :
" No, I am not made to secure the happiness of an
exceptional woman, an artist who will soon be famous,
and whom glory, fortune, and worldly successes are
awaiting. Is it not evident that I am—come let us
be frank—that I am too far beneath her ? " What
might happen when Esther at last opens her eyes,
and sees to what an illusion she has been a victim,
into what a snare I have made her fall ? All this is
shameful, abominable ; it is my place to foresee the
consequences, and resist if necessary. I will go
away, I will never see her again, and she will recover
from this incomprehensible folly. What matters my
career—I will return to the country— And yet
her love for me may perhaps be profound, inde-
structible.

VI.

Two days after, in spite of my resolutions, I was
ascending Mme. Paline's staircase. I had reflected
a great deal, and was now calm. What! upon a single word which might be interpreted in a thousand
different ways, I had built a whole romance, and it
had required two days of reflection to convince me
of my insanity. Of what use is it then to have a logical mind! Poor child, to love me !

Yet when I held in my hand the ribbon that served
as a bell-rope, I felt a slight tremor. Perhaps I was
not so entirely free from that ridiculous dream as I
had supposed. But even if I should be obliged to
leave them, do I not owe them a farewell and thanks

for the welcome they have given me? The door
opened and Mme. Paline appeared. She smiled as
she offered me her hand:

"My presentiment did not deceive me, I was expecting you. Speak low, Esther is in the studio. She
is a little better," she added.

"How glad I am, dear Madame.

"Yes, we have been talking together, she has returned to her work, and you will find her finishing
the sketch of a new composition. Oh! you will be
astonished. I do not know what is taking place in
her mind. It is not at all like her usual style, not at
all. She has given up all brilliancy of coloring; but
what nobility, what grandeur in the conception of the
subject! It is a Cain and Abel. The ardor with
which she enters into her work makes me tremble,
—you will say I am always anxious. Ah! my friend,
that is the destiny of mothers. The fact is, that
yesterday, at midnight, she was still sketching. Wait
until I knock; when she is composing, you know,
we must not disturb her too suddenly." And
with a series of little taps the good mamma murmured softly: "It is our friend Babolain, my darling,
can you receive us?"

The reply was favorable, and we entered. The
studio, as they called it, was unrecognizable: all the
useless ornaments that formerly hung on the walls
had been carried away; the young artist was working in an empty room. Upon a quantity of papers
scattered about the apartment were colossal heads
dashed off in an impetuous manner. Esther was
standing before her easel so absorbed in thought that
she did not even turn her head: "Ah! is it you?"
she said, and after a moment added: "Well, what do
you say to this?" Her mother, showing me the scattered papers, said:

"She has done all this in two days; isn't it an
unheard-of thing? You see the whole of the com-

position here—take a little rest, my dear, I beg of you, for my sake."

The young girl hastily passed her little hand through her hair :

"I will rest when I have finished my work."

"Of course ; but your health, my child ! Oh how noble that Abel is ! "

"Your health, Mademoiselle—the attitude of the Cain is really superb."

"Do you ever win in a lottery?" said Esther sneeringly.

"No, Mademoiselle, no ; I have never won any-thing in a lottery."

"I'm not surprised, for you have no luck. I ad-mit that my Abel has a fine contour, amplitude, a lofty bearing."

"He is magnificent, my daughter, he is bewilder-ing."

"He really isn't bad ; I hit upon him at the first effort ; but to make amends, my Cain Monsieur ad-mires is good for nothing : it is just Cirbec's style."

"Oh ! pray, darling, pray be careful—"

"You are too severe, Mademoiselle— Will the picture be a large one ? "

"More than life size ; do you suppose I intend to make a design for the cover of a song or a snuff-box ? "

Then she looked at me with a desperate earnest-ness that greatly intimidated me : "It is the expres-sion of the face that troubles me," she murmured, "I have my idea, but cannot produce it. I am seek-ing—seeking." She approached her mother without taking her eyes from me, and spoke to her in a low tone.

"Oh ! my darling. But I shall never dare— Do you know what Esther said to me, my dear Monsieur Babolain ? Pray do not refuse her. My daughter has just been struck by a certain expression upon

your face—it is just what she has been seeking for
ever since yesterday—would you be kind enough to
stand still one moment; long enough to make a
memorandum—to take a rough sketch?"

I thought at first that they were making fun of
me, and stood stupidly without answering, waiting until the joke should become clearer.

"If Monsieur will not do me this little service,"
said the young artist pouting, "he is perfectly free to
act as he pleases."

"Mademoiselle! I really thought you were making fun of me. Do you actually want—yet people
have very often reminded me that I was not handsome."

"It is not a question of beauty, but expression."

"Do what she asks, I beg of you," whispered the
mother, then resuming her usual tone: "Esther is
right, my dear Monsieur. Your face possesses an
expression, a character—particularly the profile. See,
my dear, what firmness there is in the flat parts." I
was resigned, but greatly excited. "Stand on that
little footstool; that's right. Don't stir, my dear
friend—yes, that is it. How kind and obliging you
are! Turn your head a little more to the left. Look
at the nail in that corner." All this was said very
rapidly, and I performed what they told me to do as
well as I could.

"Bravo!" cried Esther, clapping her little hands
with childish joy, "there is my work. At least, they
shall not say it is stencil work."

The artist took a sheet of paper, seized a bit of
crayon, and a scratching sound as it passed over the
paper immediately became audible. She bit her
scarlet lips, bent her head forward, and half closed
her eyes, or with her little finger coquettishly raised,
effaced useless lines.

The constraint I imposed upon myself was so
great, I made such violent muscular efforts to remain

motionless, that the drops of perspiration began to roll down my forehead.

"Oh! if you move, take your leave of this world." There was an irresistible charm in the tones of her voice. "Do you know that you are an excellent man, Monsieur Babolain?" she added with a blending of diffidence and affected benevolence that enchanted me.

"I really dared not impose this task upon you, al-though I wanted to."

"You are a child, my dear; do you take Monsieur for a plebeian? Come, don't say any more such fool-ish things. He knows artists well enough, is too much of an artist himself."

"Oh! Madame, pray!"

"I beg your pardon, my friend, I know what I am talking about— He is too much of an artist himself to find so simple a request strange."

"Dear me, mamma, a young girl has her little fears; one is not a termagant."

"Will you be quiet, you rogue, people will have a pretty opinion of you!"

"A poor opinion! oh! pray—can you suppose" —I murmured, trying to smile.

"But don't stir, keep your eyes fixed on your nail —Mamma, Monsieur is looking away."

The bursts of laughter escaped her lips like the warbling of a bird. Her gayety had an aggressive quality and exasperated you deliciously. She gave herself up to it completely, one might say she was passionately gay: her figure was convulsed; her eyes half closed. Through the narrow opening in the waist of her dress one could see the heaving of her neck and chest. Her little mouth opened so wide that one could distinguish her rows of white teeth glittering in their tiny apartment, which was as fresh and bright as a wet rose. Meantime Mme. Paline was saying with her usual tact and gentleness:

"Calm yourself, my love ; will you never be rational?   Really I am confused—excuse her, Monsieur Babolain, it is nervousness— Oh! dear, oh! dear, she cannot control it."

Perched upon my little stool as an angler sits on his narrow rock, I might well suffer at the thought of being so ridiculous; but I was not angry with the young girl for her mad continual laughter.   On the contrary, there was something frank and honest about it which touched me.   With a stranger she would have found strength to put a constraint upon herself and be polite.   Therefore there was between her and myself a bond whose power she felt without daring to acknowledge it.   And suppose her charming impertinence was only an attempt to conceal the truth? Who knows!   It is so difficult to read what is passing in her mind.   This strange gayety was not natural; was it really at me she was laughing so heartily?   I was only half convinced of it, and in every case I experienced a sort of pleasure in feeling myself a victim of her frolicsome mirth; I joyfully submitted to the little suffering which brought me nearer to her.

We feel pain from the needle that enters our flesh, but we sometimes enjoy it while watching the hand which pushes it in, and would not wish to be rid of the needle if at the same time the hand must be removed—

"Oh! how pleasant it is to laugh," said Esther after a moment's pause.   " You will excuse me Monsieur Babolain, won't you?   There, now I am quiet again, now I'll set to work.   Will you give me the expression if you please? "

" What expression?   I—"

" That's a droll question.   You have just killed your brother, haven't you? "

I instantly remembered Cain.   "Oh! yes, pardon me, Mademoiselle, I have killed my brother. Ha, ha!—the figment is a little—"

"Well, after this murder you can't look as if you were stringing pearls; that nail is your brother; look at it in horror and bewilderment. A baby two weeks old would understand that."

I could not tell how distressing the grimace she wanted was to me, yet I set about making it with the utmost possible good will. After an instant she suddenly exclaimed:

"Mamma, I can't do anything with that coat, that white collar, that blue cravat." I shuddered. "The costume is so commonplace that it takes away all my strength."

"That is true, my darling; let us see, what could we devise to prevent it? Your sketch is very bold, my child. Ah! if Monsieur Babolain would allow me to throw the large white cloth over his shoulders. What do you think of that? By arranging it a little—"

Esther's face suddenly brightened. "Oh! that is it, yes, certainly. But where is the white cloth?"

"In the dining-room, over the preserves. I will go and get it," murmured Mme. Paline leaving the room.

We were alone together: it seemed to me as if Esther's face was suddenly divested of a mask. She cast down her eyes and said with an air of embarrassed modesty: "You are not angry with me on account of my gayety just now. Yet, I am not malicious. I assure you, there is no need of thinking me more foolish than I am. I have my little freaks, I know very well—in short, if I have caused you pain, I beg your pardon." She looked at me very sweetly with an expression of kindness. There was more than kindness in the glance.

"Do not say such things, I beg of you," I said in my turn. I wanted to throw myself down at her feet. "I know my deficiencies; I know how offensive they are— Continue to make a little fun of me;

if you did not, it would seem as if you were longing to."

I was so deeply agitated that I scarcely noticed
Mme. Paline, who had brought in the white cloth,
and was already preparing to arrange it over my
shoulders. I was thinking, are not these singular
manners which fools cannot clearly interpret, a proof
of the most angelic frankness? Why have I failed to
understand this? Could I have lost my common
sense in consequence of wishing to explain everything by analysis and logic? Could my mind already
have become so vitiated by the theoretical study of
phenomena, that I was no longer able to distinguish
the real tenderness under these apparent follies?
Could science have withered my heart? She too is
agitated, she knows I am watching her, that each
glance of mine is like the blow of a scalpel which
can lay bare some fibre of her heart. And if afterwards—oh God! I am reasoning falsely.

"Why do you cast down your eyes, Monsieur
Babolain, you have lost a ten-cent piece."

And if afterwards, to-morrow perhaps, she should
say : " Ah, well ! dissimulation is no longer possible.
Enough of trials for you, enough of constraint for
me, let us belong to each other." If she should say
this to me, should I dare to accept—should I be worthy of it? Should I dare to blight her divine artless-
ness by contact with my analytical skepticism? I pitied myself—I found myself too strong.

Meantime Esther was sketching, sometimes im-
petuously, sometimes with care. Suddenly she turned pale, rose, snatched the sheet of paper upon
which she had been working, crushed it in her little
hands, and threw it into the middle of the room with
the fragments of the crayon.

"There, that is all, I have finished—I thank you ;
I have what I want," she said to me, and threw herself upon the cushions of a sofa that stood near.

Mme. Paline hastily went forward, and I sprang towards her, although somewhat embarrassed by the huge cloth in which I was wrapped.

" My child, my daughter, what is the matter, my dear ? "

" Mademoiselle, are you ill ? "

" Come, my beautiful darling, I am here, what is the matter ? Tell your mother, you will drive me to despair."

" Nothing is the matter, nothing, leave me."

We could not see her face, which was turned towards the wall, but we could see her clenched hand rubbing the cushions, while her foot tapped the floor incessantly.

" Let me venture to suggest a glass of water with a little orange flower, Mademoiselle."

" For Heaven's sake hush ! you will give me a nervous attack ; your voice sets my teeth on edge—sets my teeth on edge."

" Leave us, my friend," said Mme. Paline, " I do not understand this, but your presence agitates her —I perceive she is on the point of bursting into tears. Poor dear, poor love ! " she added.

I divested myself of the cloth, took my hat, and reached the door. But when I had crossed the threshold, I paused an instant, I could not make up my mind to leave her in such a critical condition.

Almost immediately Mme. Paline said in an irritated voice, " Well, what is the meaning of this nonsense ? "

" He sets my teeth on edge, that is all," replied the young girl with perfect calmness. " Tell me, mother, did you know that the sofa was ripped ? "

" Yes, Cirbec did it the other evening when he sat down."

VII.

So I set her teeth on edge—my mere presence had been the cause of this—I was an unhappy wretch, a Pariah! Had I not irritated my companions all my life? I set her teeth on edge, she could not endure the sound of my voice, my person was odious to her. And yet had she not an hour before asked pardon for her jests, had she not said to me: "I am neither foolish nor malicious." Did I not remember the loving gentleness of her voice, the almost tender expression of her glance? Was the irritation of the nerves I caused her real? The calmness with which she had spoken of it was at least strange. And that way of cutting short all explanations by remarking that the sofa was ripped, what was I to think of it? Did she know I was still there behind the door, and wish to subject me to a fresh trial?

I could not close my eyes all night. After having tossed about for several hours, I lighted my lamp and opened Dr. Virey's treatise upon women. I had read and re-read this physiological work, covered its margins with notes, and I must say that from these irrefutable statistics, these scientific documents, these luminous observations, I had obtained certain unknown quantities of great value. But now, like people who, after having cheated their hunger by reading a cook book, would give, at six o'clock in the evening, all the culinary treatises in the world for a little cutlet cooked to a nicety, I found Dr. Virey's book, which had been a most constant friend, dry and barren.

About nine o'clock in the morning I received a little note from Mme. Paline; it contained these few words: "A terrible crisis; do not come." At first I imagined that the poor child was dead, and kissed the note.

I could now account for my painful sleeplessness;

could I sleep when she was suffering? Had we not a mysterious and powerful influence over each other? She had vainly sought to escape from it, and conceal its effects, poor darling! No, no, I did not set her teeth on edge, I did more: I tortured her heart.

Half an hour after, I was in the Rue Saint Sulpice seeking in the aspect of the house some visible trace of this terrible crisis. How could these old stones remain insensible and preserve their usual appearance at such a moment! I approached the threshold of their dwelling, and suddenly fled. To merely expose her to the sight of me was to make her incur the greatest danger! How had I been imprudent, selfish enough to come here!

My heart beat violently, and I wandered through the streets, experiencing however a species of consolation, in suffering at the same time that she was, in taking my share in this horrible crisis.

I know not how it happened, but I soon found myself in the great gallery of the museum before the Rubens pictures she loved so much. Several artists were working as usual without seeming to suspect that Esther was not there. The paintings by the great masters seemed to have lost their brilliancy of coloring; a veil of melancholy was spread over the gallery, and among the various ladders and stools I wondered which were the ones she had used.

Towards evening, unable to restrain myself any longer, I resolutely ascended the staircase leading to the ladies' apartments, but in spite of my persistence was not admitted, and on the following day and the next day after that, still had the same ill-success. I was in despair, and said to myself: "It is over, it is really over, I cannot go back again since they do not wish to see me." The idea of leaving Paris returned to my mind, but the thought now caused me a pang very different from the one I had felt in the past; I could no longer reason, give an account of myself, see my mental condition clearly.

The third day, as I was making a final attempt to enter, I met Esther's mother on the staircase. "You here, Monsieur?" said she with evident emotion. Her usual noble bearing had acquired a grave and imposing dignity which overwhelmed me. It seemed as if I was about to appear before a justly irritated judge; I murmured:

"I was so anxious that I did not have courage— how is she?"

"Better, thank you; but let us go up if you please; an explanation between us has become inevitable, let us go up, Monsieur."

I followed her into a little dark room, and Mme. Paline, after carefully closing the doors, seated herself in a chair, and raised her handkerchief to her eyes, while the sound of ill-suppressed sobs became audible!

"I surprise you, do I not?" said she. "You are asking yourself the cause of my grief. Oh! unfortunate young man, why did you ever cross the threshold of this home?"

"Do not weep, Madame, I implore you." I was trembling and dared not look her in the face. "Oh! God, what have I done?"

"What has he done? You have made two lonely defenceless women wretched, Monsieur. You have—"

"But how is that possible when I would give my life to make you happy?"

"Whether the mischief was voluntary or not, matters little: and besides," she added with a heart-rending sigh, "we will not go back to that, we will not go back to that. The only thing left for me to do is to appeal to your honor, your integrity. Go, young man, go; put the world between us," and amid her sobs, while with her extended arm she seemed to thrust me back, she faltered: "Esther—Esther loves

you ! Do you understand what anguish it costs me
to make such confessions? Do you understand what
strength, what maternal love I need, to save me from
dying of shame? Oh ! go, I implore you. You see
I implore you upon my knees when I might com-
mand ; I trample under foot every feeling of pride ;
but it seems as if my head was confused ; I have no
longer the strength, no I have no longer the strength
to struggle. If the smallest remnant of kindness
still lingers in your soul, fly Monsieur, save my poor
child."

She had placed her arm on my shoulder, and was
on the point of throwing herself at my feet, while
with tears she repeated : " Save her, save her." At
last, overwhelmed by emotion, she sank fainting in my
arms.

" Let me speak, Madame, in Heaven's name let
me speak," said I, making the most tremendous exertions to replace Mme. Paline in her arm chair, for
I was by no means strong. " Calm yourself, listen to
me—the truth must be confessed, however painful the
avowal may be. I too—I—pray calm yourself." I
timidly slapped the hands of the unhappy mother,
who soon opened her eyes ; then I continued :

" Yes, I should have concealed it from you all my
life, I concealed it even from myself, but the hour
has come ; I must speak."

" Well, speak."

" I love—love, I adore Mademoiselle Esther."

" Monsieur ! "

" And my life—oh ! I am sincere ; all my life
shall be devoted to her."

" Do not go on," she said loudly, then resuming her
former low tone, continued slowly and bitterly : " He
does not even perceive the insult contained in his audacious proposal ; no, no, he does not understand it.
Oh ! Lord, give me strength to be calm. Do you not
know that an ill-assorted union, far from repairing

the evil you have done, would render it still more irreparable. The language you use Monsieur, I heard
long ago, and paid for the folly of giving it credence
by a whole life of sacrifice. My husband also implored me, threw himself at my feet. He too said to
me : 'My name and my life are yours.' I was young
and beautiful, and I, a Martignac-Corbon, married
this notary, who took it all as a very simple matter,
having paid for it with his money. My daughter and
I are not rich, I say it without shame, but our honor,
our independence, are all the dearer to us ; and you
may be sure our souls are too lofty to be dazzled by a
fortune whose charms you undoubtedly exaggerate.
You have to deal with two artists, Monsieur, and two
women of aristocratic birth."

For the first time for many days I remembered
that I was rich, and was only the more dazzled by the
greatness of soul, the haughty disinterestedness of
these two noble creatures.

So that which facilitates the happiness of other
men was causing my irreparable loss. For an instant I hated my uncle of Beaugency, whose legacy
thus destroyed my life. If, at that moment, I had
had my whole fortune in a portfolio, with what joy
I would have thrown it out of the window! But this
was not the only obstacle. I was not of noble birth,
my name was of the humblest, it was not allowable
for them to cast aside the prejudices of their rank.
My face probably expressed deep sorrow, for Mme.
Paline said more mildly :

" Perhaps fate has done all ; I will still esteem
you ; but go, go quickly."

" If there are any means— Leave one ray of hope,
Madame. Yes, it is true, I have wealth. I did not
think of it, but it is not so difficult to ruin one's self;
I can give away everything, and thus buy the happiness of being poor."

" Don't say such foolish things, noble as they may

appear. People do not resign an inheritance legally and honestly transmitted, any more than they renounce the honorable name their parents leave them. It cannot, must not be done. Would you have it supposed that the fortune you have inherited was acquired by dishonest means, and that you blush to accept it? Would not people see in your conduct either an undue pride, or the proof of a shame in which you wish to have no share?"

"Yet if I owed no one anything except myself, your daughter's hand must be deserved, I feel that fully. Yes, I perceive that at this moment I am still unworthy of her. She will be famous at some future time, illustrious, and the wealth her talent will secure will be a hundred times greater than mine. I too will labor to make myself a name. There are admirable tasks to attempt in the sciences. If I have not a brilliant intellect, I am at least accustomed to work; and one is very strong, Madame, when happiness depends upon the success of his efforts." I pressed both hands to my head, and could say no more. I heard the excellent woman murmur, "How he loves her, good heavens, how he loves her!" She soon continued, in a choking voice:

"Say no more, in Heaven's name; let me reflect; do not compel me to reply; your sentiments touch me, the eloquence of your heart agitates me; at this moment I am no longer mistress of my feelings. Ah! doubtless if I listened only to them, I should tell you to hope. What to me are the prejudices of wealth and rank! But I am a mother; I have the charge of a soul; I have no right to authorize my child to commit a folly for which the world would never pardon her; to openly defy the opinions of the society in which she ought to move. Say no more, you would perhaps persuade me. Oh! I thought I was stronger, I—I—Great heavens! I hear my daughter's step, she is coming. Open the door, do not let her suspect

anything, oh! my friend, do not let her suspect anything ; she would die."

Esther entered almost immediately. She was very
calm, and was humming a little tune with the most
perfect unconcern. How much self-control and firmness she possessed, what delicacy and dignity she
displayed in this apparent indifference. Shall I ever
reach the height of your lofty soul, noble girl ?

"You look pale, Monsieur Babolain," she said,
"it is doubtless owing to your blue cravat. Nothing
makes one look so pale as blue."

" My cravat—" I murmured in my confusion, " oh
yes, the blue—do you think my cravat ugly, Mademoiselle ! "

" Why no, not ugly, and you—"

Perfectly incapable of sustaining any conversation, I was about to withdraw, when Mme. Paline
turning towards me with solemn majesty, said :

" Well, my dear friend, offer your honest hand to
my beloved daughter, perhaps she will not refuse it."
And added in a lower tone : " If I am doing wrong,
may God judge my motives."

VIII.

Some time after the events related in the last
chapter, an elegant carriage drew up noisily before
one of the court-yards rarely to be met with in the
Rue Vaugirard, and a little man, awkward enough in
his manners, but elaborately dressed and with dain-
tily curled hair, alighted and offered his hand to two
very beautiful ladies.

The little man was myself; one of the two ladies
was my future mother-in-law, the other my adored
Esther, whom I was going to marry. My delight was
so great that I burst into a laugh every minute, tore
the ladies' laces, or stepped upon their skirts. To

think that I was going to be united by the closest
ties to these two ladies who were so proud and imposing in their regal costume !

"Isn't the first appearance charming ? " said Mme.
Paline as soon as she was out of the carriage ; " this
entrance between two pavilions, the trees, of whose
foliage one can catch a glimpse—I am sure it will
suit us perfectly."

We entered. "Is the ground floor still to let, my
child ? " continued my mother-in-law, addressing the
young woman who performed the duties of *concièrge.*
" Very well, then show it to us."

"Yes, show it to us," I repeated. I had an inde-
scribable desire to talk, to make myself conspicuous.
While the *concièrge* was shaking her bunch of keys
and noisily opening the doors, Mme. Paline, looking
around through her eye-glasses, said carelessly : "This
isn't bad ; this is the little drawing-room, where is the
large one ? "

" Madame is in the large drawing-room. The
little one is farther on, at the side of the dining-
room."

" Your large drawing-room is by no means enormous, my pretty child ; what did you say, twenty-four
feet long ?   Ah ! "

As for me, being unable to imagine that such a
magnificent suite of apartments could ever become
mine, I but feebly concealed my admiration.   Esther
said smiling :

" Pray hush, you seem as if you had always occupied a fourth floor at Pantin. This suite is reasonably handsome, nothing more."

" After all, I see only four sleeping-rooms," continued Mme. Paline.

" There are two more extra chambers, a lumber-
room, and several closets which can be used as bed-
rooms."

" Is there a stable and coach-house ? "

" No, Madame."

" That happens just right," said I gayly.

" You can't keep still a moment," murmured Esther, while my mother-in-law, after casting a glance of displeasure at me, continued with a very sly smile :

" Undoubtedly it will do very well if I sell my horses, but I am not at all decided about it."

This jest, whose sole object was to deceive the *concièrge*, wounded me deeply, for I always had an instinctive horror of falsehoods whether small or great; but I soon thought no more about it ; I was too deeply in love to search into anything. I never left my future wife, I feasted my eyes upon her every gesture, my ear was always strained to catch her most unimportant words, and if she chanced to brush against me, I was as grateful as if she had done me a signal service. Moreover, it was impossible for me to analyze my sensations, the time was actually wanting. I was obliged to run to the notary's, accompany the ladies to the upholsterer's, the fancy-goods stores — I accepted everything, found everything perfect. Nothing was too handsome or too dear, provided the selection was made quickly. And then my ideas about my income were of the vaguest ; at times I was even induced to believe my resources inexhaustible, and thus I met half way the scruples the ladies were sometimes kind enough to expresss :

" I beg of you," said I, " to do me the favor to choose for me. My taste is not good, and I should commit some folly. The worst thing that can happen will be that we shall be ruined together."

" My children," said Mme. Paline when we had re-entered the carriage, " all this is very well, but we must act prudently : economy is a necessity to everybody. Now these apartments we have just seen are suitable." , .

" I think them really princely," I observed.

"A thing may be princely and yet be only suitable. I admit they are large. Esther, do you remember your cousin Madame Salvain's large drawing-room?"

"No, mamma."

"I am surprised—although in fact you were too young to recollect it. What a charming drawing-room the de Salvain's was! But no matter. These rooms are not bad, but the price seems rather—to be sure, I shall pay a part of the rent. You know, my friend, we agreed upon that."

I felt wounded. Was this pitiful question of money to keep coming back every instant? If it could only be smothered once for all. "Madame," said I, "let all that pass, I beg of you."

"Oh! I am inflexible. If I consent to live with you, my children, it is on condition of being entirely independent, and consequently of paying my share of the rent."

"We must put mediæval paintings on glass into all the windows," said Esther, whose eyes were sparkling; "then in the dining-room an immense sideboard loaded with chased dishes and goblets. I want an organ in the drawing-room, oh! I do want an organ."

"Nothing is more simple, Mademoiselle."

"Yes, of course, but I want a large organ that will reach to the ceiling. I will paint the ceiling myself; it is splendid to compose."

Mme. Paline looked at us with an expression of infinite affection, and said, smiling :

"Ah! my poor children, I see very plainly that you will do something foolish if I don't interpose. It is necessary to calculate in arranging one's style of living, and you forget that the rent of these apartments is three hundred louis. It is enormous, especially in this locality."

"But we are in the centre of the Faubourg Saint Germain," said Esther.

· "The centre of the Faubourg Saint Germain," I repeated mechanically.

Yes, that is true, I speak of the rent because it is my duty to calculate for you; if it were not for that —I don't think the rooms dear on any other account."

"It seems to me that they are relatively cheap— what do you think, Mademoiselle?"

"I think it a mere nothing; they are a godsend: that drawing-room twenty-four feet long, and the immense chamber at the back which will make a delightful studio."

"As for that," observed my mother-in-law, "the chamber at the back is of inestimable value to us— no, really, three hundred louis is not a large price."

"I believe the *concierge* is mistaken, mamma; it is worth more."

"In that case we must make haste," said I. "The opportunity should not be allowed to escape; what do you think of it, Madame?"

"We must reflect, my children; I admit, however, that we shall find nothing so well adapted to our wants."

"Pray let me hire these rooms which Mademoiselle Esther likes so well."

"Ah! how much trouble I shall have in making you economical; very well."

"Suppose we go and look at organs, mother."

"Little goose, you know very well we have an appointment about the camels' hair shawls. Meantime, you might go and see the landlord, my friend, since somewhat against my will you have made up your mind—I think it would be well to close the bargain immediately. From there you will join us at the upholsterer's. Don't lose any time, for you know we must choose the silver at five o'clock. How many things to do, good heavens! without counting the dressmaker! Come, let us go; good-by till we meet again."

" Don't be long," murmured Esther, bowing to me
with a delicious smile.

She had winning ways which made me almost wild.

I believe that during the few days preceding my
marriage I actually had the vertigo ; I was hurried,
along and certainly had not the free use of my analytical faculties.

One fine evening in the drawing-room in the Rue
Vaugirard, which was still destitute of furniture and
sonorous as a cathedral, a notary in a white cravat,
seated before a small table, opened a large white
book, and by the light of two candles read our marriage contract, while the ladies whispered together
gayly ; then a large quill pen was passed around and
each person affixed his signature. Mine was so small
and scratchy—I wrote in that way—that among the
bold flourishes of the others it looked as if it had
introduced itself by stratagem, like an unexpected
guest who appears just at the dinner hour.

A quarter of an hour after, while Esther, Timoléon, Cirbec, Prudent de la Sarthe, the notary, and
three or four other friends were engaged in some discussion, I know not what, Mme. Paline drew me into a
corner and said :

" My dear friend, I did not wish to diminish the
generosity of your conduct by attracting every one's
attention to it. You have just made by the contract
a settlement of one hundred and twenty thousand
francs upon my beloved daughter : it is acting like a
gentleman, my dear boy. Among persons whose
hearts are in the right place a pressure of the hand
is sufficient, is it not ? "

" I was afraid it might wound you," I murmured,
and in fact I had feared that they might be offended
by my somewhat cavalier method of throwing a fortune at their heads. Was it not saying rudely : " I
am rich, you are poor." It was very embarrassing.

" In accepting everything as a matter of course,

my dear friend, I am giving you the highest proof of
my esteem. From any one else—ah! I should have
indignantly refused. As for Esther, she knows nothing about business matters, the beautiful darling, and
I assure you she did not understand a word of all
that Greek; but when she learns what it means I
foresee a storm, she is so haughty and sensitive."

"Yet it is very natural; I should have liked to
give her everything."

"Noble heart! Bear her first outburst gently,
my dear son. She will doubtless be grateful to you
in the end; but you have really played a hazardous
game."

My heart overflowed when towards midnight we
took leave of the ladies, who, since the evening before, had occupied two rooms of the large suite of
apartments. "It troubles me very much to see you
camping out in this way; you must be very uncom-
fortable," I said to them.

"Oh! no, no," replied Esther smiling, "besides,
the upholsterer has promised to make haste; will you
come to breakfast to-morrow?"

Some half unpacked boxes were strewn around
the ante-chamber, which was dimly lighted by a lamp
without a shade. Our feet caught in the handfuls of
straw that no one had thought of sweeping away;
the notary almost fell down.

"Do you know that your future wife is charming?" said Timoléon, when he found himself alone
with me in the street. "Really charming,—refined,
intelligent, witty, and rich to boot." I pressed my
friend's arm, not daring to reply. "And her mother?" he added.

"Oh! my dear Timoléon, when you know her
you will see what a choice nature she has. She be-
longs to a noble family: my mother-in-law is one of
the Martignac-Corbons, the younger branch—an artist like her daughter, but less famous of course.

No, you see, Timoléon, I am too happy—a little too
happy. If I had time to think of it I should be
frightened, but I don't think of it, consequently—"

"Consequently you are not afraid. Brave Babolain! Ah! I'm confoundedly glad of what has befallen you. Who would have said ten years ago
that you would some day—for my part, I would have
bet you would remain a bachelor."

"Yes, it is unheard-of, it is a dream, for between
ourselves — you know me well enough to be able
to judge of me—between ourselves, there is nothing attractive about me; on the contrary, I am
what people call a queer fellow. You remember at
college? And at the normal school, oh! Good
heavens! they were not entirely wrong. Ah! well, in
spite of all that—"

"You are the best of men, little old man."

"Come, come, let's be serious and speak to me as
to a brother: what reason can Esther have for loving
me, for she—it is true, my friend, she does; we are
making a—love match! I utter the word foolishly,
like a simpleton, don't I? My lips are not formed
for such expressions, and they catch in passing. Any
one but you would smile to hear me say such things.
You have never given me a greater proof of affection
than this evening, by sparing me the jests that would
have caused me deep pain. At heart, you see, I am
very sensitive; but as sensibility doesn't suit the
character of my face, I harden myself and hide my
feelings a little under an assumed air of unconcern.
I will make her happy, you shall see: my head is full
of plans. To a genius like my wife the presence of
a slower, more practical mind, will not perhaps be a
bad thing: there must be an equilibrium maintained
in life: imagination needs to be supported by analysis and critical judgment. Of course I am inferior
to Esther, oh! I don't deceive myself. Come, Timoléon, you have often been a little hard upon me, I'm

6

not reproaching you in the least, but I remember you have unintentionally caused me a great deal of pain. I had no other friend than you, you know; I loved you so much, and—in short, let us say no more about it; we have been good friends: do you remember when you came to see me in the infirmary at the school? Well, will you be one of my family now? You will advise me, you will be my brother. It shall not prevent your making fun of me a little, only do it in a low tone, won't you, on account of the ladies. We will forget the past. Let me embrace you."

From the chaos and confusion of the last hours I spent upon this earth as a bachelor, it is impossible for me to regain any distinct impression. The night before my marriage I found myself in the middle of the Jardin des Plantes, leaning upon the railing that surrounds the bears' den, and murmuring passionately: "Esther, my Esther, how happy I will make you! If you only knew how I love you, oh! if you only knew!" But alas! it was impossible for her to know, since it was only far away from her, hidden in some corner, that I dared to express my tenderness in words.

Yet on the morning of the great day, when I arrived in full dress my *fiancée* said:

"Why, Mister bridegroom, look at yourself in the glass, you are not pale, you are green."

I thought I perceived that she uttered the pleasantry to conceal her embarrassment. Diffidence sometimes displays itself so strangely, I know what it is. "I am so happy, Mademoiselle," I answered. It was a stupid reply—I thought of it afterwards—for happiness does not necessarily paint itself upon the countenance in greenish hues.

"Let us make haste," said Mme. Paline, "we must not keep people waiting, my children, Esther, my son, I shall never have the strength to endure so many different emotions. Let us go alone in the

carriage, my friend; let my daughter be mine a few
moments longer, I beg of you, and then—"

" And then we shall be less crowded," added Esther gayly. Although I feel a little ashamed of it, I
will frankly confess that this ceremony in which all
divine and human pomp united to wed—I quote the
words of the priest who married us—to wed art to
science, was a terrible ordeal to me. How could I
elevate my soul when I was shivering, cowering in
one corner of a gilded arm chair, face to face with
a crowd of people, and that huge devil of a beadle
three yards high seemed to be always on the point of
bursting into a laugh ?

As the splendors of the day slowly unfolded, a
new terror took possession of me. I had never dared
to openly display my tenderness, which had consequently swelled my heart all the more, so that I perceived with dread the approach of a moment when an
outburst would take place which I should be wholly
unable to control. When we should be alone together, what course of action was I to pursue ? Must she
not doubt my love ? After all, nothing betrayed the
feeling I had for her. Poor dear Esther! What
anxiety, what fears, perhaps, might have lurked in a
soul at once too proud and too timid to confess its
weakness.

But what joy we should experience when the
hour for mutual confidence struck; when we could tell
each other the thousand delicious little tortures that
had preceded the divine outburst of emotion !

At two o'clock in the morning, the entertainment
being nearly over, I walked noiselessly towards the
large apartment we were henceforth to occupy together. To brighten and dry the room which had
long been unused, the servants had lighted a crack-
ling fire, before which my wife was seated, watching
the flames and warming her little satin boot. At the
noise of my entrance she turned her head : " Oh !

is it you," she said with an unaccountable pout, has everybody gone?"

Naturally as the question was asked, I shuddered.

"Yes," said I, "yes, everybody, my"—I did not know what to call her, the moment was a solemn one, the slightest awkwardness might produce incalculable consequences. For greater security I did not finish my sentence; and slowly approached her with short quick steps, shaking and trembling like a child who does not know his lesson.

"Why do you keep coughing so," she said looking steadily at me.

"I don't know; it is nothing, thank you; I will attend to it."

"Oh! if it is a habit, you need not put yourself to any trouble."

I scarcely understood what she was saying to me, for I was suddenly overwhelmed by a strange transport. It seemed as if a great longing for love, which had been slumbering within me since my childhood, now burst forth. I knelt before the young wife whose heart was to give mine a home, and taking both her hands, bent my head and wept. I know not what I said amid my tears, which, far from becoming exhausted, flowed more and more freely.

At last I raised my head and cried: "Esther, my beloved wife!" while I felt impatiently in both skirts of my coat to find my handkerchief, which I needed to wipe my face and clean my glasses dimmed by my tears.

"You will forgive me for crying like a schoolboy; I cannot help it, I had a great many things to say to you but I can't remember them. You must not misjudge me, I do everything so awkwardly that people might misunderstand—I am weeping for joy."

"Yes, but other people would suppose I had been beating you, to see you in such a condition." She said this in an affectionate tone, "I am not in the least vexed. All this means that you are fond of me, does it not my dear? Well then—"

It was the first time she had ever called me dear.

"You will be indulgent, my own Esther. You— you see I am trembling in the most absurd way, I am so afraid of not finding the right words to tell you I love you; so afraid of awkwardness in caressing your beautiful hands and luxuriant hair. Will you let me kiss them? You cannot know how beautiful you are?" She tapped her little foot on the floor with a smile. " It is your beauty that awes me, and your intellect too. To say to myself : I have a wife who is an artist; intoxicated with ideal beauty—she will permit me to perceive the treasures of her heart—thoughts, feelings, everything shall be shared between us. I have made wonderful savings of tenderness since I have been in this world, my darling. You shall see, you shall see. I am addressing you so familiarly. It does not annoy you?"

" Not much, when we are alone ; but when other people are present—"

" Yes, yes, oh ! of course. How good you are ! "

" Good, how do you know? "

"If you were not, would you speak to me so gently ? I know very well there are a thousand things in my manners which must displease you, and if you were not indulgent you would make me see it."

I felt anxiously that I was becoming garrulous ; but it was now impossible to be silent and conceal my emotions. " It is too much happiness at one time," I continued. " I feel dazzled, like a man who, on coming out of a cave where he has lived all his life, looks directly at the sun."

" You are poetical, my dear friend."

"That is saying a great deal; but I should certainly become so if you would let me share your thoughts. One thing is certain ; I have always had a longing to indulge in dreams ; it is the only legacy

my father bequeathed to me. Poor man! How you
would have loved him! He was a professor too, a
professor in the college of Orleans."

"Indeed!"

"Yes, yes. He would have been an excellent
professor if he had had the ability to make himself respected by his pupils; but he was too kind,
too gentle; his moral qualities were not apparent;
everything was imprisoned in a poor little feeble body.
He was drowned during the inundation, and I found
myself all alone. It was a terrible moment, I assure
you, I can still see his motionless, lifeless body. I
would not believe it, I—"

"It is a terrible death. But what were you saying just now—about dreams, I believe?"

"I don't remember. My poor father would have
been very proud if he had lived long enough to know
you and call you 'my daughter.' I remember he
was always talking to me about—"

"We were speaking of poetry—"

"Oh! yes, I was saying that I had dreamed a
great deal during my poor life, although to tell the
truth,I have never had but one great vision : that of
being loved a little. Unfortunately—I have never
found any opportunity."

"You surprise me."

"No, never. It is probably because I was instinctively waiting for you. Yes, my own Esther, I was
waiting for you. What a fortunate thing it is to have
suffered. For, you see, past sufferings are a fortune
with which we pay for the joys of the future. Moral
laws ordain that the feelings must be properly balanced, and act as a counterpoise to each other,—a
smile is only the drying of a tear. We must have
wept in order to know how to be happy, and that is
why my present happiness troubles me, my dear little
wife. It seems as if I shall never be rich enough to
pay for all this."

" We will discuss it when the bills come due,"
she said gayly." But how tender-hearted you are for
a philosopher. Here are your eyes growing wet
again ! It's a positive misfortune. Come, dry your
tears, my husband."

She took her little embroidered handkerchief, perfumed with verbena, and passed it over my eyes with
her own hand.

" My love, my love," I murmured in her ear, " I
should like to die."

" Die ! ha ! ha ! ha ! you have a mournful idea of
happiness, and its a curious fancy to want to begin
at the end ! Why do you look at me so ? It seems
as if you had a mourning veil over your eyes."

" Oh ! pray don't fancy that. It is only my spectacles ; the refraction of light often produces—"

" You shall explain it to me some other time."
The corners of her mouth drooped imperceptibly, the
dimple in her cheek grew still deeper—" Just now, I
wanted to ask you something."

" How delightful ! What do you wish ? If it
would only compel me to make some great sacrifice !
I am yours, put me to the test."

" Then you really love me ? "

" I adore you. Come, speak."

" Well—I have wanted to ask you a long time ;
by granting the request you will really give me pleasure."

She bent her face so near mine that her curls
brushed my cheek : " Wear a pair of eye-glasses instead of those frightful spectacles ; " she said, bursting into a little laugh, " will you do that for me ? "

And as I murmured in some little embarrassment :
" Why did you not tell me so before ? Good Heavens,
it was such a simple matter ! " she continued :

" Because really these spectacles give you something like the air—I am not offending you—of a sexton
or an alchemist. But I will say no more, for you are
sensitive."

" I was not aware of it. How little one knows
ones self! Oh! I beg of you, tell me everything you
think of me. Since your husband has ridiculous peculiarities, let us make fun of him, it is the surest way
of curing him."

The door opened with a crash, and my mother-in-
law suddenly entered the room.

" You here ? " she said, turning towards me as I
knelt at my wife's feet. " Fear nothing, my Esther,
your mother is here," and making a sign to me to
leave the room, she added: " I want to speak to you,
Monsieur."

I followed my mother-in-law, as in duty bound.
When we were alone in the little parlor, where the
candles where just going out, she turned and, pressing her hand upon her heart said to me :

" You have made me ill, really made me ill. Why,
Monsieur, what fiend possesses you ? What do you
conceal beneath your apparent simplicity? What
sort of a man are you ? " Her eyes expressed terror.
" What society have you frequented, merciful God !
What society has he frequented to have the hardi-
hood to deceive us so ? "

" I do not exactly understand," I murmured greatly agitated ; " some one has doubtless been slander-
ing me; explain yourself, mother."

" Oh! do not use that sacred name. Do you not
feel that a mother's heart is bleeding at this moment,
the pride of noble birth is roused to indignation.
Why the very savages would respect the last moments
of a young girl's timid fears ; they would blush, upon
my honor, to enter the nuptial chamber, as you have
just done, before the bride had received her mother's
blessing. Above the written law which may perhaps
authorize,—don't interrupt me—which in some cir-
cles may perhaps authorize such brutalities, there is,
Monsieur, the law of honor and good breeding, and
this holds sacred the threshold of the temple where

the weeping girl sheds a last tear and bends her head to receive her mother's blessing. But all this is of no consequence to you ; having the text of the law on your side, you care very little about killing my Esther."

Although I felt a certain respect, I will even say a species of admiration for Mme. Paline, it seemed evident that maternal love had blinded her strangely ; so I said with great frankness :

"You are mistaken, mother."

"Ah ! at last you throw aside the mask. This is what was concealed beneath the diabolical candor you assumed in order to deceive us more completely."

"Oh ! Madame, no—let me—"

"And now you are raising your head again, you intend to trample upon my heart."

"But your mistake—"

"See the insults he hurls into my face ! I had not suffered enough, oh ! God. The very day he tears my Esther, my life from me. I ought to have expected it."

"What insults ? I, insults ! Calm yourself, mother."

"No, I had not suffered enough under my husband's yoke. Strike, Monsieur, overwhelm me, finish your work, crush us under your iron hand, drive me away now, drive me away, I have neither husband nor brother to defend me. You are a tiger. But upon my soul I would rather have you so. At least, you are no longer a hypocrite."

"I am in despair, pray listen to me."

"No, Monsieur, I will not listen to you. You will not force me to do so, I hope. No, my daughter, I will not leave you alone, defenceless, I will struggle— yes, Monsieur, I will struggle—"

She could say no more, and closing her eyes, sank into a chair. I was beginning to lose my wits : had I not after all committed some act unworthy of a good man ? My intentions were pure, it is true, but I might be mistaken. Unfortunately there was no time to analyze my conduct.

Meantime Mme. Paline's condition was really alarming; nervous tremors shook her whole frame; her beautiful arms were writhing convulsively.

" Forgive me," said I, although she did not seem to hear me, " forgive and listen to me." It was, alas! a nervous attack; she was subject to them. Her teeth chattered, and the whites of her beautiful eyes appeared between her partially opened lids; it was positively terrible. I took her hands, besought, implored, humbled myself, confessed my crime; she did not answer, and the symptoms continued to increase. Suddenly, —necessity is the mother of invention—I had an idea; I ran into the dining-room which had been left in great disorder after the entertainment of the night before, poured out a glass of water, dipped a napkin into it, and hastily returning to the poor woman, who must be relieved at any rate, slapped her face briskly with the wet cloth.

Although very ill, she started as if under the influence of an electric shock, rose instantly, and hurled at me a glance in which contempt and fury were only too clearly depicted.

" Brute, fool!" she said in a hollow tone—and then left the room, while the slamming of the door of her chamber was distinctly audible. I stood bewildered holding in one hand the half empty glass, and in the other the dripping napkin. " If only Esther has not heard this scene ; she is so sensitive," I thought. A clock in the neighborhood struck three ; I put down the articles I held in my hand, and walked noiselessly towards my wife's room, at the door of which I cautiously knocked. A little diplomacy is sometimes necessary. I did not think of telling her a falsehood, but I wanted to conceal a portion of the truth. I knocked a second time more loudly, but again received no reply. I even tried to turn the knob ; the door, which was double locked, resisted my efforts. Then a feeling of indignation overpowered me ; I reproach myself for it, for it was utterly useless, and I ought first of all to have sought out the causes of what was befalling me ; but I was still young and proud ! I should have liked to knock again, call, force an entrance, and perhaps might have done so if I had not been afraid of exposing myself again to the anger of Mme. Paline, who would certainly have come at the noise.

My overcoat had been left hanging in the antechamber ; I took it, wrapped myself up in it, and returning to the drawing-room where the old sofa from the Rue Saint Sulpice had been placed, threw myself upon it. Strange, when there, I experienced a sensation of comfort ; I felt relieved, like a man whom necessity compels to defer a difficult enterprise until the morrow.

As I felt my head sink gently among the cushions, I remembered the day when Esther, lying upon this very sofa, had plucked at them with her little white hand, while I could see her breast heave under the velvet folds of her huge wrapper.

I had just awoke and was in the act of untying the silk handkerchief in which I had enveloped my head, when my wife suddenly entered the drawing-room.

" What did you do last night," said she, " my dear, what did you do ? My mother has passed a horrible night. How did you forget yourself so far as to proceed to brutality and violence ; for my mother speaks of brutality and violence. Can you not, if only from affection for me, restrain your passionate temper ? "

I was just preparing to have a friendly explanation with Esther on the subject of the locked door, but, on perceiving evident traces of great vexation upon her lovely face, was completely disarmed.

" Do not grieve until you have listened to me, my darling," said I ; " there is—"

"Oh! hush," she replied putting her hand over my mouth. " Would you have me doubt my mother's word ? She has told me all. Alas ! I know very well that men consider it a point of honor never to yield, and prefer to push energy to injustice. You do not reproach yourself you say, but—"

" I have said nothing which could—"

" Have the honesty not to distort facts. Who will believe, my dear, that my poor mother, who, although she has suffered so much, is so kind and in- dulgent, could be in her present condition without any reason whatever ? She loved you so truly. Is not her sensitiveness in everything relating to the affec- tions the clearest proof of her tenderness ?"

" Certainly. But this is exactly what happened. My darling, do not—"

" You must perceive that all explanations from you would be simply an indirect accusation."

" I accuse your mother ? "

" Then you see you regret what has occurred."

" Of course, but I can't understand what—"

" You cannot have courage enough to acknowl- edge even an involuntary wrong, to go to my mother simply and frankly and express your regret. You can- not, the very next morning after our marriage, sacrifice your pride ever so little for my sake. Ah ! well I know you can do all this, and—you will, won't you ? "

No words can describe the tenderness of the glance she cast upon me. It would have been monstrous to resist her entreaty. I hastened to offer my apologies to Mme. Paline, who accepted them without any very great reluctance. This little incident had no annoy- ing consequences, but it made me perceive that I must now act with great caution if I wished to avoid wounding any one's feelings.

IX.

Meantime the utmost confusion reigned in the large suite of apartments in the Rue Vaugirard. While men were bringing, piece by piece, the monumental organ which was to occupy the back of the drawing room, the locksmiths were removing the windows to facilitate the insertion of the Gothic painted glass. Upholsterers were taking away the carpets and hangings arranged for the wedding day; painters were putting up their stagings to transform the ceiling into an azure sky strewn with golden stars; and in the midst of all this, boxes were being unpacked and bales opened. Thanks to the indefatigable activity of the ladies, who traversed Paris from morning till night and made a quantity of purchases, packages of every kind and all sizes were arriving every moment. They were set down haphazard,—here, there and everywhere, one above another,—but especially in the dining room, which had become the central storehouse. There were piles of gilt dishes among bandboxes, glasses under packages of linen, clothing, pictures, easels, muffs, and engravings crushed under kitchen utensils. All this was so mingled with straw and paper that at first sight it was impossible to distinguish anything. I should never have imagined so many things were needed to commence housekeeping. Yet they still piled up the goods, and the tide continually rose higher. What vexed me was that my papers and books were lying at the very bottom under the chaos in the dining-room. But I received packages and paid bills with an enthusiasm which was certainly very natural—for within the last two days Esther had permitted me to perceive the affection she felt for me. I was the husband, the companion of this superior being who, seeking the beautiful even in the most ordinary affairs of life, could take pleasure only amid the splendors of art, surrounded by the magnificence of gold and silk. There must be veritable marvels in these packages.

My natural indifference to comfort and luxury was now actually painful to me. Was it not the sign of an intellectual coarseness which was doubtless indelible? I was anxious about it. With that exception, no cloud obscured our horizon. It is true I watched my slightest gestures, my most unimportant words with the greatest care. It must also be mentioned that the ladies were always out.

What delighted me was that my wife was beginning to trust me, and I detected the first symptoms of a great moral intimacy. One evening, while she was unrolling her hair, she said to me :

" I made one great mistake, my dear, when I drew my Cain. We give way to perfectly absurd raptures. That sketch can never satisfy me ! Come, you know me well enough now to appreciate me, do you really think the barrenness of that design can satisfy me ? "

It was not only love, it was friendship, a blind confidence in my judgment. If she had known how ignorant I was of this grave question of color and design ! If she had dreamed that the two words had not even a definite meaning to me ! And yet at this moment I imagined I understood everything: nothing was more simple, clearer, plainer. I answered earnestly.

" Of course the sketch cannot satisfy you, my darling, it cannot satisfy you ; it is beneath your powers."

" You talk foolishly. It is neither above nor beneath them. Stop, look here, my hair is not unbecoming raised in this way,—I merely say that drawing is not my forte. You see I have the Venetian temperament—color is my life."

" Could you not always dress your hair in that way? You look so pretty ! "

" That wouldn't hold—yes, the Venetian temper-

ament. I feel it, I—after all, perhaps it might, I
must try with large pins. Do you know what would
suit this style of hair dressing admirably. A shower,
a profusion of pearls."

" Do you think so ? Well, there is nothing impossible about that."

" You're a spendthrift. You know very well I
wouldn't put any pearls that might happen to come
along upon my head, and an ornament which would
suit me would cost too much. No, no, let us be reasonable, and for the present think of nothing but the
decoration and furnishing of these rooms ; it is a serious matter. And then, taking everything into consideration, wouldn't it be infinitely wiser to have a
horse and carriage ? In so retired a situation as
this, it would be a safeguard : we may want a doctor
suddenly ; what could we do ? Lose two whole
hours in looking for a hack while one might die
twenty times over ? The mere thought makes me
shudder. My mother is not so well as one might
suppose. Her health must not be trifled with."

What I particularly admired in my Esther was
her power of imagination, and also the aristocratic
ease with which she discovered fresh windows to
throw money out of. Reduced to my own resources
I was crushed under the burden of my wealth without being able to find any means of lessening its
weight. " But you always have a calash at your orders," said I.

" Of course, we hire it, and it's horribly dear.
And you—you must spend an immense amount in
cabs."

" I. No, I never take a carriage."

" Indeed ! But this is not all : we must consider
that a coachman will be like a second footman, and
one male servant is quite insufficient for this household. If you want to kill Joseph, you need only
compel him to continue the work he is doing. But

I'm talking foolishly. The master of the house must decide these important questions."

While talking thus, she had continued to arrange her hair. " Well, I declare, this does hold very firmly. How do you like me with it dressed so? It is becoming, isn't it ? "

" You are charming," said I enthusiastically.

She came up to me and taking my head between her hands, as one would a child's, exclaimed :

" Don't be silly enough to buy me pearls, at any rate. You know nothing about them, not even where to find them, while I am familiar with all the good places. Well, come, won't you kiss me ? "

What would I not have done to deserve such happiness? Yes, yes, she should have a carriage, servants of her own, and I would see her pass in her brilliant equipage. She must be queen by luxury, as she was by genius and beauty. She should have pearls, diamonds, ornaments ; her room hung with satin should be a temple worthy of her. How could I have compelled these two women to ride in a hack until now !

Soon the Venetian temperament of which Esther had spoken recurred to my mind, and I perceived that I actually had no idea as to the meaning of the words. Yet I could not remain in ignorance of questions so indispensable to our mental unity, to the community of ideas and emotions which was to unite us. What did people mean by color and design ? The holidays gave me plenty of leisure, and I resolved to study the subject. I purchased Dr. Brücke's book, procured *La Chromatique, et la Chromatographie,* by George Fied, and Newton's Optics, and was soon completely absorbed in my task. It was a positive delight. To satisfy at the same time my longing for work, which had always been the pivot of my life, and prove my affection for her by a study which brought me nearer to her !

Unfortunately, in the huge apartment filled with workmen and packages, it was impossible to find even a single little corner where I could work at my ease. After having broken several plates in the dining-room before regaining possession of my books and papers, and been driven successively from one room into another where the uproar still pursued me, I resolved to take possession of a large trunk in a small store-room opening from the ante-chamber, and intended to be used as a fruit-room. It was at this door that my good Timoléon, who had quickly become the familiar friend of the household, knocked every day.

"Good-morning, little old man," said he; "are the ladies at home? You're at work; don't disturb yourself."

And when the ladies saw him enter they always cried with a merry laugh: "Ah! here he is, he has come just in time!" He really had the art of making himself useful—indispensable; he drove nails, told stories with wonderful spirit, moved the furniture, or, climbing a step-ladder, wrote on the wall with a piece of chalk, signs dictated by Esther.

"Make a straight line," said she. "Very well. Now write in the middle of the left hand panel—red brown with a dash—dear me, how slowly you write!"

"It's because the ladder shakes, Marquise." He was so full of gayety that his jests never wounded the feelings—"A dash of what?"

"Of cobalt. That's right. Trace another line about fifty centimêtres from the first, and between the two write carved wood. Very well. Now in the right hand panel put—cloth of gold with black and red branches. Come down quick, and see the effect."

"To tell you the truth, my dear Marquise, I don't perceive that there has been any very material change in the appearance of the wall within the last five minutes."

7

"You're a Bourgeois, you have no faith. Come
into the studio and help us arrange the pictures."

Timoléon played such amusing pranks and told
so many interesting anecdotes, that the ladies forgot
to go out, and we soon heard the clock in the Carmelite church strike seven.

"Do you think there would be any harm in my
asking you for some dinner?" murmured our friend
with an affectation of diffidence.

"What a joke, my dear Monsieur Timoléon!
What have we for dinner, my daughter?"

"Oh! dear me. Why I forgot to order any;
didn't you think of it, mamma?"

"Certainly not, my darling; I sent the cook to
the upholsterer's."

"And Joseph is at the dentist's having a tooth
out."

"A tooth! The whole thirty four must have
gone; he has been away ever since noon. We are
in a pretty plight." They were shouting with laughter.

"This is delightful, ladies," cried Timoléon; "I
don't know of a more artistic situation. Have you
some butter, eggs, a little saffron, and some fresh
fish? I excel in making *bouille-à-baisse.*"

"Come, let us be serious," said my mother-in-
law, turning to me. "Run to the nearest restaurant,
my friend, and meantime we will set the table."

"That's it, bravo!" Esther clapped her hands,
turned up her little cuffs, and bounded over the piles
of packages, followed by her mother, dignified and
smiling as ever, who murmured:

"That charming Timoléon, what a flow of spirits!
How lively he is!"

When I had discovered my boots, found my hat,
and hunted up my cravat, I took myself off and returned half an hour after escorted by a waiter carrying an immense basket, while I had two bottles under

my arms and a corkscrew in my watch pocket. They hastily opened the basket and out came everything the proprietor of the restaurant had chosen to put in. The strangest of dinners was the consequence: no soup, but a lobster, prawns, a monumental pie, three rolls, and not a drop of water. Timoléon was brilliant, the ladies were almost exhausted with laughing, and everybody pulled at the piece of canvas which, for want of napkins, they had spread over their laps.

I know not why, but I felt chilled by this wild mirth, lost all appetite, and found it impossible to smile. It was not merely restraint and embarrassment that overpowered me, but actual sadness.

It was very natural they should make a little sport of my piteous face, and I was not at all surprised; but they increased my embarrassment without making me any the more lively. When the meal was over, Esther seated herself at the piano, and Timoléon taking me aside, said:

"Now listen to me, my dear fellow, I can assure you that you are making yourself perfectly ridiculous with your contrite airs. I tell you so because we are old friends. You are hurting these ladies' feelings terribly."

"Do you really think so? I had no intention—"

"I'm sure of it. It's your own affair, you know; but pay attention to it, little old man."

"I am in despair, Timoléon. Try to set the affair to rights, my friend. You know how to explain everything. Tell them I can't help it, that I had the headache, that I am ill, tell them anything, but above all, that they must not feel hurt."

As days and weeks elapsed, I experienced at rare intervals a certain sensation of anxiety. I was more in love with my wife than ever; but the feverish excitement of the first few moments was beginning to decrease; the bewilderment caused by the sudden transformation in my whole life was somewhat calmed;

I was beginning to feel the earth under my feet, and at the same time the tastes and habits of former days sometimes plucked me by the sleeve. Occasionally, amid the disorder which was continually changing its form without diminishing, I remembered my little bachelor's room, small and bare, it is true, but so well arranged ; my table, my books, my papers were all close at hand. Ah ! I would have given much to live pleasantly and quietly, without any parade, in a suite of modest little rooms where intimacy is easy and one feels at home. It seemed to me that amid such surroundings I would have had more of my wife's society. When I was walking along the street, and saw on the third stories of houses windows with very white curtains, adorned with gilliflowers, I could not turn my eyes away from them. How much at their ease the people up there must be !

There are souls of different powers of flight: some delight in great enterprises, vast designs ; they need room to unfold their wings, and the endless fields of fiction and the ideal soon become a necessary space to them. The impossibility of the vision attracts them ; they look it in the face without trembling or shuddering, like eagles which gaze at the sun. These are privileged beings, and doubtless necessary to the moral equilibrium of the world. But side by side with these birds of lofty flight how many sparrows there are which never go above the roofs, and are obliged to live happily on crumbs left forgotten here and there. I was born a sparrow, made to flutter two feet above the ground in unfrequented lanes bordered with hedges.

My pride was no longer wounded by it, though I might have sometimes dreamed of the heights of heaven. But I was troubled that so great an obstacle should separate me from Esther. Yet should I have loved her so much if nature had made her less different from me ?

I examined this question under all its aspects. What I could not deny was the ever-increasing restraint that I was compelled to impose upon myself in order to share the life and pleasures of the ladies. The interminable adornment of the suite of apartments, the everlasting presence of workmen, the incessantly modified plans and projects tortured me. It was useless for me to try, I could no longer conceal it from myself.

The carriage and horse had been purchased–a magnificent animal, whose impatient prancing made me shudder; and an irreproachable coachman, who intimidated me quite as much, had increased the establishment of servants. He was a reserved, grave, but very handsome man, dressed with studied elegance, and was gifted with a wonderfully aristocratic air. When in the presence of this person I felt the necessity of maintaining my position, and even forced myself to address him authoritatively, as my wife and mother-in-law did. I had noticed their distant manner and thoroughly aristocratic mode of uttering the sentence : " Louis, you can bring out the carriage for a two hours' drive," the gesture which emphasized the order, and their way of turning the head as we do when we call some one very far below us. I had analyzed all this, but when the moment for imitating my model came, I felt an unconquerable shame ; it seemed as if I was going to commit an infamous action. Why humiliate this man who, physically at least, was greatly my superior ? Might he not have believed that I was jealous of him ? Then I used a thousand little circumlocutions.

" Could you be ready at such an hour ? " I said.

I avoided calling him by his name, which seemed arrogant in my position. " You will do the ladies a favor by being punctual. Farewell." And I went away with a smile. While I spoke to him in this way his silence, his imperturbable seriousness dismayed me. What sorrows, what moral tortures might be in the heart of this man, who was certainly not in his proper station.

It was impossible for me to pass him like a milestone without speaking to him; and whether he was washing the wheels of the carriage in the courtyard, harnessing the horse, or mounting his box, I cried: "Ah! you are washing the wheels," or else: "You will find it very warm to-day."

This was not proper. Mme. Paline, whom nothing escaped, gave me to understand it clearly; but how was I to do otherwise?

It was the same with my other two servants. At times I would actually have liked to take their places to avoid the sight of their servility, which I begrudged myself. If either rose at my approach, I said in a low tone: "Pray sit still, is it worth while to trouble yourself?"

I analyzed this impression and ascertained that it contained a great deal of pride: the respect of these worthy people seemed like a species of sarcasm; their purchased deference contrasted too violently with the numberless jests whose object I had been all my life. I was conscious of being still more ridiculous beneath the plume with which they adorned my head. How many times I have waited until the coachman or footman had left the courtyard or the ante-chamber, in order to go out without fear of being saluted by them!

Yet I should have been indignant if they had not showed the ladies the deference and attention I did not want for myself. When I heard the roll of the carriage as it entered the courtyard, and saw my wife and her mother in their rich dresses leaning back among the cushions, I trembled with pleasure. I raised the curtain and pressed my eyes against the window pane, watching the slightest shades of variation in their haughty grace of bearing. I did not say

to myself: "They owe everything to me." I have
never had such base feelings in my heart. I was very
far from reckoning upon their gratitude, since I was
well repaid by the pleasure the sight of them afforded; but I was proud of them and would have liked
to have them received with public enthusiasm on condition of remaining an unknown spectator behind my
curtains, dressed in the frayed coat in which I was so
comfortable.

Under a thousand pretexts I took refuge in my
little corner, for there only I felt really at home. In
vain my poor Esther had given me a dressing-gown
of gray damask with greenish branches and sleeves
à la Véronèse, then very fashionable in the world of
art. In vain did she bestow upon me Indian slippers
ending in slender points ; I always avoided putting on
this costume, which weighed upon my shoulders like
a leaden shirt. I decked myself out in it two or three
times for breakfast, but I was always so constrained
and ridiculous in these magnificent ornaments that it
was impossible to make me put them on again.

X.

The vacation of several months which had kindly
been given me on the occasion of my marriage was
at last drawing rapidly to a close. I say at last, for
in spite of my love for my wife and my respectful affection for my mother-in-law, it must be confessed
that I was looking forward with great impatience to
the time of resuming my course of lectures. More
and more incapable of sharing the life of the
ladies, and ignorant of all the usual occupations of
wealthy people, I was suffering keenly from my en-
forced idleness, which compelled me to lead a most
pitiable existence. "My mind," I said to myself,
"needs the healthful and substantial food of science,

exact analysis, inflexible reasoning. Thus alone can
I arrive at the intuition of the arts; I must know
how to proceed, to go from the known to the unknown. If I am foolish enough to throw myself with
bent head, without compass or guide, into the chaos
of sentimental impressionability, I may compromise
everything."

But how happy and light-hearted I felt when I
found myself once more in my large black gown, and
had drawn from the little green box where it was repos-
ing my professional cap, magnificent though somewhat worn. It seemed as if from the depths of the little
box I had regained my self-control. My colleagues
congratulated and shook hands with me, and these
trifles delighted me. The class-room looked cheerful, pleasant to the eye—the good, hospitable, sonorous class-room, with its walls decorated with a beautiful, solid, yellow tints; its freshly white-washed
ceiling destitute of gilt stars. I felt at ease,—at
home; my eyes wandered approvingly over the ink-
stained benches, the grated windows, the grayish
floor. Even so the warrior, returning from a distant
and glorious expedition, pauses with deep emotion
before the walnut trees and thatched roofs of his native village, which have been witnesses of his past
life. It even seems to him that only when confronting
these cottages and this steeple, do his military successes assume a shade of heroism.

In like manner, while I was lecturing with the
boldness of a man who will neither be interrupted
nor opposed, my position as a husband and master
of a house became dazzling, radiant.

With my regular daily employment, order and
calmness were restored to my life. Labor, by re-
awakening my energy as a professor, turned my
thoughts from the thousand cares which had obtained
too great an influence over me.

I loved my family none the less, but my individuality asserted itself a little more. Often when the ladies' conversation rose to those realms of art which I had never been able to enter, far from persisting in following them, I quietly glided away in thought and reflected upon the lesson for the next day, or some new demonstration; or else suffered myself to float quietly back at the will of my memory towards the years spent at school, which were by no means so dark as I had supposed.

"When I have the honor of speaking to you, son-in-law, it would be civil in you to do me the favor of answering," said Mme. Paline suddenly.

"I beg a thousand pardons. Yes, of course, you are right. I was thinking—"

"Oh! I thought you were asleep. You must take some bitters; your blood is getting thick."

In spite of these warnings I took refuge more and more in a world of my own; and while with the ladies, led a life entirely apart from them. From time to time, when conscious of my absence of mind, I actually felt remorseful. Then I entered into the life of the family again as if by a rebound, burst out with all sorts of questions about furniture, servants, dresses; found the most astounding adjectives to apply to everything that surrounded me, and in my eagerness to pay my debt of admiration almost always overshot the mark and wounded the ladies deeply.

I believe that at this time I was positively unbearable. Yet I loved them with all my heart; but one cannot wholly change his nature. Ah! if they had been able to understand with what delight I gave up the management of the household to them; with what joy, from the depths of my shell, I gazed at their luxury! There was no portion of the establishment whose fashionable appearance I did not observe with pleasure, even to the servants, since I no longer considered them mine. But they could not read

my feelings.   Yet I was sincerely touched, cordially
grateful to them for their kindness when they ush-
ered me into the beautiful study which had been
prepared for me, showed me the table covered with
green velvet where I was to work; the immense arm-
chair, carved like the rose window in a cathedral
where I was to sit; the lion skin on which my feet
were to rest; the Byzantine lamp suspended from the
ceiling; the Turkish sabres and Circassian pistols
that adorned the walls.   Is ingratitude, selfishness, a
natural vice?   I do not know; but that very day I
settled myself permanently in the fruit-room, arranged
my books and papers on the shelves, placed in one
corner a little table and a straw chair, double-locked
the door of this sanctuary, and put the key in my
pocket.

After having taken this great step I felt the joy
of the freeman who has asserted his independence
once for all.   And yet I swear that I worshipped
my wife.

About this time the great drawing-room was put
in tolerable order; the walls upon which Esther was
going to execute some paintings remained bare, it is
true, but the gothic arm-chairs, the ottomans, the Ori-
ental carpets, the tables and chandeliers were placed
in regular order, and the ladies began to receive.
Contrary to my expectations, there was an immense
crowd at once, and on the very first day I had to greet a
Polish lady who was an inimitable violinist, an Italian
count, two Wallachian artists, and a Prussian major
who sketched landscapes and played on the bassoon.
These entertainments really promised to become
very brilliant.

"How do you happen to know all these people,
my darling?" I said to my wife; "you have not travelled a great deal."

"It seems, my dear, that the little fame I have is
enough to attract all Paris; I cannot help it.   It is

the way of our artist world. People know already
that I intend to execute some decorative painting,
and many inquisitive persons undoubtedly come on
that account. I have even been obliged to show
them my sketches. In teaching, you have none of
these annoyances, you are not conspicuous like us.
Well, they are the inconveniences of the profession."

"Do you know that when you are in your drawing-room you seem like a queen surrounded by her
court! If I were jealous! ha! ha! ha! you are
handsome enough to—you know very well I am only
joking. But I really was not aware that your genius
was so famous."

"See what comes of not reading the papers,
Monsieur le savant: the *Ferme-Modèle* has devoted a
long article to me, which is by no means badly expressed."

"And you have told me nothing about it! Then
success and fame at last crown your efforts. Ah! how
happy I am, my dear Esther. Artists need glory, renown, triumph. I understand that fully."

These receptions thenceforth appeared to me under a new aspect; they were proofs of my wife's
genius, and although I was forced to conquer a
thousand feelings of repugnance, I considered it a
duty to put a good face upon the matter. I tried to
be as unobtrusive as possible, for I knew perfectly well that these artists did not come to see me,
but had merely been attracted by my wife's talent;
it was therefore her place to do the honors of her
house; my part was an entirely secondary one, and I
rejoiced over it in my heart. Yet I neglected no exertion to aid Esther in the discharge of her delicate
duties, sought to find a civil word for every one, and
hidden in the window corners, talked enthusiastically
about the only subjects which could interest them, my
wife's genius and decorative painting. It was no
slight labor. Although I set to work with great energy

to fulfil my task, it was evident that it was a heavy
one, for Esther, passing near me one evening, said :

"Your cravat is untied. But tell me ; I am
ashamed, my poor friend, to make you sit up so late;
you rise very early ; at least don't feel obliged to
drain the cup to the last drop ; if you slip out quietly
no one will notice you."

"Nothing escapes your attention, my angel. I
talk continually to keep myself awake, but I am actually dying to go to sleep."

"Don't put yourself to the slightest inconvenience,
I beg of you."

What! even in the midst of this entertainment
where every one was doing homage to her, she
thought of me. "What a kind heart!" I said to myself as I beat a skilful retreat.

The license granted by my wife gave me all the
more pleasure, because I was unaccustomed to sit up
late, and twice already, on the mornings after these
entertainments, had not risen in time, and reached
the college five minutes late, which deeply humiliated
me. I had a religious respect for punctuality. I remembered an alarm clock I had purchased in the
country at the beginning of my career, and to avoid
another accident, resolved to make use of it as I did
then. So I set the little article very carefully, put it
behind the curtain, and kept myself awake to warn
Esther, who would certainly understand the necessity
which compelled me to adopt this course.

But the devil ordained that at the moment she came
in I should be sound asleep. The next morning,
precisely at half-past six, I was suddenly roused by a
terrible uproar with which I was no longer familiar ;
and while my conciousness of the truth was slowly
coming to me, my wife, rudely wakened, screamed :

"What is the matter? Oh! dear, what is the matter?"

"Calm yourself, my darling, it is nothing," I said

smiling to reassure her more fully. " See, Esther, it's only a little alarm clock. I meant to tell you about it last night; but I fell asleep. I am very sorry, darling, and I beg your pardon."

These conciliatory words, accompanied by the noise of the accursed machine, far from soothing her, only excited her nerves still more. " Blockhead!" she cried, making the most despairing gestures, while from the next room, which was occupied by Mme. Paline, was heard the confused sound of a voice screaming in tones of distress. Soon the partition resounded with the blows dealt upon it, and all the bells in the house began to ring.

Trembling for the result, I sprang out of bed and hastily dressed by the faint light of dawn which was beginning to steal into the room. My mother-in-law would make her appearance directly, the servants were already running to the spot—I heard the distant sound of doors.

" My darling, it is true, I confess, I have been ridiculous. I ought not to have drawn the string out to its full length, but your mother is very wrong to be frightened."

" Don't insult my mother. Oh! how wretched I am."

I noiselessly left the room, holding my cravat in my hand, and found myself face to face with the chambermaid and cook, who came up rubbing their eyes.

" It is nothing," I said soothingly, "nothing at all."

I had committed a folly, but could it be supposed that a mere act of heedlessness would entail such baleful consequences.

The fresh air completely restored me. While walking on at random, I thought to myself: " It is evident that the culture of the arts puts the brain into a peculiar condition. Cannot an over-powerful imagination be scientifically considered a disease?

A sublime malady, of course, but none the less a disease, a want of equilibrium between the nervous and muscular systems. I ought to have warned her. The slightest unexpected impression agitates, disturbs her, and it is this excessive impressionability which renders her so charming and gives her her genius. How, in this world, everything logically obtains a counterpoise! If I had not had a temperament and tastes entirely opposed to hers, I should perhaps have been indifferent to the delicate sensibilities of this exceptional nature. In electricity, opposite poles attract each other, similar ones repel. Is not the effort we make to understand each other the firmest bond which could unite two beings? What is tenderness if not a succession of unsatisfied feelings of curiosity? What is moral communion, except the incessant familiar interchange of dissimilar ideas and impressions? The eternal law of the universe wills that this state of things should be. Marriage is a salt, and in every salt there is an acid and a basis. Now would it not be very wrong for one of these elements to complain because its neighbor has not the same qualities as itself, when this dissimilarity is the cause of their union?"

"My poor Esther! it is very provoking that I should not have warned her!"

When, about eleven o'clock, I re-entered the Rue Vaugirard, my first thought was to inquire for the ladies; but before I could receive a reply, bursts of laughter echoed from the drawing-room, and I recognized Timoléon's voice. I rubbed my hands with delight.

This dear friend always came just at the right moment; undoubtedly his irresistible gayety had repaired the mischief I had done. I entered with a smile upon my lips, but the ladies rose gravely. "Come to your work, my child; let us withdraw," said Mme. Paline, who, as she passed me, hurled at me

a glance whose haughtiness expressed the utmost
contempt.

"Heaven bless you and your striking machines,"
said Timoléon when he was alone with me.

"Ah! do you know that? It is true, my dear fellow, I ought to have warned her, but I fell asleep."

"No, you see, little old man, there is an order of
things which you don't understand. You are all of
a piece, logical, square, straight as an I. To you, a
man of bronze with joints of steel, all fastidiousness,
all physical and moral shades of difference are ridiculous weaknesses. You know but one meaning in
words, one form in ideas."

"Listen to me, my friend, allow me to tell you—"

"I don't want you to tell me; you are a material-
ist. The vague anxieties of the soul, its confused aspirations, its inexplicable sensibilities, all that consti-
tutes the nature of women, especially women who are
artists, is a closed book to you. Mme. Paline, whom
you will some day blush for having despised—"

"I not appreciate my mother-in-law! Oh! Timoléon."

"I understand. Well, Mme. Paline said to me with
tearful eyes: 'I esteem my son-in-law, but I fear
him, he frightens me.' And indeed, with your way
of analyzing every emotion, treating the soul as a
subject for anatomy, you are very capable, although
a very good fellow, of making these two poor women
wretched."

"What are you saying? You are joking, of
course. They made wretched by me! Why, what
have I done to them?"

"Can one enumerate the thousand needle-pricks
which in the long run wound as deeply as a blow from
a dagger? Besides, I know very well you are not
conscious of it, little old man."

"You do not know me. I am very sensitive, I assure you."

"Let me alone: You are a stoic—and then, you see, where there is no religion there is no sensibility."

"I have done everything in my power to gratify their tastes and make them happy."

"There, see how you put your fortune above everything else. We know of course that you are rich, and that materially you do things very well: grand pianos, cathedral organs, dignified coachmen, carriages, upholstery, furniture. There you are in your element, it is clear, distinct, can be weighed and measured."

"I think you are unjust, Timoléon, and you are causing me great pain."

"Do you suppose your conduct gives me none, and that if I did not love you with all my heart I should have the courage to tell you my opinions so frankly? Besides, this doesn't prevent my defending and excusing you to the ladies; but it is useless for me to try: is it possible that two such impressionable creatures should not perceive the care you take to isolate yourself from them, to remain indifferent to everything that interests and occupies them? Do you suppose they do not notice the air of disdain with which you talk about one thing when they are speaking of another, and cut short every question relating to art by some commonplace remark. Why are they always alone like two poor widows? Why do you affect to be a stranger in your own house, and leave the whole burden of ordering and managing everything to these ladies? In short, why do you prove by all possible means that you consider them inferior beings, which is totally false? When I think that you have not even asked to see the rough draughts of the pictures your wife is going to paint! Come, old boy, is this affection?"

"But I worship my wife, I swear it; I love her with all my heart, and am ready to make every sacrifice for her."

" Sacrifices again. Why that's all admitted ; you fairly crush them with benefits —— are you satisfied ? But if my words wound you, let us talk of something else ; I have told you all this with the sole object of doing you a service, and because my convictions, my ideas—my religion, let us say the word—forbid me to remain indifferent to the misfortunes of others. Now, believe me, you are overlooking happiness; you have never noticed the two estimable beings who live with you, or rather you have never seen them except through your abominable mathematical instruments. Try to judge them with your heart."

" You are a true friend, though somewhat severe ; but I thank you none the less. Give me your hand, and then I will tell you the whole truth. You are going to breakfast with us ? "

" The ladies have breakfasted, at least. they have eaten as much as their agitation allowed."

" Ah! I was perfectly insane last night, I confess."

" And I took a cup of coffee to keep. them company. Besides, I am late, I have an appointment—apropos of that ; I was forgetting that I have a favor to ask you. But after the conversation we have just had, will you do me a favor ? "

" Oh ! pshaw, my dear fellow, I can't allow that joke to pass. What right have you to doubt my affection ? "

" None, my little old man; so I shall apply to you. In two words, the matter is just this : I am in pressing need of two thousand francs to-day."

I could not help starting, for the idea suddenly entered my mind that perhaps I did not have that amount.

" If you can't lend me the trifle, don't inconvenience yourself, I will go to that clever Vilser."

" Not at all; why, see how angry you are getting."

" Well, you look as if you were trying to find an
8

excuse. I'm speaking to you frankly, with my heart in my hand. No, I prefer to go to Vilser, devil take it. You treat me as if I were importunate."

"Indeed ! "

"You're not conscious of your rudeness. I don't bear you any grudge for it, because I know your ways; but how do you suppose those two poor women, who have thinner skins, can help being utterly crushed ? "

I turned towards a small ecritoire, and rummaged the drawers.

"Ah! fortunately I have almost as much as you want. Here are seventeen hundred francs."

"I should have preferred two thousand, but give them to me, eight, nine, ten, five and two make seven, it is all right."

"It is impossible for me to lend you more, this is all that is left of my sixty thousand francs."

I pretended to be perfectly calm, but I was strangely agitated. It was the first time in my life that any question of money had disturbed me so.

"But you are unreasonable," said Timoléon with great gentleness; "I know very well that to set up housekeeping in this style requires a considerable out-lay. It's only a little breach which—"

"It is not the only one, I remember now."

"With a little economy you will make it good. Your mother-in-law seems to be such a skilful house-keeper."

"Yes, certainly. The ladies have been obliged to make a number of little expenditures—indispensable ones—so they have drawn upon the treasury without much calculation."

"Then they have the key of the cash-box ? "

"Of course. Do you suppose I dole out money to them by the crown piece ? I put a certain sum into this drawer and look at it occasionally; or else the ladies tell me, and I replace the money when it is necessary. The plan has always succeeded very well.

If I had pursued any other course I should have hurt their feelings—and been ashamed of myself. Have we not the same interests! I will go to the notary's for more funds some time in the course of the day, that's all."

"I'm sorry for it; but you see, I have this note due. You are not in love, old philosopher?"

"Not in love! I'm passionately in love with my wife, you know very well."

"You're wisely, reasonably in love; you never commit any follies. I allow myself one. It must be confessed that this time the princess is worth the trouble. Dear little angel! I have never seen any harm in it in my life; oh! well, I wouldn't have believed a poor uneducated child could have so much frankness and purity, such noble aspirations. No, indeed, I have never had my soul more expanded. Now we are on the subject, tell me exactly what I owe you in all, little old man. I want to settle it, I hate to have debts of long standing."

"Oh! there is no hurry about it," said I consulting a little note-book I kept in a special drawer under lock and key. "You owe me in all twelve thousand two hundred francs."

"You're very exact. Oh! you're right; I admire you. How it does roll up, it is surprising! Twelve thousand two hundred. I will settle it at once, my dear fellow."

"Whenever you choose; but let us say no more about it."

"No joking. I shall attend to it without fail. Well, good-bye, little old man."

"Sixty thousand francs," I murmured while breakfasting. "Why, it is confusion, it is ruin—where can the money go?" I saw a gulf yawning at my feet. I had often been troubled by vague anxieties, but had always deferred until the morrow the care of analyzing this uneasiness, which seemed to me a token of a

narrow, despicable soul.   Face to face with so prodigious an expenditure, my petty plebeian instincts of
economy and system suddenly awoke, it was necessary to examine the evil thoroughly and apply a remedy, for it was impossible to remain in such a situation.
I was grateful to my kind Timoléon, who, by his unexpected borrowing, had opened my eyes and compelled me to adopt some definite course of action.
Therefore, after breakfast, I went to the studio where
my wife and her mother were sitting.   I was resolute,
but very calm.

Esther, holding an immense palette, her hair
dishevelled, her eyes beaming, and her hands concealed under long gloves, seemed to be in the act of
seizing some inspiration.   The furniture was loaded
with drapery, cartoons, and engravings.

"I hope I am not disturbing you, ladies," I said
gently.

Mme. Paline's only reply was a little dry cough,
which reminded me of the deplorable incident of the
alarm clock.   How difficult it would be to get at the
financial question !

" My dear Esther, my kind mother, I have come
to make my apologies for my awkwardness this morning, and—"

"Oh ! don't say another word about it ; it would
end by setting our teeth on edge.   You are in my
light, my dear, you see I am working."

" True," I said more boldly, " excuse me.   The
idea of my standing stupidly directly in your light.
And you, mother, I hope you will pardon this ridiculous little accident."

" I should never have dared to make use of that
adjective, but since you employ it, it meets with my
approval : ridiculous indeed, extremely ridiculous.
Let us stop there.   You have noisy habits of early
rising to which we shall know how to submit.   You
were not late this morning—I hope your young lads

studied well. It would oblige me if you would not crush the engravings on that chair by sitting down upon them."

"Ah! I beg your pardon. I crush the engravings, I stand in the light! What *is* the matter with me to-day?"

"Why nothing extraordinary, it seems—"

I turned to my wife: "Oh! this is the sketch of the—for the drawing-room. You have worked very industriously, my darling, and are beginning to put on the colors."

"Yes, I am beginning to put on the colors." The two ladies exchanged pitying glances. I felt that I had indeed spoken like a veritable plebeian. I was always wounding them by my awkwardness and inadvertence; it must be confessed that my mind was preoccupied by the money question. Thus I perceived it was necessary to compliment her upon her work, but what was I to say? I could distinguish nothing in these sketches but a perfectly unintelligible confusion. Yet I wished to make myself agreeable in order to lead the more gently to the fatal explanation. Fortunately, an interesting recollection recurred to my mind:

"What astonishes me," I said eagerly, "is that the light constantly coming from the left side does not annoy you horribly."

"We stand so as to prevent the colors from shining."

"It would not surprise me if this custom was the cause of grave errors in the appreciation of colors."

"That is a new idea; and why, if you please?"

"On account of the sclerotic light, my darling." Sure of interesting them deeply by this little scientific detail, of which they were doubtless ignorant, I had, I believe, pronounced the word sclerotic with a certain emphasis. The two ladies began to laugh; but I was not much disconcerted, for I knew very well I was

right. I continued: " It must first be observed that the
light which reaches the back of the eye does not enter
only by the pupil ; the sclerotic coat, otherwise called
the opaque cornea, or the white of the eye if you prefer,
and which in you has such a delicate tinge of blue—"

" You are very complimentary."

" You will understand, in an instant : the sclerotic
coat and the vascular tissue underneath both permit
a large portion of the external light to pass."

"Oh! dear, what *are* you saying to me ! " asked
my wife with comical terror.

" Perhaps it is very interesting," observed Mme.
Paline ; " let your husband continue his lecture, darling."

" I will not go on if it is disagreeable to you."

" On the contrary, I already feel the greatest sympathy for this sclerotic coat."

"Little rogue," I continued : "a large portion of
light then passes through the sclerotic coat and the
vascular tissue—"

" Beneath, it is understood."

" Beneath, of course. Now this light becomes
tinged with red in its passage through the membranes
of the eye, then spreads out diffusely over the retina,
and, in consequence of its color, diminishes the retina's susceptibility to red."

" You will break my heart ; but what can I do to
help it ? "

" There would not in fact be any inconvenient result if this sclerotic light entered the eyes equally ; but
as in painting you always have the window on the left,
it follows that much more enters the left eye than the
right ; and consequently, in artists, the retina of the left
eye is less sensitive to red than that of the right."

" That is unfortunate ; and then ? "

" Then ! Dear me, why that's all. The equilibrium between the two eyes might perhaps be restored

by the aid of spectacles with glasses of different colors."

"You're secretly in partnership with a dealer in glasses, there's no doubt about it, and you want to sell your wares."

The financial question was receding farther and farther. By a fortunate accident my mother-in-law gave me an opportunity of returning to it.

"My dear son-in-law," she said with great affability, "I have just received some bills, I don't know exactly what they are—for hangings, furniture, etc. You will see. I must point out to you in regard to the coachmaker's account, that the prices were agreed upon between the man and myself. All the papers are yonder on the table—but go on with your little lesson, I beg of you."

"I have finished." Then muttering to myself : "It must be said, it must; come Babolain, be a man."

"Do these bills amount to a large sum ? " I asked in a smothered tone.

"Look yourself, my friend ; the whole collection is over there—you're stepping on my dress ; take care ! "

I began to look them over, and in the first place read : "Byzantine lamp in enamel, fifteen hundred francs. Original drawing attributed to Véronèse, nine hundred francs."

I was bewildered, and felt a tempest raging within me and ready to burst forth. "What!" said I, "that hideous old night lamp in the next room cost fifteen hundred francs, when I have lived for a whole year on the same sum ? Where are we going ?—this is frightful. My good mother, my dear Esther, reflect. We are lost, ruin awaits us, if you do not pause upon this fatal declivity. What! not a bill paid ! Then for what have the immense sums I have placed in the drawer been used ? For what ? It is the very madness of extravagance and improvidence. These apartments, which surpass in luxury the abodes of

princes, these horses, these carriages! It is bound-
less, it is a gulf, an increasing indefinite mathematical progression."

The silence that surrounded me like an icy mantle soon produced its effect : my tongue faltered, the
words came with difficulty, and at last I stopped
short, bewildered by my own audacity.

"I see I was not mistaken in regard to you, Monsieur," murmured Mme. Paline with sovereign dignity. "Do not be afraid, your interests shall be protected; I will pay all the expenses that have been
incurred here from my own property. You hear me.
And now you can withdraw."

It was utterly impossible to resist the authority
of such a deportment. I was advancing towards the
door in great agitation, when Esther, seizing me by
the arm, cried : "So you want a separation. You are
not satisfied, miserable man, with having broken our
hearts by a thousand tortures, a thousand mortifica-
tions, you want to taste the joys of the tiger; that is
what you want."

With her eyes flashing, her nostrils dilating, her
lips half parted, her face almost concealed beneath
the luxuriant hair that had fallen from its bonds, she
was exquisitely beautiful—I could not help it—I
turned, and suddenly clasping her in my arms, cried :
"My Esther, my love—I—I am a very poor man!"
and hurriedly made my escape.

While on my way to my lawyer's I thought to myself: "Yes, I am a very poor man. Nothing is more
contemptible than to upbraid another with a benefit,
and upbraid with such violence." The more I reflected upon my inexcusable outbreak, the baser and
more despicable I found myself. It was through
weakness, foolish pride, and awkwardness, rather
than tenderness, that I had allowed these two poor
women to become involved in a course of mad expenditures of whose consequences they were ignorant;

would not a word have been sufficient to open their eyes before their improvidence had become a habit? I had never been ignorant of the fact that they needed to live in an atmosphere of luxury, surrounded by delicate and refined pleasures. I knew they were not accomplished housekeepers, economical and attentive to the petty details of every-day life, but enthusiastic, lavish, poetical, incapable of calculating and foreseeing; and was it not precisely those very qualities which had attracted me to them? Had I not enjoyed their magnificence and prodigality? Piteously, it is true, and like a miser; but, after all, had I not enjoyed it? And now that I was obliged to pay for the expenditure I had encouraged, my avarice raised its head, and in pious indignation I appealed to morality, to the holy domestic virtues. If I had even made this money—but it had fallen to me from the skies. How can I ever understand these great poetic souls soaring through space, I who trudge along in the path like a timid beggar, having no other horizon than the pebbles in the road?

Yet a faint, almost smothered voice to which I did not wish to listen, but could not help hearing, said: " Is happiness so far away? Would they not have been contented amid plainer surroundings? Were you not born, fool that you are, for the calm and quiet joys of a laborious, orderly life? Your wife should be a simple, economical, prudent girl, having no other ambition than to nurse her children and govern her household, and then perhaps you might have become a distinguished savant ; instead of being the pitiful husband of a woman of genius, you might have undertaken one of the noble works of which you dreamed when you were poor ; and people would have hailed you on your way as they greet one who has fulfilled the task Providence marked out for him." The voice spoke to me thus ; but far from heeding it, I thought: " How skilful man is in deceiving him-

self! What is there in this humble, narrow life which
seems to me like an ideal vision, except the desire to
amass wealth ? Should I have such thoughts if I were
not an egotist and a miser ? But, by Heavens, I will
tear these passions from my heart;you shall no longer
have to blush for them, my Esther; I will no longer
be an obstacle to your genius and your glory!"

And I proceeded on my way to my notary's with
the energy of a man who rushes forward to storm a
breach.

XI.

I returned from the notary's with my pockets full
and my mind somewhat calmed. I had decided upon
my course : I would mortgage my vineyards, sell a
small farm, and obtain as much advantage as possible
from my title of professor by giving private lessons.
I was convinced that, unconsciously to myself, I had
been basely jealous of Esther's fame. True, I could
not prove this jealousy by facts, but disgraceful feelings know how to conceal themselves so skillfully
within the deepest recesses of the heart ! Yes ! yes !
I had been jealous of my wife's superiority, and I
would punish myself for it.

While awaiting the time—which would not be
long deferred—when she could sell her works for
their weight in gold ; when she should obtain the fortune her genius assured her, I wanted her to have all
the material pleasures money procures ; I must honestly provide her with the luxuries which were neces-
sities to her. If either must be sacrificed to the
other, it was only just that it should be I—I without
genius, without wants, born for obscurity. And besides, the idea of imposing upon myself, for her sake,
a heavy task of which all the world would be ignorant, greatly consoled me. I should thus compel her
to accept, without her being able to help it, the fruit

of my labor. It would no longer be money fallen from the sky, but money I had earned, and earned with painful toil.

Scarcely had I re-entered the house when I went towards the little room where the chest of drawers stood, to deposit in them the contents of my pocket-book. Although I had rung the bell without any special caution, and had not thought of hushing the sound of my steps, the ladies, though the study door was half open, did not hear me; for in spite of my presence they continued their conversation as if I was not there; and it was this very conversation which made me understand the full extent of the wrong I had done them:

"Knowing himself to be rich," said Esther, "he believes himself intelligent; that's perfectly natural. We seem fools to him, nothing more."

"Do not utter blasphemies, my love."

"And I, who had dreamed of marriage as a communion of enthusiastic feelings, a constant soaring towards the pure regions of the ideal, find instead of this, a shameful and dishonoring slavery, the subjection of my soul to the will of a being inflexible as steel."

"Your father was the same, my love; I know what people suffer!"

"It's enough to kill one!"

"Yes, it is indeed; but I am here, my child. And in the first place, I will have our situation perfectly clear; I will compel him—yes, I will impose the shame upon him, I will compel him to accept the payment for my board, which hitherto I did not dare to offer, out of consideration for him. I will pay him as we pay an innkeeper, a common tradesman, a shoemaker."

"Let us behave like Christians, mother."

"But what would become of you, my dear, if I should die? what would become of you in this hell?"

"I should find an invincible strength in the love

of my art. Oh! I feel it; all the ardor of my soul bears me towards painting, towards that passion for the beautiful which is devouring me. Oh! God, it is through suffering that genius is purified."

"You are worthy of all admiration, my poor angel."

"Henceforth I shall devote myself to religious painting; that alone can harmonize with my mood now. I will paint sorrow and resignation in impassioned touches. My Abel was, I see, a successful effort, only I sketched with siccatives, so that I was mistaken about the causes of my failure. Color is for bright, happy souls; to be a colorist one must have the sun in nature and in the heart. Those fair days have passed. An austere style, pure, simple drawing will console me. Yes, for the next exhibition—I still have a fortnight—I will make two allegorical figures, on a golden background, in the style of the ancients. It shall be: Despair supported by Religious Feeling; a group. I see, I feel it. I will paint Despair from myself, to dispense with models, and you will sit for Religious Feeling, won't you, mother? My career is beginning anew. We will see what the name of poor Esther Paline, the fool, the enthusiast, will become. Will you go out with me, mother, I am stifling!—and then we'll go to the gilder's to order the golden background."

"I will order the carriage. What misery! Great Heavens!"

"And we will return through the Champs Elysées."

"Especially as we must go down the Rue Royale for the chandelier."

While making due allowance for the exaggeration natural to artists, I saw only too clearly by this conversation how deep was the suffering of these ladies. Chance inflicted a harsh but salutary lesson! I took a secret vow that it should not be useless to me, and that I would do all in my power to rehabilitate myself in their eyes and regain their affection.

From that day forth I was attentive to everything, and anticipated their wishes to the best of my ability; unfortunately I usually guessed wrong. I eagerly interested myself in everything they liked, overwhelmed them with attentions, and made them a thousand little presents. On leaving my lecture-room I rushed to Chevet's to get the early fruits, of which Mme. Paline was very fond; at other times I purchased rare flowers to fill the drawing-room—in short I did the very best I could.

They accepted everything with a cold politeness that greatly distressed me. I was conscious, it is true, that I did not set about it properly; I did not know how to offer my gifts; they never came just at the right moment, but too soon or too late; and they could-read in my attentions the efforts I was making to render them more attractive. One would have said my conduct inspired them with a species of distrust, and repelled them from me. My violent outbursts had certainly caused them to feel less repugnance than my present humility and dull submission. They no longer hated me; but I wearied them. I had a proof of it one evening. There was company at the house—I was very tired, having worked ever since early morning, when my mother-in-law approached, and smiling kindly at me, which she had not done for a long time, said:

"Son-in-law, your dear little wife is very ill. ¡ Oh! don't be alarmed; it is nothing dangerous, but she needs rest, perfect quiet, a few nights of sound sleep will doubtless restore her."

"You really think it will be nothing serious? My poor Esther! Perhaps she sits up too late."

"Perhaps she is awakened too early; besides, it is the doctor's advice. You leave the house at daybreak—"

"Yes, I am so busy—"

"I have no intention of censuring your acts; they do not concern me, but your early departure and the noise it causes trouble her very much. It would be prudent for her to avoid all kinds of disturbance for some time; where shall I have your bed made?"

It seemed as if I was going to be ill, so violent was my agitation, yet there was nothing unnatural in Mme. Paline's words.

"In my little study, if you please; there I shall disturb no one."

"In the fruit-room? As you please. Will you give me the key of that boudoir?"

"Thank you, I am going there myself."

I could not accept this banishment without having an explanation with Esther, bidding her good-night and embracing her. I waited until every one had gone, and then knocked at the door of her room.

"I am very much obliged to you, my dear," she said instantly, "you won't have very good accommodations in that little hole, but then you have a fancy for small corners."

"It is you who are concerned in this matter, my darling; so you are very ill?"

"I am very tired, that's all. I am working too much on account of the picture I want to finish."

"But what a piece of imprudence. To execute a work of so much importance in a fortnight!"

"That is another question. It is certain that I can no longer sleep. It is because I am feverish, and because—without any disrespect to you—you snore like a hero."

I would have preferred anything, even her anger, to this little remark so gently uttered.

"But you should have waked me—told me: nothing in the world is more intolerable—"

"Waked you! Do you suppose that is an easy matter? When you are sound asleep, and you generally are, you would be insensible to the reasoning of a boxer. Besides, when, after a sleepless night, I am just beginning to get a little rest, the reveille sounds for you, and the noise—you must understand it. Come, don't look at me in that melancholy way; I'm not vexed with you, but I need—a vacation; there, that is the truth. Kiss me, you see I'm not vexed with you; good-night, my dear."

"Good-night," I murmured. I was about to press my lips to her forehead, and, as she bent her head, I kissed her hair.

The idea that, unconsciously to myself, during my slumber, I had imposed upon her a torture perfectly unendurable to a nervous woman, haunted me. And in spite of all, she had had the goodness not to make me a single reproach! Ah! if she could have read my heart, seen with what eagerness I vowed to redouble my attention and homage! But the misfortune was, that I did not know how to make myself understood, I seemed to be imprisoned in an accursed armor I could not cast off. If she could have realized the strange joy I felt for several days in watching the drawer empty with increasing rapidity, and saying to myself: "At least they will not accuse me of avarice." If she could have seen the effort I was making.

Thus the fruit-room became my sleeping chamber. I was, of course, very unhappy; and yet one sometimes has strange impressions—the feeling of independence I experienced within those four walls was not without its charm. I was away from her, it is true, but I was more free to think without fear of displeasing her, by looking at or approaching her, of irritating her by an indiscreet question, or the shrill tone of my voice. In fancy, I could gaze into her face, take her hands, cover her with kisses, press her to my heart, and I no longer trembled for the consequences of my boldness. In fact, I possessed her

more completely. And in the evening — these follies
return to my mind—when I embraced my pillow, murmuring: " Good-night! my Esther, good-night! my
love," I imagined I could see her smile, and was
grateful to her for it. And in the morning at daybreak, while I hastily ate a bit of bread and some
chocolate, I talked to her aloud without fear of wak-
ing her, told her my most secret thoughts, discussed
mathematics, and she did not yawn. I reckoned before her the number of my lessons, consulted her
about the means of making them still more numerous, told her of the money I had earned, calculated what it brought us in per day, per hour.
" You see you can play the princess, my little darling," I said, embracing her, and it was evident that
she was not indifferent.

Yes, I was very happy in that little fruit-room, and
thanks to my habits of analysis and criticism, I had
the good fortune not to let a single one of these joys
pass without testing and squeezing it like an orange.

One day, when I was returning from the college,
walking very quickly along the walls and carrying
under my arm a huge bundle of books and papers, I
heard Timoléon's voice behind me.

" Have you turned peddler, little old man? What
has become of you—what are you doing?"

" I am busy—I—I have a great deal of work to
do," I replied. " How are you?"

" To judge by the size of your baggage, your occupations are by no means trivial. Are you beginning the famous work—you know—the book you intended to write?"

" No, oh! no—that is, yes; I am thinking of it,
but in short—you have just come from the ladies?"

" Of course, and I hoped to meet you there, but
you are becoming impossible to find. I said to Mme.
Paline just now: ' Where have you hidden my friend,
in what closet have you shut him up? Have you

sold or exchanged him?' I saw at once I should try in vain to make them smile. Your prolonged absences grieve those two poor women deeply."

"Is that true?" I asked suddenly; "did my wife speak of me to you?"

I should have liked to confess that I was working for them ; that, having been occupied ever since early morning,I had breakfasted on a roll bought at a baker's shop I passed. But was not confessing this to him to make a parade of devotion, when I was only doing my duty, nothing more. And then, in Timoléon's eyes, it was coming down from my little scientific pedestal. Besides,I saw plainly that he considered me a hypocrite,who wished to conceal his conduct.

" Listen to me, my little old man : I have already told you so once before—you are in a miserable way; on pretext of important occupations, you neglect your family. Your mother and wife weep and lament over it, mourning has entered the household. All this must be changed. Ah ! let me speak, or I shall no longer trouble myself about anything. The two poor women need some lively amusement ; it is absolutely necessary to arrange a little entertainment, a fancy ball, for instance : when all Paris is amusing itself masquerading, committing all sorts of follies, why the deuce should they remain yonder alone in their convent in the Rue Vaugirard?"

" But, my friend, perhaps you think that—"

" I merely think you remain for whole days absent from your home ; that you scarcely re-enter it at meal times. Is this true or not? "

" Yes, it is true, but—"

" Oh pshaw ! there are no buts. Facts are facts. A man who loves his wife doesn't act so. I tell you this frankly, for my heart really bleeds when I hear those poor ladies murmur. 'What does he do? Why does he desert us in this way? What habits is

9

he forming away from his home? With what people does he associate? Why does he envelop himself in mysteries? Does he not believe in anything, even God? You are not behaving well, my dear fellow."

I could no longer conquer my emotion, and replied:

"There are no mysteries in my life, Timoléon. I work very hard, that is all. I am giving—hum, hum, I am giving a great many lessons, being a little embarrassed just now."

"What, embarrassed! You're joking, I suppose. Embarrassed with your fortune? Do you happen to want to remind me that I haven't settled our accounts? You shall be paid, my dear fellow—confound it, of course you shall be paid."

"Timoléon, my friend, my old schoolmate, pray don't imagine that." His remark wounded me deeply. Then I had again been acting very badly for the best of men to believe me capable of such feelings! "Do not desert me," I continued, "you know how awkward I am. With you it is very different. You are right, we must amuse my wife, give a ball, a masquerade, certainly—there is no doubt about it. Their health, their happiness must take precedence of everything else. You will arrange all this, won't you? But believe me, I have told you the truth: I give lessons because I am short of money."

"Don't say a word about it to those two poor women, at least, it would hurt their feelings! What a humiliation! They could not endure it. But how did you get so reduced? Have you been making unlucky speculations?"

"Yes, that is it. I have been speculating."

"In a word, you've been gambling—you're a gambler! oh! poor creatures!"

"No, I am not a gambler; it is an accident; you know how such things go? An investment—people may be mistaken. Don't say anything to them; the misfortune will soon be repaired. You swear you won't say anything to them."

" Yes, of course I swear it. Should I tell them that to kill them ? "

" Thank you, you are always very kind. You won't forget the little entertainment ? I have no time to attend to it."

What a good idea that was of Timoléon's ! What an experienced man he was, and what an excellent friend. On the following morning I could see the effects of his benevolent intervention : the idea of the ball was like a reviving balsam. Esther, exhausted by working upon her large picture with the golden background, was suddenly re-animated, and gave herself up without reserve, with all her artistic enthusiasm to the preparations for the ball. Meantime the little entertainment, which was at first to be only a party of intimate friends, gradually assumed a ceremonious character which made me uneasy. The list of invitations lengthened every moment, and already three workmen were installed in the drawing-rooms cutting and nailing almost day and night. Timoléon gave directions for everything, and never left the house ; and every evening, when I came in, I noticed with great pleasure the eager activity of the ladies.

" At least they are happy and have not reproached me even once," I said to myself ; " what does the rest matter ? "

My dear wife, gay, joyous, active, running hither and thither, flying into a passion, laughing heartily, thinking of everything, anticipating everything, was like a general on the eve of a battle. I said to myself : " She is much better ; she will be perfectly well, and there will soon be no necessity for the regimen she is now compelled to follow." Oh ! God, what a joyful thought !

" I'll wager you are thinking of going to bed, my little old man," said Timoléon clapping me on the shoulder ; " it is ten o'clock."

I did not wish to let the extreme fatigue I always felt at this hour be perceived. "Why so?" I answered. "Look, my friend, see how pretty my wife is! She doesn't appear to be ill now, does she? How fresh and blooming she is!"

"I had not noticed it; yes, it is true, but you are longing to go to sleep."

"You are making fun of me, Timoléon. Come, give me your advice frankly, a friend's counsel, as they call it. Do you think I ought to—wear a fancy dress?"

"Why, of course, that is indispensable."

"Ah! but really, seriously, *is* it indispensable? The thought occupies my mind a great deal. I never wore a disguise."

"I shall disguise myself entirely. One must be like the rest of the world."

"Shall I be very ridiculous? If it really must be, I will do it. I have thought of nothing else for the last three days. Oh! I should very much prefer not to—you understand, being a professor—"

"What you say is absurd. You are not obliged to appear as a savage, put feathers on your head and curtain rings in your nose, my little old man. Take a historical costume, something dignified—in a word, a dress suitable for the master of the house. It is a mere formality. I'm no more disposed to play the part of a merry-andrew than you; besides, we shall have a gay circle, and eccentricities would be inadmissible."

"Will there be a great many people? Are not the ladies afraid? It is very perplexing—you say a historical costume."

"You know of course that every one nearly or distantly connected with the arts will want to come to this ball; these are the unpleasant consequences of fame."

"True. And you still think that, in spite of the

number of guests, I must wear a costume ? Then I
must reflect upon it. I am so busy."

" Ah ! yes. How do your lessons progress ; are
you satisfied ? "

" Yes, yes, perfectly satisfied."

" Well, so much the better."

The great day arrived. A row of huge lamps was
smoking in the freshly-sanded courtyard, and in the
drawing-room a squad of footmen dressed as mediæval mendicants were lighting the candles and arranging the benches ; while the orchestra were taking their
places, and the ladies were under the hands of the
hairdressers and costumers. I shut myself up in the
fruit-room, double-locked the door, and put on a pair
of black silk knee-breeches, somewhat too long for
me. I was pale, agitated, sad enough to weep, and
yet I could not have explained why. When I had
adjusted the knee-breeches tolerably well, I turned
towards my little bed on which were spread a black
doublet, a short black cloak, gloves of the same
color, and a chestnut wig with long hanging curls. I
took the candle and gazed at these things with a sort
of despair. " Why did I choose the costume of
Charles the First ? " said I to myself. " I was wrong :
I should have been more at my ease and more concealed under Richelieu's large cloak—though to be
sure, the cloak is red, and red attracts attention. The
members of the Council of Ten also wore a cloak, it
seems to me, and a mask besides. A mask ! Why
didn't I think of that ? I should be concealed. The
executioner also wore a mask — that would have
been repulsive, but I should have been sheltered."

While saying this, I thought of all the accidents
which might still prevent my being present at the ball.
Who knows ? I might slip on the floor, break a leg,
or merely get a sprain. Yes, but how much trouble
that would cause the servants, who were already so
busy. I might swallow a bottle of brandy, a cruet of

vinegar, some drug—I drove away all these foolish thoughts, which were not proper for an honest man, and arranged the wig over a brow damp with perspiration.

This royal costume was not at all appropriate for me. Yet I had explained my delicate position to M. Babin, and even requested permission to speak with him in private for that express purpose.

" I am absolutely obliged," I said to him, " to attend a fancy ball next Friday, and although I never—"

" Madame Esther Paline de Martignac's? Yes, Monsieur ; it will be a very magnificent entertainment ; we have made several costumes for it ; pray sit down."

I started as I heard my wife called by her maiden name, which of course she signed to her paintings, and was on the point of saying to M. Babin : " Excuse me, I am that lady's husband, and my name is Babolain, formerly a pupil in the normal school, now titulary professor of mathematics in the college of Saint Louis." I had been on the point of saying this, but I did not dare. " My tastes and my career, Monsieur, I will even say my social position, would not lead me to disguise myself ; but as I have had the honor of telling you, I am absolutely compelled to do so, therefore I come to you in all frankness to ask you what costume is best — most suitable, I mean ? "

" There can be no possible hesitation : in your case, which often happens—"

" Ah ! indeed ; does it often happen that people are obliged to wear a fancy dress against their will ? I pity them."

" It happens constantly, and then there is nothing to propose but the costume of Charles the First. It is dignified, historical ; we have recommended it a hundred times to magistrates, physicians, lawyers— and we have never had any complaint of it."

"Then I will decide upon the dress, since you assure me—I am not a lawyer."

"Allow me to take the measure."

"Nor a doctor—it will be plain, will it not, and as dark as possible. I should not wish to be conspicuous."

I went away somewhat cheered by a few kind words from Monsieur Babin, and it was thus that I found myself, not from any excess of pride, but by the force of circumstances, dressed as a king of England. Moreover, I must say that with the exception of the knee-breeches, which were too long, all the garments were very well made.

When I was ready, had put on my orders, and gummed on the mustache and the patch that completed the costume, I looked at myself in the little glass with mingled terror and compassion. "How I must love you, my Esther, to get myself into such a plight!"

The idea also occurred to me that I ought to have shaved off my whiskers, which, I don't exactly know why, hurt my feelings.

Meantime, for at least ten minutes, I blew my nose, coughed, put on and pulled off my fringed gloves, murmuring: "I am ready—have I forgotten anything? No, I am quite ready;" and upon a thousand pretexts I deferred the moment when it would be necessary for me to leave the secluded fruit-room and brave the glare of the candles. At last the rolling of carriages echoed from below—it must be done: I rushed out, and without looking around me entered the large drawing-room blazing with light—as a poor actor pursued by hisses and rotten apples might have done. My great cane annoyed me, as well as the hair of my mustache, which tickled my nose.

"At first I did not see my mother-in-law, who, waving her fan, was giving the mendicants their last orders. She was dazzling, powdered, elaborately dressed, decked

with plumes, and so completely at home in her costume of a marquise of the days of Louis XV., that I
was bewildered.

"Good gracious, my dear friend," she cried, ill concealing a burst of laughter, "what a queer idea it was
to muffle yourself up in that dress?"

"I am very ridiculous, am I not?"

"Why no, I didn't say that: it is just the first
moment. You know one must get accustomed to it.
Take care of your cane. Why, it is a regular paschal
candle. Ha! ha! ha!"

Madame Paline was interrupted by the entrance
of guests, who succeeded each other in constant succession. I greeted the first with great energy, but
soon perceived that all were total strangers to me,
while I was equally unknown to them; and therefore
it was useless to longer undergo a torture no one
could appreciate.

I had been concealed in an out-of-the-way corner
for some minutes, when a murmur of surprise and
admiration ran through the crowd. I moved forward
and saw Esther, my own wife, who was making her
triumphal entry. I almost fell backward; never in
the most fevered visions of my youth had a creature
so strangely beautiful appeared before me. But
was it really Esther who stood yonder in the guise of
that great Venetian lady, with the golden hair, milk
white skin, and indefinable look, at once gentle and
terrible? By what magical art had she thus transformed herself? A shower of pearls and precious
stones was scattered over her hair and covered the
rich brocade skirt which, raised — I gasped for
breath as I looked at all this—raised on the hips, revealed scarlet breeches; and while the waves of velvet and flowered damask swept behind her like a sort
of royal mantle, her neck, her shoulders, her swelling
bosom, her exquisite arms—destitute of any ornament, free from all constraint, were displayed with a

confidence the malevolent might have taken for boldness ; but I knew very well that this excessive lack
of modesty was only the innocence of genius.

All heads bent instinctively, and she slowly advanced showing her beauty without the least embarrassment, and smiling at the eager, curious glances
which seemed like ardent caresses.

I too approached with outstretched neck, parched
throat, and trembling limbs, supporting myself on my
long royal staff, and murmuring in my agony : " Yes,
I recognize her ; it is she, it is my wife.   Oh ! God,
how beautiful she is ! too beautiful ! "   Why could I
not turn them out, kill, murder this crowd of strangers, clasp her in my arms, bear her away with me far
from the world into a desert—and destiny ordained
that the moment I longed for her most fervently was
the very one in which a new gulf yawned between us.
I felt an emotion of mingled terror and rage.

She returned, waved two or three persons aside,
and made a sign to the musicians in the orchestra,
who were waiting for her order to begin.   At the mo
ment the instruments burst forth all together, we
found ourselves face to face.   I could not control
myself and said to her in a low tone :

" Oh ! how beautiful you are, my darling.   I love
you, I love you."

" Keep out of the way, my dear, keep out of the
way."

I could not be angry with her, for she was right ;
but the words pierced my heart like a nail.   I saw a
nobleman of the time of Louis XI. with an aquiline
nose, flashing eyes, and princely bearing, approach,
offer his hand, and lead her to a place in the quad-
rille.   Then as the throng crowded around the
dancers, I was elbowed and pushed out of the way,
and saw nothing but the backs of these people who
were smothering each other to look at my wife.

I sat down in a window corner, for I was bewil-

dered; everything was swimming before my eyes.
Two Swiss girls, with their hair dressed in long braids
passed by, and one said to the other :

"Let us go away; we ought not to have set foot
in this house."

In spite of my agitation, I thought I recognized
the daughter of the head of my college.   I also saw
confusedly the ladies' coachman and footman coming towards me.   The sight restored my self-control ;
I wished to avoid the eyes of the servants, so I rose,
and gliding through the midst of the crowd, not without difficulty, reached, at the end of the suite of
apartments, a small, dimly-lighted room no one had
yet entered.   I put my cane in a corner, sank down
upon a sofa, and gave free course to the tears that
were stifling me.

I had perhaps been there a long time when I
heard the sound of footsteps behind me; I raised my
head, and in the opposite mirror saw a Charles the
First, also armed with a large cane and wearing silver
fringed gloves.   He seemed overwhelmed with sorrow, and I should have taken him for my own image,
if he had not been much taller than I, and much more
robust in every way.   We greeted each other with a
wan smile, and Timoléon for it was he, sat down beside me pressing my hand affectionately.

"Have you seen my wife, have you seen her ? " I
said with an emotion I could not control.

"I noticed her, yes, I noticed her ? " Strange, his
voice trembled almost as much as mine.   "She is
having an immense success.   There were so many
people around her that I could not pay my compliments to her.   It is a magnificent ball ! "

We remained a few moments without uttering a
word, both gazing at the figures upon the carpet.

"You know all those people yonder ? " continued
Timoléon with an expression of anger very unusual
to him.

" Not ten persons, my friend, and you ? "

"No more. But what the deuce?—you are at
home, why aren't you in the drawing-room ? It is incredible, and extremely indecorous. Zounds, you
owe it to yourself to do the honors, to see what is
going on in your house—it is different with me : I
came here to sit because I have a terrible headache.
And then your wife herself received me in a very distant manner."

" You must not be angry with her, you know she
has a great regard for you; but at such a time— She
is lovely, isn't she ? "

" Yes, yes, oh ! yes."

" Perhaps you are like me, you think her too
beautiful; it isn't her fault; but after all, she is too
beautiful. If you had seen her when she came in !
It scorched one's eyes, my dear Timoléon. Everybody was agitated, I saw that—well, what I experience
is a selfish feeling, I know, but I can't help it; all this
causes me terrible suffering; I should like—you can't
understand what I feel—I should like to break everything here."

" Calm yourself, my good little old man; the
master of the house ought not to get into such states.
Your eyes are red, you are as white as a pocket-hand-
kerchief, and you have lost one side of your mustache."

" What difference does it make ? I care for nothing, you see, nothing but her. I know very well I
have none of the qualities necessary to please her,
but I love her, is it my fault, I love her madly. She
might have chosen a more unobtrusive costume—"

" She ought to have done so, Babolain; upon my
honor she ought, out of respect for herself and consideration for you ; for after all, she bears your name,
which is an honorable one. There is no getting
over that, she is married."

" We must not be too severe. I am sure she did

not intend to annoy me.   She has the imagination of
a great artist, of course ; she rushes on without reflection towards what seems beautiful—the illusion, the
enthusiasm of the vision—but at heart she is the
purest of women; you do not doubt it at least, my
good Timoléon, you do not doubt it."

"Pick up your mustache, there it is, over by that
foot-stool—you enrage me, you really enrage me by
your absurd mania for approving of everything.   No
indeed, it isn't enough to be honest at heart, appearances must also be preserved.   To how many evil
suppositions, injurious interpretations, may not your
wife's insane conduct have given rise ?   It is the whim
of a spoiled child, an artist's fancy—is that what you
are going to say ? "

"Exactly, Timoléon, that is what I wished you to
observe."

"Well, I allow the wildest caprices and follies, but
on condition that people shall bear these consequences alone.   Husband and wife are mutually responsible for each other, they are one before God and
man.   Are marriage bonds a mere jest ?   Oh ! Heavens ! "

"Calm yourself, I beg of you ; your friendship for
me makes you exaggerate matters enormously."

" If the sacred respect for family ties is not enough
to check the vagaries of the imagination, where
will they stop ? "

" Yes, yes, that is what I was thinking; but don't
let us allow ourselves to get into a passion, and let
us try to analyze all this. When a woman is more
beautiful than others—"

"She is compelled to use greater care to keep at
a distance—"

" The impertinent scoundrels who—I mean what
I say—who contaminate her with their gaze."

"Certainly. She ought to force them to show her
the respect of which she is worthy."

"For after all, Timoléon, there are costumes and costumes—it is the—I don't know whether you have noticed, it is the waist particularly that—"

"That has excited your indignation. Oh! my poor little old man, how fully I understand what you must have suffered."

"I know perfectly well how all this happened: she could not resist the pleasure of showing her beautiful arm a little, and then by degrees, without dreaming of any harm—perhaps she did not think people would notice her so much."

"You are absurd. Did she put on that wig with the golden shades, and those pearls, by accident? Did she paint.her face by accident?"

"Are you sure she has painted her face? Yet she is beautiful enough without that. Oh! God, why, she is insane! And that skirt raised on the hips. Did you notice it, Timoléon?"

"Yes. Is it accident again that raised that skirt? Listen to me, Babolain, believe your old friend, for our acquaintance is not a thing of yesterday."

"No, indeed;" said I warmly, pressing his hands, "it is not a thing of yesterday, but not until to-day did I know all the goodness, affection, devotion in your heart. You are my friend, my only friend."

"We will talk of that another time. Now be a man, go back into the drawing-rooms; your place is there, and not here. Zounds! the master of the house must not hide himself, and at certain times the husband should appear."

"I know it, Timoléon, I know it, but see how ridiculous I am in this dress."

"Well, what then? If any one has the ill-luck to smile when he sees you, spring at him and use violent measures. When you have cuffed one, the others will be submissive. If they are not, I'll take charge of them. Come, Babolain, come with me."

The clock in the Carmelite convent had just

struck six in the morning, everybody had gone, and the bluish light of dawn, entering the ball-room, was struggling with the yellow rays of the expiring candles. The flowers and plants, drooping and withering, hung their heads mournfully; several tables were still loaded with the remains of the supper. Esther, her hair and dress in disorder, animated, trembling with excitment, more beautiful than ever with her paint half brushed off, was pacing up and down the room. I was seated on the end of a bench following her with my gaze. I was feverish, and my eyes were burning. She paused, burst into a gay laugh, poured some champagne into a glass, and raising her arm high into the air, while the strings of pearls clashed against each other, said in a ringing voice:

" Let us drink to Venice the beautiful. Will you, husband mine ? "

I swallowed at a single draught the contents of the cup she offered me.

"It was splendid," she continued, " confess it was splendid, oh! king without enthusiasm." She went towards the organ, played a few chords, sang two or three notes at the top of her voice, and turning towards me, said : " Are you pleased with your wife's success, say, king of England, are you pleased ? I am a queen too, queen of beauty, queen of painting; I am a sovereign in the world of art. Behold my transports! behold my triumphs! Ten years of an obscure life for ten minutes of this dazzling reign ! Did you see how they all looked at me ? It is a fine thing, my dear husband, to attract all Paris to one's house by the mere prestige of one's name and genius; to see all heads bow, to say to one's self they are furious; Cirbec is foaming, Prudent de la Sarthe and the others are ready to burst with rage, and yet they bow all the same. Ha ! ha ! ha ! "

She was standing very near me, erect and motionless. I took the bare arm that hung by her side and

glued my lips to it; I must have burned her; she did
not seem to notice it—but I,who for hours had been
longing passionately for this kiss, trembled from head
to foot, and it seemed as if a fire was suddenly kindled in my veins.   I felt I was going to share the enthusiastic transports of the adorable wife who was at
last mine ; I was alone with her, the agony of the
evening vanished as if by enchantment—with infinite
caution I passed my arm around her waist, and murmured ;

"You cannot know how I love you, my Esther—
my darling, I have been very miserable all this evening."

"You were afraid of seeing me eclipsed, weren't
you?   There, you are a pretty good husband; rather
a funny king of England, but that makes no difference."

I kissed her again, as smiling and gazing into vacancy, she said in extremely voluble tones:

"Eclipse me! oh yes! You saw the Polish lady,
and the two Russians,and the little Countess de Ripan-
era, and all the others with their real diamonds—well
come and compare notes, my love! Mine are false,
but come and compare. I am a daughter of Venice,
my beauties, ha! ha! ha!"

I felt wounded: was it possible that my wife, the
divine creature before whom every head bent, had
worn false diamonds like a mere actress, a common
adventuress! Was it possible this great artist had
cause to blush! My honesty revolted at the thought.

"Yes, my little king, you know very well they are
false. Have you ever bought me real ones? I never asked you for any, I don't ask you now."

"And why shouldn't you have them? These
Polish and Russian ladies are not your superiors, my
love—I want my Esther to walk with head erect, I
want her to be the most beautiful, the richest—brilliant, worthy of admiration ; I want no one to be able

to look her in the face without casting down his eyes."

I was losing my self-control entirely—I was intoxicated with love, and any words seemed fitting to express my transports.

"Who is so worthy to wear jewels as you?"

"Don't talk so foolishly; you don't know the value of these things; the smallest diamond rivière is worth twenty-five or thirty thousand francs."

"Well," I had no longer any knowledge of reality: "If you want that sum I will give it to you, you know all I have is yours."

She suddenly took my head between her hands, and embracing me with a sort of transport, cried:

"Do you want me to adore you?"

Then she resigned herself to my embrace.

XII.

Adore me! It was a mere form of speech of course, a sort of affectionate joke; but what a delightful way of joking! People do very wrong to despair and complain: never had my wife shown me more real kindness and affection than during the few days that followed the ball. When I brought her the thirty thousand francs in a portfolio lined with white moire antique, she was on the point of refusing it. It was too great an expense, she said, the folly must be given up—I was obliged to urge her, and almost get angry. She had an excellent heart and possessed true solid qualities.

Towards the end of this exceptional week, on my return from college, I saw Mme. Paline, dressed in black and evidently under the influence of some violent emotion. She was waiting for me.

"My dear friend," said she, "I have a great misfortune to tell you; be brave, it is a hard blow for

Esther particularly, poor child. Her *Despair sus-tained by Religious Feeling* has just been refused admittance to the Exhibition, excluded, cast aside, yes, cast aside."

"What, again! Those two figures on a golden background? Oh!"

The oh! was uttered without indignation, for to tell the truth, I felt a sort of relief. I had at first feared a much greater misfortune. "It is incomprehensible: refused again! and at the very time when she is receiving the tribute of general admiration."

"Yes, it is an academical infamy. See to what a degree of meanness jealousy can lead these imbecile, stupid old men." After a short silence she continued with dignified indifference: "I must also tell you something of which you are probably ignorant. Your wife has been in a delicate situation about six months, I don't know whether—"

The sentence was scarcely finished when, springing towards Madame Paline and clasping her in my arms without the least caution, I covered her with kisses.

"Esther about to become a mother," I cried; "oh! that makes amends for everything. About to become a mother! My dear mother—oh God!"

"Why, son-in-law, you're losing your wits, and —you are stifling me, you are certainly crazy."

"What happiness! My darling, my Esther! Do you know whether it is a boy or a girl?"

And, almost in spite of myself, I began to embrace my mother-in-law again, until, red with anger, she was obliged to beg me to go away.

Had I been wrong in believing in the future, in the joys and intimate relations of family life? I had certainly gone through some sorrowful scenes in the past, but what delight was in store for me.

"Where is Madame?" I said to the lady's maid with the tone of a major, and on being informed that

Madame was in the studio, hastily entered. Esther was lying upon the sofa weeping, with her face hidden in her hands. I ran to her, and taking her in my arms without thinking I might displease her, cried :

"Is it true, my Esther, tell me, is it true ? "

"Yes it is the truth, the wretches, the cowards ! " Her little hands were clenched and her great eyes flashed with an expression of bitter hatred. "They won't undertake the struggle in open daylight, the honest struggle in which they know very well they will be conquered. Cirbec, who licks their feet, has helped to deal the blow. Cirbec, a mannerist, a flash in the pan, a coward ! Ah ! they don't fear the rude scrawlers, the brawlers of the palette. You want balderdash, gentlemen, but no ! I will not yield. You shall have war, since such is your good pleasure, and a terrible war. When people try to crush me, I will defend myself ; I will make an outcry."

She said all this so rapidly that it was impossible for me to put in a word.

"Of course," said I as calmly as possible, "of course this is provoking, my darling ; but you won't die of it if the devil is in it ; and these gentlemen—"

"The scoundrels ! "

"That's what I mean—these scoundrels will not deprive you of your genius." Then, unable to help smiling, for my heart was full of sunshine, I added : "What your mother told me—you know ? is it true ?"

"What ? What did mamma tell you ? "

"That you would soon be a mother."

She turned her head away, the corners of her mouth drooped, the pink nostrils of her little nose dilated.

"Well yes, and what of it ? Ah ! you set my teeth on edge, you drive me wild. Go away, I hate you. Go away, you'll give me a nervous attack." She tossed violently on the sofa.

"Pray keep quiet, you do not know that such movements are very dangerous."

Upon ordinary occasions I should never have spoken to her with so much authority and abruptness; but at this moment I had extraordinary courage.

"I shall be calm when you are gone," she murmured.

"Then I'll go at once. The least imprudence may entail terrible consequences."

Nothing could divert my thoughts from the new feeling that had taken possession of me. One would have said that only now had I found my real vocation. The pivot of my life was changed. The idea of this child, whose coming colored the future with unforeseen tints, pursued me everywhere. I talked about it to everyone. I could not bridle my tongue, and gradually accustomed myself to refer all my thoughts and actions to this single object.

If it is a boy, I thought, he will undoubtedly inherit from me the critical judgment and gift of analysis which are my only peculiar qualities. His mother will transmit to him that power of idealization, that artistic penetration, which elevates the character, enables one to generalize, to separate the principle and law from amid the chaos of things seen in detail. Moreover, he will have Esther's beauty, her admirable ease of manner. These are very great advantages in life. Now, gifted in this way, a scientific career will naturally offer itself to him : he will enter the university, but with great ease ; his mother's celebrity will procure interest for him. Then by a stroke of genius he will spring into the realm of pure science : a discovery, a book, will place his talent beyond question. He will execute the great task of which I have dreamed ; I will give him my advice if he asks for it, which is by no means certain,—for of course he must consider me a dunce. Ah ! I won't be angry with you, my dear boy, what does it matter !

I shall enjoy your triumphs, I shall be your father,
that title cannot be taken away from me. Some fine
learned name, which would look well in print, must
be found for him. But suppose it was a daughter.

This thought troubled me greatly. Not that I
was less disposed to love her than her brother,—but
she, like her mother, would need surroundings worthy
of her, rich luxurious surroundings, and afterwards a
large dowry. Why had I not understood that it was
my duty to transmit my uncle Babolain's fortune, of
which I was only the trustee, intact to my daughter?
I had committed more than an error, a positive
crime. I ought to have checked the ladies in their
extravagance, they would have understood all this,
would have commended me, thanked me afterwards.

From this time a passion for economy took possession of me. I bought a large account-book, and
began to calculate; but at the same time that I ascertained the enormous breach that had been made
in my fortune, I perceived it was impossible for me
to lessen my personal expenses. My daughter's fate
was therefore entirely in the hands of the ladies;
how was I to impose upon them another style of living? I felt that I was mean-spirited. Especially at
this time, when they were greatly agitated in the
midst of a violent conflict, how could I speak to them
of the thousand petty details, the thousand necessary
reforms prudence and economy required! It was
with difficulty that I could say a word to my wife.
The young fiery Tambergeac, art critic for *La Ferme
Modèle*, now spent whole days in the Rue Vaugirard.
Thanks to his merciless pen, a most violent article
had been issued against the Institute; my wife's name
had been made prominent; the outrage of which she
had been the victim had served as a text for the ar-
raignment of these "gentlemen of the *Pont des Arts*."

People met at Esther's house at appointed
hours, disputed eagerly together, and made plans for

the campaign, for the question had gradually assumed large proportions. The matter was no longer confined to mere conversations between a few discontented people, but had increased to eager discussions in which the future of French art was directly concerned, and whose avowed object was the downfall of the Institute. This was severe, but apparently just. Several bearded painters, warm partisans of a radical revolution in the world of art, had been introduced by the indefatigable Tambergeac, who, petted and flattered, had his plate at the table, and a cushion under his feet. Was it a measure in behalf of neatness, or a proof of the great esteem in which he was held?

In the centre of the largest drawing-room was an immense table covered with papers and pens, wafers enamelled the carpet, and the furniture was loaded with newspapers. It was evident that the ladies were at the head of a formidable party which would stick at nothing. Esther bought a bell with an ivory handle, and tried to draw up a memorial which that confounded Tambergeac was to sign. Every evening when, after my day's work was done, I found myself in this club, surrounded by eager, excited people shouting themselves hoarse; I fancied myself under the influence of some nightmare. I approached my wife and said softly:

"You are heating your blood, my love; you are scorching your poor blood. In your situation—besides, my darling, you should be attending to the little one's wardrobe."

"What, do you advise the soldier to abandon his post, to desert in the presence of the enemy?"

"No, no, but you will soon be ill, and—"

"Are not we, I and my friends, the defenders, the true soldiers of the holiest cause? Is it not insulting Divinity itself to deny high art, or oppose its free development? Is it necessary to give you proofs, to

quote texts? In the moral life of a nation, everything is mutually dependent, is linked together.
What is, I ask you, this tumult which shakes the
throne ? "

"You have undertaken a mission full of nobility
and grandeur, I am sure, though I have never studied
these questions."

"Then hush! Our conflict has for its object the
triumph of the soul over matter, and if it was possible for you, who have no faith, to understand the fatal
consequences of religious indifference—"

"Yes, I know, but you are heating your blood.
Children have been born with the germs of disease
because the mother heated her blood. And then
you see," added I timidly, "perhaps it is not God's
will that the Institute should be reduced to powder."

"Do you not know that your jest is sacrilege ? "

"In this respect," said Mme. Paline, "I am entirely of your opinion, my child. Your husband's
words are indecorous in the last degree ; but on the
other hand, I think you and your friends, as you
doubtless ironically call them, are embarking upon
a democratic career which I confess is repulsive to
my instincts. Besides, all these people who come
here are indisputably slovenly."

Esther took too much pleasure in launching thun-
derbolts at the wretched Academy under Tambergeac's name to calm down immediately. Thanks
to my wife's more and more violent attacks, the
Ferme Modèle attracted so much attention that its
fiery critic came to the house one night with a bandage around his head, a compress over his eye, and
one hand in his vest. The night before he had received two severe blows and several strokes from a
cane from a son of a member of the Academy, who
had been especially insulted by Esther.

"My dear friend," cried my wife, taking the
wounded man's hand, " you have a noble heart ; you

are my only friend, and I will avenge you : hand me a
pen."

In these words the generosity of her enthusiastic
nature was depicted in all its completeness. The
young critic expressed his gratitude to the best of his
ability, but gave her to understand that he was powerless to struggle against the determination of his editor—to give up all literary and artistic polemics. The
meeting at Poissy was about to commence, and the
Ferme Modèle must devote itself entirely to the special
study of cattle raising. It was certainly a great dis-
appointment, but I was delighted.

" Wouldn't this be the right time to attend to the
clothes ? " I ventured to say, rubbing my hands.

I did wrong to show my satisfaction so openly.

Two or three days after, about eight o'clock in the
evening, my dear good wife gave birth to a beautiful
little girl. It is impossible to describe how charming
the child was ! I wept, I laughed, I hugged everybody—I even shook hands with the coachman, addressing him as my friend. Suddenly it was discovered that my daughter was entirely destitute of clothing, and, for the time being, they wrapped her in
napkins. The following morning I entered the
ladies' carriage and drove to a linen draper's, whom
I was obliged to rouse. On the way I could not help
singing, sat first on one side and then on the other, and
it seemed as if my delight could not escape the notice
of any one. The passers-by must be saying to themselves : " Look, there's Monsieur Babolain, professor
of mathematics, whose wife has just presented him
with a little daughter."

" Mademoiselle," said I to the shop-woman, " pray
make haste; my little girl has absolutely nothing to
wear. Thank you, Mademoiselle ; I haven't time to
sit down. We were taken by surprise."

" Such things sometimes happen."

" Indeed ! Please give me the best of everything.

There was nothing to make us suppose they would
be needed so soon. Did I tell you it was a girl? Oh!
give me whatever you choose."

One thing after another was piled into the carriage, which was soon full : embroidered bands, cash-
mere shirts, wonderful leading strings, hats with
feathers, etc. While returning to the Rue Vaugirard
I tossed over these pretty things, smoothing the
hats and kissing the caps, in which I fancied I saw my
little girl.

"It is impossible to make a more absurd selection," said my mother-in-law at once. I could not
help laughing, I was so happy. "Are you not afraid,"
continued Mme. Paline, turning to the doctor, "are
you not afraid my son-in-law is attacked by some bad
fever? He bewilders me."

"We'll see about that by and by," he answered
laughing. "Just now the most pressing necessity is
to have a nurse, and I am going to choose one."

"I'll go too," said I. "Two are not too many to
make such a selection, and besides, I am something
of a physiognomist."

"Very well, come. Is your carriage at the door?
And besides, between ourselves, the patient needs
rest."

I perceived that he was not sorry to take me
away ; in the outburst of my joy I must have made
an intolerable bustle ever since the night before.
When we were alone in the carriage I said :

"Doctor, I want to thank you for what you have
done for me. You are an excellent man, my friend,
my dear friend—I beg your pardon, but I can't help
calling you my friend. You must excuse me ; I am
really intoxicated with joy."

"That is perfectly natural. It is unusual to have
so little cause for anxiety on the birth of a first
child."

"That is true; it is my Esther's first child; I

didn't think of that. My head is turned inside out. Let me shake hands with you, doctor. I am more agitated than any one else would be, because I have more reason to rejoice that an indissoluble sacred bond has come to sanction our union : you are not ignorant that my wife is a great artist : she has refined tastes, noble aspirations. The mother and daughter are both, I may be permitted to say, most admirable characters. As for me, I am thoroughly commonplace ; I am talking to you with brotherly frankness, doctor. Ha ! ha ! ha ! When the mind has long been habituated to exact analysis, it is difficult for it to enter the kingdom of imagination, so that—in short, the first days of our married life were, I must confess, somewhat painful — I had been as poor as Job all my youth— And stay, this is a very natural, very curious thing : now that another horizon is open before me, now that the future smiles upon me, I feel an indefinable joy in recalling the sorrows—the little sorrows, of course, of the—"

Suddenly I let down the front window and pulled the coachman's coat. I had just seen my friend Timoléon, looking grave, pale, and careworn, and no longer walking with his usual haughty air.

"Do you know the news, my dear old friend ?" I said as he approached.

"Yes, Babolain, yes, I know it. Heaven has blessed your union by sending this little angel. I will pray for you all ; I will try to pray."

"What ! you don't rejoice ? What is the matter, my dear Timoléon, what is the matter ? Come and choose a nurse with us."

"No, no, I'm in a hurry ; good bye." And he went away.

"Doctor, I'm very much afraid my friend may be seriously ill ; I've already noticed that he has been very much changed for some time—I was telling you that I was as poor as Job when my uncle, who lived in Beaugency—"

" Here we are at the Place de l'Estrapade : let us get out, the office is here.   It is settled that you are one of my colleagues."

We entered a small room with a low ceiling, pervaded with a very strange heavy odor.   A clock made of shell work stood upon the mantel-piece, and on the wall hung two framed engravings; Napoleon at Saint Helena, and Joan of Arc in a cuirass.

A fat lady in a plaid dress, whom one would have taken for some old corporal of dragoons retired on half pay on account of too great obesity, appeared, rang a bell, and eight or ten nurses carrying their babies entered and stood ranged in a semicircle. The examination was conscientious.   The milk gushed forth under the doctor's hands in long white streams that at first nearly reached me.

One of the nurses having been selected, the poor woman urgently requested that her trunk should be sent to her new master's address, gave her child a last embrace, and entered the carriage, where we found ourselves alone together, the doctor having been compelled to leave us and continue his rounds.

" Take the back seat, my good nurse," said I, "and beware of the draughts.   You are not cold ? Wait, I'll raise the window ; it's always safer— And now let us make haste."

It seemed as if my daughter must find the time very long and begin to be impatient.   When the nurse was seated in the back of the carriage she raised her apron, felt for her pocket, and having drawn out a huge blue and yellow plaid handkerchief, wiped her eyes with the extreme edge of one corner without unfolding it, and uttered a heavy sigh.

" Why do you cry ? " I said sympathizingly. " Were you sorry to come with me."

"The child was very fond of me; it makes me feel bad all the same."

I was very much touched by the simple words.

How had egotism been able to blind me so far as to make me forget that this poor woman was a mother, and I had just torn her child from her! Why should the peasant's son be sacrificed to the professor's daughter? Is it possible that the world contains creatures poor-spirited enough to be able to love their children only when at a distance from them! And I am making myself an accomplice of this social monstrosity! The nurse gained such grand, moral proportions in my eyes that I said, with a shade of respectful embarrassment:

"Madame, pray believe that I understand what you must suffer, and I assure you shall always feel the truest, the most sincere gratitude for the service you are about to do me."

She removed her handkerchief and looked me steadily in the face.

"Ah! I know very well, my good friend," I continued, "that such sacrifices cannot be repaid with money." She moved restlessly to and fro on the cushions of the carriage, and answered in a very energetic tone:

"Then I shall go back to the office. Why did you say twenty crowns a month? Before everybody, too! Twenty crowns with sugar and coffee—I've got witnesses. Tell your man to drive back to the office."

"You misunderstand my—"

"What are you talking about? I don't like double-faced people—I've got witnesses."

"My meaning, my good friend, and your suppositions hurt my feelings."

"When have I hurt your feelings? When have I done you any harm? Come, I want to go back to the office. When one has milk — what did the doctor call it ?—'Savory milk' he said—that's the very first quality, and when a body has such milk as that, there's not much trouble in getting one's twenty crowns with sugar and coffee."

"But I'll give you twenty-five, my good friend. You see you misunderstand me. And I promise you as much more in presents. I shan't be ungrateful, I assure you."

The worthy woman still gazed at me with increasing astonishment. Then suddenly mollified, she murmured in a low tone, in which a slight shade of distrust still lingered:

"Then why did Monsieur use so many words?"

She was right, but I had intended to act for the best.

XIII.

I was the happiest of men: my little Valentine—this was my daughter's name—had welcomed her nurse Marianne with an excellent appetite, and the good woman confessed that she was very comfortably settled. Mme. Paline was extremely kind to me. As for my Esther, she recovered rapidly, and I must say that she had never been more beautiful. Enveloped in clouds of muslin and lace, she had already received a number of visits, and was inspired with a most ardent affection for her daughter. She had her brought to her from morning till night, covered her with knots of ribbon, and actually wanted to curl the few hairs on the back of the little one's head.

I wasted a few days in enjoying the pleasure of looking at her, but the feeling of duty soon returned and I resumed my heavy toil with ardor. It was more necessary to earn money than ever. I arranged a sort of class which enabled me to give six or eight lessons in a single hour. Moreover, having heard that an editor, then very enterprising, intended to publish a sort of scientific dictionary, I offered to perform a portion of this great work. What would I not have done to make good the money losses I had suffered, and gain a dowry for my little daughter? From time to time my pride awoke, and I said to myself, ' I might have been a man of learning, entered the Institute, earned honors, titles, left a noble work to posterity; and here I am reduced to trade in science'—I was foolish, for after all, is it not as honorable to be a good father as a great scholar? Was not my little Valentine the most beautiful of all works? and what would my titles, my learning, matter to her by and by? Would she love me the more for them? Certainly not.

Meantime the labor spent upon the dictionary, to which I devoted my evenings after the well-filled days were over, and which I often prolonged far into the night, fatigued me terribly. I had fits of dizziness that greatly troubled me, and felt pains in my chest which alarmed me. What would happen if illness compelled me to rest? Meantime, in the midst of my toil, I committed the error of leaving the ladies very much alone and neglecting myself. "You are growing slovenly," said Madame Paline. And indeed she was right: my clothes were more worn than was proper. I heedlessly came in without a cravat, and forgot to shave. Without being aware of it, absorbed as I was in my work, I gradually fell into the habit of living away from my family. I breakfasted in a modest little restaurant not two paces from the college, that I might lose no time; and my classes frequently would not allow me to return to dinner. The ladies on their side, overwhelmed by the thousand occupations celebrity entails, were rarely at home.

Matters were in this condition when, one Sunday

after breakfast—we happened to be all assembled in the same room—a little man with a hooked nose was announced by the name of Isaac. He had, in fact, all the external characteristics which distinguish an Israelite.

"Madame," said he, casting an inquisitive glance around the apartment, " I'll go straight to the point, as one ought to do in addressing an artist of your talent. I should be glad to enter into business relations with you, and have come to inquire what price you ask for your last picture. *Despair pursued by—by—*"

"Sustained by Religious Feeling."

"Yes, Madame, exactly. The painting possesses very superior qualities, a pure elevated style. Please tell me your price."

I was not surprised by this proposal, I was convinced that sooner or later fortune and fame would reward Esther for her efforts ; but I was very glad, for I was always thinking of Valentine's dowry. Madame Paline, seeing that my wife hesitated, answered :

"You are rather late, Monsieur ; my daughter has already refused several offers for this picture which has made quite a sensation, and I should be the first to use my influence over her to prevent her disposing of it for less than three thousand francs." I was entirely ignorant that such offers had already been made for Esther's painting. Monsieur Isaac did not seem surprised.

"I don't think the amateur whose agent I am will be deterred by that sum. You say—"

"I say three thousand five hundred francs without the frame," replied Mme. Paline with dignified firmness.

"I misunderstood you"—I had also misunderstood —" however, in concluding this matter, there is one little condition to which my patron attached a certain degree of importance : M. le Comte de Vaugirau

—I have no special motive for concealing his name—
would like to have Mme. Esther de Martignac "—I
always felt a positive pang when I heard my wife
called by her artist's name—" promise to reserve for
him, on conditions she will mention herself, the three
pictures most nearly completed."

" I will think of it," said my wife.

" But it would be much easier, my child, if the
Comte de Vaugirau would, visit your studio. You
have a number of very beautiful sketches, a number
of partially finished pictures."

The Jew highly approved of my mother-in-law's
suggestion, and everybody was satisfied.

This visit had considerable influence over the ladies' mode of life. From this day forth, I saw scattered through the suite of apartments in every direction, canvasses signed in large characters and covered with sketches whose boldness was really remarkable. How could any imagination be fruitful enough
for all these productions? Once, in the courtyard, I
received a bow from M. le Comte, who was just getting into his carriage which was loaded with my wife's
sketches. This passionate lover of pictures was tall,
wore long moustaches curled up at the ends, and his
whole bearing was distinguished by an air of aristocratic elegance. The members of my family were
never weary of praising the generosity of his conduct.
I was even shown a wonderful box in which he had
given Esther the price of her last pictures.

Unfortunately, I became more and more absorbed in my work; but I saw clearly that my wife, surrounded by homage and success, was giving herself up
rather too much to the happiness of making herself
admired. I could not reproach her ; after all, it was a
very natural weakness. She had won her reputation
at the sword's point, it would have been pitiful for
me to be surprised that she was a little proud of it.

One thing caused me deep sorrow: just in proportion as, rising above prejudices, she accepted the sometimes singular expression of a worship of which she was worthy, the memory of the past seemed to become unendurable to her.

She took very little notice of her daughter, and I guessed from trifles that my presence irritated her more than ever. One would have said that by excluding me from their life, into which however I had neither time nor skill to enter, they wished to free themselves from an intolerable yoke.

It happened that the room in which my wife worked became too small, and I was told it was absolutely necessary to hire a studio, somewhat expensive, it is true, but very large and light, in the neighborhood of the Quai.

I had the courage to interpose and speak of economy. " Perhaps the great drawing-room might do," I suggested.

" Why, don't you understand," replied Mme. Paline very dryly, " don't you understand that all hard labor is impossible in the neighborhood of a crying child ? "

Yet my little Valentine seldom cried ; it was impossible to find a better or a prettier child of her age. Still, my mother-in-law might be right. My wife's incessant labor was different from mine, and required complete freedom from interruption. She loved Valentine in a different way, better than I did, perhaps ; if she had not worshipped her, would she have toiled with such ardor to secure her future ? Did not her efforts replace the caresses she had no time to give her ? Poor Esther ! Can one have a great intellect without also having a large heart ? My dear wife tells me nothing, says nothing about her business matters : she has the modesty of heroism.

" If I have spoken of economy," I added, " it is because I am always thinking of our little girl."

" And of yourself too," replied my mother-in-law.

" But don't be afraid. When you married my daughter your instincts did not deceive you, it is an excellent thing ; and if you were ruined, you may be sure you won't be allowed to starve."

She said this with such a strange smile that I did not exactly understand her.

" What do you mean ? " said I.

"I? nothing; I am joking. Good bye, I must go out."

It was not until afterwards that these words and many others recurred to my mind, and it became evident that my presence had made them suffer terribly for a long time. Alas ! how could I have perceived it? They suddenly began to pay me most unusual attentions. Seeing that I was suffering from weak eyes and a pain in the chest caused by the excessive amount of work I was compelled to accomplish, they said a thousand kind words to me. One day, when they were going out in the carriage to dine in the city, I heard Esther say to the cook: "Remember that your master does not like his meat well done, and see that the dinner is good." These attentions, to which I had never been accustomed, made my eyes fill with tears.

Besides, I was more in love with my wife than ever. When she went out I lay in wait to see her, cautiously drawing the little curtains back from the window to admire her at my ease. Her beauty had increased wonderfully of late : I was awed by it ; she now seemed to exceed all ordinary bounds : a slight degree of embonpoint gave her whole figure a fullness and dignity whose charm was irresistible ; besides she had suddenly acquired a new and wonderful art of dressing. I did not know how to express the admiration all this inspired ; but she, anticipating my remarks, kindly explained how simple and economical the toilettes I thought regal really were. She had purchased such and such

lace for almost nothing, thanks to an exceptional opportunity ; and the jewels, the precious stones, the
cameos, in which she daily appeared, had been
bought under similar circumstances. In short, by all
the little confidences she bestowed upon me, I was
convinced that she was acting like a wise and prudent economist. It was a great relief to me.

Months elapsed in this way, the ladies, notwith-
standing their worldly life, continuing to overwhelm
me with attentions and consideration that bewildered
me ; and I loving and admiring my Esther at a distance, while I resumed the life of laborious study
which had an indefinable charm for me.

One evening, about eight o'clock, when I came in
to go to work, I saw on the table such a huge pile of
proof sheets to correct, that a momentary feeling
of discouragement overwhelmed me ; and while
lighting my lamp, it occurred to me that this evening the ladies were to be present at the first performance of a piece at the Opera-Comique. The package of proof sheets was really enormous ; I had
not set foot inside of a theatre for nearly a year.
The idea of surprising the ladies took possession of
me, and I hastily dressed. I must have been losing
a great deal of flesh lately, for my coat seemed to
hang around me. When I had finished tying my cravat, I went to tell the nurse, kissed Valentine, who
was sound asleep, and went away humming a tune.

Unfortunately the hall was full, and it was only by
paying twice the usual price for a seat that I obtained
with great difficulty a little stool in the embrasure of
a doorway. It was in the midst of the interval between the acts ; there was great confusion in the room,
and at first, suffocated by the heat, and dazzled by
the lights, I could distinguish nothing. I noticed
however, that my two neighbors were smiling as they
looked through their opera glasses in the same direction. "She is really magnificent," said one. "It's

her assurance that I particularly admire," replied the other, and they whispered together, laughing heartily.

I also glanced in the same direction and saw on the lower floor, near the left hand passage, several very fashionably attired gentlemen, who, with their backs turned to the hall, were standing before the corner box talking very gayly with the people within, whom it was impossible to distinguish.

Besides, I cared very little about what was going on there. I had come to the theatre to meet my wife and her mother, who undoubtedly on a night when mere stools cost such exorbitant sums, must have taken very inferior seats. I carefully examined the second tier of boxes, and then the third, but in vain; and was thinking of crossing the orchestra to inspect the portion of the building hitherto concealed from my eyes, when I saw my friend Timoléon, hidden under the shadow of the right hand gallery as I was under the left. His arms were folded, his eyebrows drawn into a frown, and he was gazing intently at the closely surrounded box, which seemed to attract general attention.

At that moment the bell of the theatre was heard, and all returned to their seats; the famous box on the first floor was unmasked, and I recognized my wife and my mother-in-law leaning back amid waves of silk and lace, and beaming with smiles. A gentleman about forty years old, with a pair of mustaches curled in military style, whom I thought I recognized as having seen somewhere before, had remained alone before the box. The signal was given, the orchestra began the prelude, Madame Paline made a graceful gesture of invitation to the elegant gentleman, and the latter took a seat between the two ladies, who moved apart that they might not obstruct his view of the stage.

The sight made me feel a violent heart-burning, and my brow suddenly became damp with perspira-

tion.　As I turned to take out my handkerchief I saw
Timoléon, who was also wiping his face, and evidently very much agitated.　Why was my friend hiding in
that dark corner—why was he so troubled and restless ?　I was about to rush towards him to have an
explanation of the mystery, when the curtain rose
and the words : " Sit down, sit down," murmured on
all sides, forced me to be silent and motionless.

I wanted to listen to the piece, but it was impossible for me to hear a note or understand a single
word.　I was constantly watching Esther and her
mother.　What was there peculiar about them ?　It
seemed to me as if their manners, their gestures, and
even their toilettes were singular.　Was I the sport
of a illusion, or was my wife really transformed ?　How
does it happen that all these people surround her and
talk to her with such familiarity, while I—　Am I
not her husband—　And Timoléon, why is not he
near them ?　I am crazy, I am absurd, I am acting
like a child.　Instead of reasoning, I am wandering.
Could I have lost my faculty of analysis ?　Let us
look at the matter coolly : what is there surprising
in the fact that a woman who is justly celebrated
should attract attention when she shows herself in
public ; that she should be surrounded by respectful
homage ?　Do I not know that for a long time the most
distinguished persons have considered it an honor to
be admitted to her studio, that she moves in a circle
of society entirely unknown to me, and that all this is
perfectly natural.　But then why am I so agitated ?

The plaudits that from time to time echoed
around, suddenly roused me.　I should have liked to
go to the box, but dared not.　It seemed as if everybody must know me and would say, pointing their
fingers at me : " That ugly little man with the pale
face, crooked back, white cravat like a justice of the
peace, red eyes and blue spectacles, is the husband
of the great Esther Paline, the magnificent woman

yonder." "And why did you come here?" said I to myself, "you proud, foolish fellow? Why did you come if you did not have the humility to remain in the shade that is proper for you, exulting in a triumph you cannot share because you have not earned it. Were you not happy in your old coat, bending forward under your lamp near your sleeping child, working for her as well as you were able? What madness has impelled you to leave your proper sphere? Yes, of course. Esther is triumphant, radiant, admired— And yet she is my wife, and I love her," I added, crushing my hat. The interval between the acts having come, I hastily went up to the first floor and, pausing, began to read the placard hanging on the wall in a frame. "I ought to go," I said to myself, "I ought to go;" but I gradually approached the box in which the aristocratic profile of the gentleman with the mustache was dimly visible through the half open door. After having vainly tried to button my gloves, I gave two little raps. "Come in," said Esther, who was laughing gayly. I entered; the ladies turned, and my wife, with a sudden blush,—was it caused by surprise or displeasure,—could not restrain a low exclamation.

"Oh!" said she, fanning herself violently, "oh! it's you. Good-evening."

My mother-in-law, who was excessively flushed, but majestic as usual, seemed indignant. The five or six gentlemen who were again assembled around the box were silent, raised their opera-glasses, and stared me coolly in the face. My situation was horrible. I felt that I was utterly ridiculous, smiled foolishly at everybody, and made a number of little bows around the circle. "Be dignified, natural, don't show the least affectation," I murmured between my teeth. Then bending towards Esther, I said to her:

"I thought I should please you by coming to bid you good-evening, my dear. Does the play amuse you?"

She did not answer, but leaned back in her arm-chair, and said in a loud voice, with the air of a queen :
" Gentlemen, my husband."

A profound silence followed, and it seemed to me that every one was smiling ; but before my agitation gave me time to analyze the nature of the smile, the gentleman with the mustache, bowing with extreme courtesy, murmured :

" Madame de Martignac, do me the favor of introducing me to Monsieur ; I believe this is the first time I have had the honor of meeting him."

" My dear, le Comte de Vaugirau, who worships painting," she said with great volubility.

" Monsieur le Comte, I am charmed—"

" No more so than I, Monsieur, I assure you. Do you still devote yourself to sculpture ? "

" You are mistaken, Monsieur le Comte, I have never devoted myself to sculpture."

" Ah! I beg pardon a thousand times. At one of the last exhibitions I admired a very beautiful bust, signed Martignac, and naturally supposed—I was mistaken."

" De Martignac is my wife's name. I love the arts—"

" That is a matter of course."

" Doubtless, but I have no talent for them."

" Ah ! so much the worse. Madame de Martignac. A thousand pardons, Mlle. de Martignac, I ought to say, or rather : Madame—Madame—"

" Madame Babolain, Monsieur le Comte."

" Ah ! yes, Monsieur Babolain. I'm delighted to make your acquaintance. Have you any children, Monsieur Babolain ? "

" Yes, Monsieur, I have a little daughter," I murmured. And I felt such a violent pang in my heart that I stopped short. There was something veiled under the excessive politeness of this fine gentleman which made me suffer terribly. Was it scorn—pity ? I could not tell ; I did not feel insulted, but I suffered. By what right did he speak of my child at this moment?

The interval between the acts being over, each of the gentlemen bowed to me, and I found myself alone in the box with Esther and Madame Paline. I did not conceal it from myself; the sole cause of the excessive civility of which I had just been the object was the high esteem in which Esther was held. It was to the husband of the great artist that all these attentions had been shown, for personally I had been as foolish and ridiculous as possible all the evening.

I was not sufficiently a man of the world, was not sufficiently master of myself, to behave with this ease of manner. I must certainly have annoyed the ladies greatly by arriving in this way without being expected, and even imagined that they would make some remarks on the subject; but contrary to my supposition, they thanked me for coming in the most charming terms. Yet my wife said in a low tone, in a voice of tender reproach : " My dear, you have left Valentine at home alone."

I did not know what to answer. She was right: how many accidents might have happened during my absence ! Would the servants know enough to come after me, to call the doctor in time— The orchestra began to play, and I took refuge in the back of the box, which was quite dark. From that time I was more at my ease and tried to analyze my feelings as I had been accustomed to do. I was ashamed of the part I had played so badly, I was aware of having been a pitiful creature : I ought to have done this, said that. Now that I was no longer on the stage, I once more regained my clearness of thought and saw plainly. But while I gazed at my wife's admirable beauty, I confusedly distinguished opera-glasses turned towards her from the main hall, and thrilled from head to foot with emotions of pride. " Yes, yes," I thought, "look at her all of you, admire her, enjoy her works, be proud of winning one of her smiles, but I have had her first tender caresses, I have understood her; she has already loved me. I have a child who is a pledge of our mutual affection, a child who will have her genius, and whom we both fondly cherish. My wife, yes, my wife."

While an actor was announcing the author's name, I rushed into the gallery, ordered the cloaks to be brought, and helped the ladies put them on; I tried to be as free from awkwardness as possible, and Heaven be praised, got through my task without accident. I offered Esther my arm, slipped a five-franc piece into the box-keeper's hand, and thanked her with a smile for her civilities.

Was it the result of chance, or was my wife's presence the cause? I do not know, but it seemed to me as if the vestibule was crowded with people waiting to see us pass. Besides being troubled at the idea of going through this throng, my sight was too poor to enable me to distinguish the faces clearly. A sort of lane was formed; it seemed to me that people were bowing to us; at all events, I also bowed right and left, until drawn on by the ladies, who had a horror of being stopped, I found myself sitting opposite to them in the carriage.

" How do you like the piece?" said Esther in a voice that rang cold and clear as crystal.

" Oh! it's admirable," said I; " pardon me, I answered you without thinking. The truth is, I didn't understand a word of what was being played; but what a triumph you had, my darling, what a triumph!"

" I? I didn't notice it. Tell Joseph to drive a little faster." But what was Timoléon doing hiding in the shadow like a conspirator, I thought, drawing up my legs that I might not crush the ladies' dresses.

XIV.

One morning, two or three days after the first night of the piece at the Opera-Comique, as I opened the door of the dressing-room where the college professors put on their gowns before going into the class-rooms, I heard loud bursts of laughter. Being a little late, I hastily entered, and the laughing instantly ceased. One of the gentlemen, who had evidently just been reading an article aloud, threw the newspaper carelessly on the table, and began to fasten the collar of his gown. I had undoubtedly interrupted something very interesting. I soon found myself alone ; the paper was still there, I took it up and instantly saw a heading that excited my curiosity greatly. It was couched in the following words: " *The·Artist Wife.*" Unfortunately the signal for the lecture sounded ; I hid the paper under my gown and carried it into the class-room. There, although interrupted every instant, I could devour this abominable piece bit by bit.

The author of this study of manners, for such it was, had pictured in repulsive terms a type of womanhood which might have been taken as describing general characteristics, but was in reality the caricatured portrait of Esther. Exact particulars abounded ; special details, scarcely veiled, left no doubt whatever in regard to the writer's intentions. Not only was the talent of the artist wife very slightingly judged, but the boldness of her extravagant style of painting was looked upon as a barefaced means of attracting eyes and hearts, a strange mode of obtaining notoriety, to which justice must at last be done; so that after having read thirty lines of this atrocious article one was convinced that it was alluding to some bold, artful courtesan. To complete the picture, the husband's portrait was added, a grotesque fawning fellow, living on the crumbs of the banquet, not even having the modesty to remain unknown, but appearing from time to time.

The first feeling I experienced was one of unmitigated disgust. These are the bitter fruits of fame, this is what it costs to surpass one's rivals. To what degree of baseness can jealousy push some foul souls! I cared very little for the insults heaped upon myself; the very excess of these calumnies rendered them senseless and harmless; I did not feel injured, I scorned such mire; but she, the irreproachable artist so passionately devoted to her profession, thinking only of the pursuit of the beautiful, impressionable and sensitive, like all refined natures, how she would suffer in reading these infamous lines! I was in agony.

When my lesson was over, I went to the dressing-room, and in the presence of all my colleagues, said :

" Gentlemen, I had the curiosity to read the paper you apparently found amusing, for you were laughing very heartily when I came in here before I went to my class-room."

While I was speaking, one after another went out through the half-open door. " This article, gentlemen, is an infamous thing, a succession of monstrous calumnies which I should despise if they attacked only myself, but being levelled at a person whose honor is entrusted to me, whose character must remain stainless, I cannot endure them, and beg you to explain them."

Two or three of the gentlemen who had not yet left the room, shrugged their shoulders slightly, and without raising their eyes, made their escape. This destroyed the composure I had maintained up to this moment. " You are cowards, gentlemen," I cried. " I said it, and I repeat it ; you are cowards ! "

" Come, Babolain, calm yourself ; you see there is no one here," said one of my colleagues, who, con-

cealed by the door of the wardrobe, was hanging up
his gown and cap. I turned and recognized the professor of rhetoric, a very distinguished young man
who had graduated from the normal school with me.
" Are you there ? " said I. " Do you understand
nothing about what is happening to me ? What! do
gentlemen who know me seem to approve of such in-
famies by their silence, and pretend not to hear me ! "

The idea occurred to me that my colleagues had
perhaps wished to make sport of my emotions, and
doubtless the next day would come to meet me, hold
out their hands, and apologize. " If they wanted to
mystify me," I added, " they have, without intending
it, cruelly overstepped all bounds. I don't think I
am excessively sensitive, but—"

" Babolain, we are old acquaintances, and no one
can hear us ; let us speak frankly : you know very
well that what you are now doing is useless ; why do
you make all this outcry ? In certain positions—I
don't judge you, mind that ; but in some situations
people keep quiet ; if I hurt your feelings, I regret it
—I'm right, believe me."

I approached him, ready to burst into a fury, and
said in a hollow tone : " I wish you to explain yourself instantly ; I insist upon it ; ah! you are smiling at
the base slanders like the others, ah ! you like the
dirty—"

" Let me alone ; you are perfectly ridiculous."

" No, I will not let you alone ; no, this matter no
longer concerns me. Ah ! if I were only the sole
person whose character was at stake. But it is my
daughter's mother, my wife, who—"

At the word wife he clapped me on the shoulder : " You haven't strength to play these parts—"

I paused an instant, I was suffocated. What mo-
tive had my old schoolmate for crushing me so ?
Had the poison of calumny glided into every heart ?
What was I to do, what could I say, where should I

find help? Yet I must defend my wife, plead her cause, prove, persuade— I succeeded in calming myself a little, took my companion's hand in my trembling fingers, and entreated, conjured him: "Tell me what people think—what you think yourself; I know nothing about these scandals! Everything people can say is false, you see. I swear it is false. This comes from the Institute—I will tell you all, my friend. You will perceive of what hatred my wife is the object by the mere fact of her great genius. You cannot know how implacable are the conflicts people enter into in the world of art—drawing, coloring, light and shade. It is a reign of fanaticism, and jealousy from preference attacks the most refined natures, the most lofty minds."

I saw plainly that he was touched. It was because I spoke from my heart. At that moment I felt an outburst of love for my wife which it is impossible to describe. I was her only defender against all these attacks, and the idea inspired me. I felt elevated, freed from my fetters; I was tall enough to rise to her height, to rescue her; for the first time in my life I was protecting her.

The professor of rhetoric looked at me a moment with a very peculiar expression; and putting his books under his arm, said: "Your innocence exceeds all bounds, my poor fellow," then glancing at his watch: "I'm somewhat hurried, I will leave you."

"And in a dastardly way, like all the others," I cried, giving myself up to an outburst of the most violent rage. Having taken off my gown, I was in my shirt sleeves with my cap still on my head, and I repeated with the most energetic gestures: "Coward! yes, coward!"

"What the deuce—have you gone crazy? You are making me angry at last. Is it my fault if Madame Babolain makes herself the talk of all Paris?"

"Wretch, oh! wretched liar!" and as I uttered

the words I sprang at his throat. The door was thrown violently open, and five or six persons rushed upon me ; I struggled like a madman, striking blindly at everything around me, but the pain of being feeble and powerless was to be added to my other sources of shame. I was mastered in an instant. " I'll kill him ! yes, I'll kill him ! and all the others," I murmured.

" Put on your coat, Monsieur," said the proctor gravely, " and cease this scandal. Have the kindness to withdraw, Monsieur Babolain, or you will be obliged to do so by force. Go at once."

I was compelled to obey, and was escorted to the door of the college by two men who had been summoned for the purpose. When I was in the street I sat down on a stone ; I was like a drunken man. So I had angered everybody without convincing any one ; I had compromised my dignity as a professor without result. The slanders would circulate more rapidly than ever, thanks to my clumsiness ; I must be the most foolish of men, not to be able to prove what was perfectly plain. I saw my poor Esther holding out her little hands to me imploringly, and saying: " In the name of our child, defend me ; everybody is attacking me ; my dear husband, you are my only hope."

This thought reanimated me, and I began to walk on haphazard, with my eyes fixed upon vacancy, and my fists clenched. Soon I noticed that I still held the scandalous paper in my hand, crushed and rumpled, it is true, but nearly intact. It was a ray of light. At the first glance I found at the top of the page the address I wanted, got into a cabriolet, and twenty minutes after was knocking at the door of the *Lardon, a Journal of Literature and Art.* In a very narrow room, divided by a partition of lattice-work adorned with placards, was a large table covered with printed papers, among which a gentleman with an extremely bald head and a very weary air was rummag-

ing. The atmosphere was very close, and pervaded
with a smell of stale tobacco smoke and beer.

" Monsieur," said I without the slightest preamble, " I have come to demand satisfaction for the
abuse and slanders your miserable paper contains."

" Pray sit down," replied the bald man smiling,
" I don't exactly understand what you mean. Against
which number do you make these grave charges ? "

" Here it is, Monsieur, look." And I threw the
fragment I still held in my hand upon the table.

" Oh ! I remember perfectly ; but there is nothing
in that number except an article entitled *An Artist
Wife ;* and I see nothing personal there, not a name,
not even an initial ; it is merely a study of manners in general, a type in which any one who chooses can recognize himself, but which is no one's
portrait."

" You have lied. Madame Esther Paline is plainly designated in that article. It is against her that
these anonymous slanders are directed ; have the
courage to confess your infamy, of which I will have
an immediate and complete retraction."

" And who are you who speak with so much authority ? "

" I am Monsieur Babolain, professor of mathematics in the college of Saint Louis, and husband of
the eminent artist whose fame you vainly seek to
tarnish."

" Her husband ! Well, Monsieur, I'm sorry for
you ; " then turning towards the grating he said, raising his voice : " Are you there, Henri ? Come here."
A short man with a cigarette in his mouth, disordered
hair, and flashing eyes, suddenly appeared, and my
surprise was great to recognize in this personage the
fiery Tambergeac, the implacable native of Toulouse,
the invincible bulwark of criticism. At last, then, I
should meet an honest man, who was independent
and just, and therefore ready to help me ; I held out

my hand to him. But without responding to my ad-
vances, he struck a dignified attitude in front of the
table, and said :

"It is vain for you to attempt a system of intimi-
dation here, Monsieur, which is beyond all bounds of
propriety. It is a sacrilege to limit the sacred freedom of criticism, and this paper, I would have you
to know, is an independent tribune where people can
speak according to their consciences."

"It is for that very reason that I appeal to your
fair dealing, your memory, the regard you have always shown for my wife."

"A truce to useless words, Monsieur. Admit, if
you choose, that I am the author of the article in
question, not a line of which will be expunged: I assume
the whole responsibility. The time is at last come
to drive the money-changers away from the temple,
to purify the arts, to do complete justice."

"You are either a fool or an arrant rascal, Monsieur Tambergeac, miserable lackey of the Institute!"
I uttered this insult haphazard, without understanding its meaning very clearly myself, but imagining
it would sting him. The effect was speedy. The
gentleman from Toulouse buttoned his coat: "The
contempt your situation inspires saves you from an
immediate chastisement, Monsieur. I shall expect
your friends to-day."

"For what purpose, scoundrel?"

"To make an arrangement with them as to the
best way of slitting your ears." And he disappeared
behind the grating.

That evening I returned to the Rue Vaugirard at a
very late hour. My good friend Timoléon, who, for
reasons which I did not exactly understand, had
positively refused to be my second, had shown the
utmost devotion in every other respect; seeing that
the meeting was inevitable, he had kept me shut up
in his house all day, to prevent my getting into any

other scrape, he said, and taken upon himself the difficult task of the arrangements and discussions. He came back about ten o'clock in the evening, dripping with perspiration, and found me seated before some soup and a cutlet which had been brought from some neighboring restaurant, and I had found it impossible to taste. He told me the result of his labors : everything had gone off as well as possible ; the arrangements for the duel had been very easily settled. Tambergeac, who was convinced of my awkwardness and inexperience, and moreover very eager to carry out an affair which, without the least danger, would secure himself the benefit of a scandal, Tambergeac, I say, was intractable. We were to fight early the next morning with swords, in a spot admirably adapted for the purpose, just behind the race-course of Montrouge : a dispensary student and a young ensign were to be my seconds.

I confess that when I heard all this I felt chilled to the very marrow of my bones. The fever which had sustained my strength during the first part of the day was completely calmed, and I saw the seriousness of my situation clearly. I had never touched a sword ; my sight was wretched, and I was not ignorant that my awkwardness was exceptional. Were there not very great chances that I should be killed ? Yet my predominant thought was not the fear of death, but the dread that I should not be equal to my duty when on the ground, and might behave like a coward.

I returned home under the influence of this feeling, lighted my lamp and began to arrange my papers, pausing in my work, from time to time, to eagerly swallow large glasses of water. At daybreak I went into Valentine's room ; she was sleeping peacefully in her cradle. I wanted to kiss her, clasp her in my arms, but was trembling so violently that I was afraid I should wake her ; was there any reason why she should be disturbed because I was going into danger ;

would it improve my situation in the least? I leaned
over my little daughter and murmured in a low tone :
"It must be, my precious darling, it must be.
This matter concerns your mother's honor and our
own. I must defend you both. If I should die, it
would be a misfortune; but you don't know me very
well yet; your sorrow would soon be over—still, you
would not forget me too quickly. Do you remember
when we played on the carpet? We've had very pleasant times together, my poor love."

The clock struck five. I hastily dressed, took
down a little picture of Esther which hung on the
wall and put it in my pocket ; then with a parting salute to the house I might never see again, went cautiously out.

We were the first to arrive at the place appointed.
"It would have been better, Monsieur," said the
young ensign, "if you had worn boots with heels.
What a lovely morning—will you allow me to lend
you some military gloves? I have a pair that are
just the thing—flexible and thick : see, this doesn't
confine the fingers, and the weapon is supported.
You don't know your adversary's game, Monsieur? "

I thought of my wife and daughter who were both
sleeping at that moment. " I hope my absence has
not been noticed yet," I said to myself. I dared
not answer the officer lest the trembling of my voice
should betray my state of mind, so I slightly shrugged my shoulders and affected the utmost indifference. " Faith, I'm like you, I don't want to know
my opponent's game, one is all the more prudent and
watchful. Not very long ago I had an affair with a
fellow of whose method I was entirely ignorant. As
I put myself on guard, I said to myself, 'one of two
things, either this fellow is—' "

The soldier's story was interrupted by the arrival
of the art critic, who bowed to us and immediately
took off his coat. We were ready in an instant.

12

Strange, when I saw my adversary's flashing eyes, threatening face and shining sword, the necessity of fulfilling my duty loyally to the end impressed itself so forcibly upon me that all agitation ceased, every fear vanished; it seemed as if some fatality surrounded me, some superhuman power commanded me to chastise this scoundrel, and the sense of the justice of my cause rendered me invincible. As soon as the seconds had measured the swords and retired, I clenched the hilt of my weapon firmly and advanced rapidly upon my enemy to kill him.

Tambergeac grew very pale, and hastily retreated until stopped by a fence, when he stretched out his arm and turned his head aside. I felt a strange chill sensation in my chest, my limbs tottered, everything began to whirl around me, and I sank upon the ground.

"The time is false, but it is a good thrust," said somebody.

Meantime my opponent had thrown himself upon me, crying:

"Oh! God, gentlemen, I have killed him. How did I do it?—This is terrible—I wished him no harm, gentlemen, none at all."

It was impossible for me to utter a word—I fainted.

XV.

When I again opened my eyes I gazed around me for a long time like a man who has suddenly awaked in a strange country; then by degrees the fog in which I was enveloped dispersed; the forms of things, which were at first as confused and undecided as the outlines of a wave, grew clear; and with strange surprise I recognized the fruit-room, my books, and the narrow bed on which I lay. I wanted to feel the coverlid with my hands, touch the walls to confirm the im-

pression received through my eyes ; but found I had
not strength even to raise my arm.   Meantime a pale
woman whom I recognized by her white cap as a Sister
of Charity, was watching me earnestly.   Beneath the
mild and benevolent gaze, I felt reassured, my memory returned, and I recollected my wound, the duel,
the horrible scene that had caused it, and all the rest.

"You are better," said the Sister, who hád approached me ; "do not speak.   You are still too
weak."

I muttered unintelligibly, "Where is my wife—
and my child?"

"Don't be anxious, my dear Monsieur, the little
one is very well; she will come in and kiss you when
she gets home from the Luxembourg."

"My wife?"

It seemed as if the Sister did not wish to hear;
but seeing that I was still questioning her, she replied
with a faint blush:

"Madame is not in just now ; come, come, calm
yourself, or the doctor will scold us."

I was too much accustomed to Esther's absence
to be surprised that she was not at home.   Yet I
should have liked to have given her my first glance
when I regained my consciousness ; I felt that there
was now a new and indissoluble bond between us—
that of the blood I had shed to defend her.   My poor
wife, how she had suffered during the crisis !   On
seeing me in this condition, she must have said to
herself: "If he should die, it is I who have killed
him."   In anticipation I consoled her, held out my
arms to her.   But why was she not here, it would
have done me so much good !   I was making these
reflections when the doctor entered, accompanied by
Timoléon ; his cheeks were hollow, and there was a
look of despair in his eyes.   My old friend came up
to me and pressed my hands, while the doctor said
with a radiant face :

"I can boast of having brought you back from a long journey, my dear Monsieur; for more than a month you have been obstinately endeavoring to glide into the other world. Thank God! the danger is now over."

"And my wife?" I faltered, looking at Timoléon.

"She'll soon be back again, my friend; the ladies were obliged to go into the country for a few days. They thought your sickness would be less severe of course."

"Yes," added the doctor with a peculiar expression, "it was absolutely necessary. I ordered their departure on account of an attack of bronchitis, which required a change of air; but calm yourself, what a man you are! I assure you there is no danger, it is a mere precaution."

"You are perfectly sure?"

"Why, of course. Don't be disturbed, keep quiet," said the three persons at my bedside in the same breath. They smiled at me and I smiled too.

My strength rapidly returned; but as I grew better, my wife's absence and persistent silence seemed more and more incomprehensible. Every day I asked about her—at last Timoléon said:

"My dear friend, since the truth must be confessed to you, I fear the ladies won't return as soon as I expected. They went much farther than I told you."

"But where are they? Speak, I beg of you."

"They are in Italy. Doubtless they would have been less hasty in taking their departure, but you know how eager an artist's imagination is. Your wife received commissions for several important works, which she could only complete there, and you know that for a long time she has had an ardent desire to visit the museums of Italy. The study of the great masters is a capital question—"

While saying this, Timoléon was choosing words in great embarrassment. I had remained perfectly bewildered, with my eyes fixed on vacancy, and my hands clasped. After an instant's pause, I murmured, without intending it : " She is very cruel. And suppose I had died—what would have become of our child ? She did not think of all this, I know very well—her art takes complete possession of her. It is too easy for us who know nothing of the transports of genius to tax with ingratitude these privileged beings whose mission is not to nurse the sick, but to create magnificent works which are the glory of the human mind. Could they produce their master-pieces if their pursuit of a single object did not render them insensible to the thousand details of every-day life ? It is we who are guilty, we commonplace mortals, who, through instinctive jealousy, want to cling to their wings and find in their souls our petty, trivial virtues, which could not exist there. She causes me great sorrow by going away ; but after all, what does that matter, if she can paint one picture the more ? "

" Oh ! you are sublime," exclaimed Timoléon.

" If people are sublime so cheaply, you are sublime too."

" I—I am a miserable wretch, a scoundrel, a coward. If you knew what I really am, you would be ashamed to have held out your hand to me."

" You are joking. Yet this is not the time."

" Yes, I'm joking : I am wrong. When Madame Paline went away, she gave me this letter for you, and I promised to deliver it, my dear friend. I have not read it, but whatever it may contain, promise me to be calm. You will be brave, won't you, you'll give me your oath."

He opened a drawer and placed a pile of papers in my lap.

" There is your mail," said he ; " there are a great many proofs to correct, as you see."

He pressed my hand and left the room. I instantly recognized my mother-in-law's writing, broke the seal and read the following lines :

"MONSIEUR :

"Your last mad act caps the climax of
the tortures we have endured ever since bonds which
are unfortunately indissoluble have united you to
my daughter." I stopped short, turned the letter in
every direction, again examined the signature, and
then resumed : "Too long, Monsieur, have I excused
you, believing you unaware of the suffering you
caused us ; but now doubt is no longer possible ; you
had premeditated everything, calculated everything
in advance ; you had set yourself the task of smothering the enthusiasm, the glow of the artist's soul under the heavy burden of your truly oppressive individuality. Pardon me if any offensive expression
slips from my pen ; my despair does not allow me
time to choose my phrases, and I wish to tell you what
I think at once.

"To attain your object more surely, to complete
your work of destruction, you cause scandals to
spring up, call to your aid the publicity of I know
not what discreditable papers, and even lose your
self-respect so far as to cross swords with low people,
doubtless in the hope that some of the disgrace of
such an adventure will be reflected upon your wife's
brow and my own. We have in our blood, Monsieur,
a hatred of certain base actions and cannot endure
them near us. You wish to become famous too, to
win renown by force ; you are at liberty to do so ; but
do not depend upon my daughter's reputation as a
stepping-stone on which we will allow you to mount.

"My daughter, by my advice, has used your name
very little hitherto ; henceforth she expects to forget it
entirely. We break all ties with the past. Overwhelmed with broken illusions, suffering from a thousand blows, bleeding at a thousand wounds and with
our brows crimson with blushes, we go to seek at the
sacred springs of art, rest and forgetfulness. May
God forgive you, Monsieur. We leave your roof

with empty hands, contenting ourselves with our few personal effects; for we want to deprive you of even the shadow of those pretexts you have been skilful in transforming into a scandal. Let it be clearly understood that your wealth, however great it may be —we do not wish to know—is not a chain strong enough to keep us under your authority.

" My daughter, who approves of this determination, joins me in signing the present letter.

" ESTHER PALINE DE MARTIGNAC-CORBON.
" EVELINA DE MARTIGNAC-CORBON."

I could not turn my eyes from the fatal sheet; but it was useless to fix my attention, it was absolutely impossible for me to understand its meaning clearly. I was in the midst of a nightmare, whose reality appeared only in the most confused forms. The only thing that seemed plain was, that they had gone away hating me. I called Valentine, and when I had her in my arms, passionately kissed her cheeks, her forehead, her hair, her little hands and her clothing. I looked at her as if I saw her for the first time.

" I have no one but you now, my darling," said I. " How shall I love you without making myself hateful ? " And I clasped her so closely that, doubtless, being terrified, she called her nurse. " Yes, yes, carry her away," I said eagerly, " she must not be frightened."

I mechanically opened another letter ornamented with a huge red seal; it contained the following lines :

" *To Monsieur Babolain, Agrégé des Sciences, Professor of Mathematics in the college of St. Louis :*

" MONSIEUR,

" Upon the report of your principal, and according to the vote of the council of the Univer-

sity in the session held upon the third of this month,
His Excellency the Minister of Public Instruction
has decided that you should, until further orders, be
suspended from your office and placed on the unat-
tached list:

" His Excellency, Monsieur, regrets that reasons
of great importance, which it is doubtless needless to
recapitulate, compel him to adopt a measure whose
severity ill harmonizes with the pleasant associations
formerly left by you in the minds of the body of professors."

This was signed and countersigned.

" So everything is crumbling around me ! I am
accursed ! " I exclaimed.   " But after all, what have
I done ? For what crime am I hunted down in this
way ? " In an outburst of rebellion and despair, I
crushed the papers lying before me, hurled them
upon the floor and trampled them under my feet.
" Heartless creatures, you have plundered me, and now
that I have nothing left, now that I am without strength
and without resources, you fly from me as if I were
a mangy dog only fit to be killed ! Genius ! genius !
Does it concern me ?   Do I know anything about
your wild fancies ? Why should I be the expiatory
victim of your genius ? To satisfy you, I must also
be deprived of the possibility of repairing the evil
you have done me, and that my ruin may be complete,
you wrest from me even the nails with which I
might scratch the ground. Oh ! you may hate me, for
I hate you too. I will efface the memory of your
passage through my life, as we brush mud from our
clothing. Hatred for hatred, scorn for scorn, that is
justice, and I will prove it to you when you return."
Exhausted by this fit of passion, I sank upon my bed.
" They will never come back, since they detest me.
Is it their fault ? Is not one always guilty when one
makes one's self odious ? Who compelled me to plun-
der myself for them ; did I not do so of my own free

-will, from a mere feeling of selfishness? I was proud of them; my pride was flattered when I saw them brilliant and admired; of what use is it to threaten Providence? Would God be just if His logic were not inflexible? Can He change moral laws for me? Have I not been blind and mad, ridiculously vain to believe myself agreeable? And yet she has felt real affection for me at times—I cannot refuse to believe proof; she has loved me; yes, yes, I remember."

"It will be useless for her to protest, to curse me," I thought; "this great artist has given herself to me, and of the past, which she is powerless to destroy, I retain a most living proof—our Valentine, my sweet little angel."

I rose, picked up the papers scattered over the floor, and seating myself before the table, eagerly began to correct my proof-sheets.

When Timoléon returned, he surprised me in the midst of this task. Pausing on the threshold he held out his arms to me:

"Pardon me, Babolain," said he, "I did not have the courage to remain near you while you were reading those letters, whose contents I guessed only too easily. My poor friend—my brother! I have spent all this time in the Carmelite church— You are wretched, are you not? You must take refuge in prayer, open your heart to God; in Him alone you will find strength to resist the blow that is overwhelming you."

I know not why Timoléon's eager sympathy was painful to me. Why had he besought the aid of Providence; why did he advise me to do the same? Did God need so many idle words? What could I tell Him? should I seek to deceive Him by decking myself out in my woes before His eyes? Should I be pitiful and ridiculous enough to ask Him to stop the course of His justice, and was it not the only prayer

worthy of Him, to accept His inevitable sentence and
bend the head without prayer or pleading?

"What is done is done," said I, casting down my
eyes, for I was by no means sure that I could look
him in the face without bursting into tears. "Let me
correct these proofs; you see I am very much behind-
hand, and the people at the printing office will be furious. Never speak to me again of what you know,
will you? Never, never."

"Sorrow glides over without hurting you," he said
with a shade of irritation in his tone. "You don't
know what we suffer, we who have less hardened
souls. But your indifference frightens me, I assure
you; if the philosophical skepticism which takes the
place of everything else to you produces such effects
upon hearts, I think it is repulsive, and I pity you."

"I am not indifferent, and it is useless to pity me,
Timoléon."

"I excuse no one; but indeed, I can understand
many things now! So you don't suspect, heart of
stone, that even as I talk to you I am suffering the
tortures of the damned? I'm disturbing you—good-
bye," said he.

"Good-bye, Timoléon, good-bye."

My life was to begin anew, that was all. I had deceived myself; I had been mad; my pride had intoxicated me. I had believed myself able to marry a
woman who was my superior. The point in question
now was to see if I had the material for a father in
me. That became a fixed idea. I imagined myself
in this new character; my ugliness, my physical defects, etc., would no longer be obstacles, and besides,
I was conscious of possessing treasures of tenderness and devotion for my little daughter.

I dismissed the servants, sold the horse and carriage, and began to set my affairs in order; but as
fast as I paid back bills, fresh debts, of which I knew
nothing, seemed to spring from the ground. There

was something incomprehensible and exorbitant about them. Was this a gulf in which our last resources would be engulfed? "Oh! God," I said in despair, " if we should have nothing left ! "

At the same time that I was settling my affairs, I resumed my labor with desperate eagerness, to finish the heavy task I had undertaken. Morning, noon and night, I went to Valentine's cradle, lowered the curtain, re-adjusted the coverlids, listened to her breathing. It always seemed to me as if some danger threatened her, and her life depended entirely upon my care and watchfulness.

Often too, I wandered through the large suite of apartments, whose disorder reminded me, only too clearly, of the ladies' hurried departure. It caused me deep sorrow, and yet I sought a thousand pretexts to return and remain amid the furniture and hangings. Must I not bid them farewell? For I should soon sell them ; I would separate myself from these scenes of luxury which were not fit for me ; and I sat down upon the sofa, where she sometimes used to lie. I opened the piano and paused before the wardrobe ; rummaged in every corner, searched the shelves, and if I chanced to find a bit of ribbon, a pin, any trifle that might have belonged to her, hastily wrapped it up and carefully concealed it.

She sometimes appeared before me so distinctly that I felt actually frightened, took refuge in my room and double-locked the door.

One day, some recollection returning to mind, I remembered the Jew Isaac, the picture-dealer who had so greatly appreciated my wife's talent. Perhaps this man still had some painting signed by Esther in his shop. At all events, it was possible that he had kept up his business relations with her, and could give me information of her whereabouts. After hesitating a long time I went to Isaac's shop, and when I had looked at some sketches, said to him : " I believe you have had several of Mme. Esther Paline's pictures."

I saw at once that he did not recognize me. He smoothed his chin like a man who is trying to remember something.

" Esther Paline—Esther Paline ? "

An instant after, he smiled brightly.

" Oh ! yes, I recollect perfectly. One of the pictures made a good deal of stir ; M. le Comte de Vaugirau bought it, ha ! ha ! as well as many others. I've got them all up stairs."

I felt chilled.

" So, Monsieur," I stammered, " you have a great many of this artist's paintings."

"Everything she has done, probably. When Monsieur de Vaugirau went to Italy a short time ago, he left the collection with me."

I clung to an easel to save myself from falling. "To Italy—to Italy ? " I repeated in my agitation ; " that is impossible."

" What did you say ? "

" Nothing—I said nothing, on the contrary, I was thinking—ah ! to Italy."

The Jew looked earnestly at me, and said in an insinuating tone :

" Madame Esther Paline is an artist of great originality ; some of her sketches are — amazing. Would Monsieur like to see any of them ? I would sell them at a very low price."

"Oh ! no, I have not—my situation will not allow me to buy—on the contrary, I was going—pardon me, I am a little out of breath—I was going to offer you three of this lady's drawings which I happen to have."

Isaac's expression changed completely.

" That's a very different matter," said he, " totally different."

" Would you buy these sketches, Monsieur ? "

"No indeed," and he burst into a sneering laugh. "They are very interesting sketches; the first inspiration of the artist."

"Don't urge the matter; you see I'm loaded with Esther Paline's pictures, and the paintings are absolutely worthless to me with the exception of the frames. You must perceive I'm not quite crazy enough to increase the number—beg pardon—I'm just going to breakfast."

I suddenly drew myself up to my full height, as if I had received an electric shock.

"You speak very contemptuously of works which have excited enthusiasm and admiration."

"Between ourselves," replied the dealer impatiently, "Madame Paline's pretended talent has never existed, and her painting is far below mediocrity. A fuss has been made about her as well as a great many other pretty women, with whose success art has absolutely nothing whatever to do; you know that as well as I, Monsieur."

"It is not so; it is false," I cried, struggling like a wretch condemned to the stake, whom the flames are just beginning to reach.

"It must be confessed you're a very odd stick," said the Jew, bursting into shouts of laughter.

"And why should M. le Comte de Vaugirau have bought all these pictures if they were valueless?" My tone was threatening.

"Ha! ha! ha! Why, what do you want me to say? M. le Comte undoubtedly had excellent reasons—these things don't require any explanation."

"You have lied! you are a knave!"

"What! what! Be good enough to take yourself off at once."

I wandered through the city like a bewildered hare pursued by a pack of hounds. I suddenly crossed the street and then went back again; stopped without any reason, jostled against the passers-by,

stared around me without seeing anything, and then
continued my way, while the Jew's voice still buzzed
in my ears.   If this scoundrel had told the truth,
what was the woman I had married, of what infernal
play had I been the laughing-stock?

But how could I believe in so many horrors?   It
was all false, I was the victim of abominable impos-
tures.   While struggling against the proof that clutch-
ed my throat, I said to myself: "We will go away.
We will pack up to-morrow.   I will break, burn everything they have touched; my child must be snatched
from these accursed scenes before they have made a
lasting impression upon her mind.   Valentine must always be ignorant of these falsehoods.   We will take
refuge in some corner of the world far from knaves
and liars.   We will live for each other, and perhaps
the memory of these evil days may in time be effaced.

But alas!   we cannot do away with a portion of
our existence at will.   All the thoughts and emotions
of life cling together, and are interlaced like the
links of a chain.   Memory is disobedient to the com-
mands we wish to impose; recollections are ever-
watchful foes, and if for an instant we succeed in
driving them from our homes, they take up their
abode without, watch for us, haunt our walks, twine
about us, and the circle of the past whirls around the
old man with the more violence, the greater the efforts he makes to fly from it.   Life is not a succession of naked facts; around each are woven the feelings, the fancies, the impressions of every kind which
have preceded or followed it, which have been its
cause or effect; and this brain-work, these illusions,
these mirages, with which we have swaddled our acts,
soon mingle with them; so that afterwards we can
no longer recollect the act without at the same time
remembering its surroundings, its swaddling bands,
its bark; it appears to us ready clothed, and we are

powerless to separate what we have done from what we might have done, the real from the imaginary, the object from its image. This is why we love certain things in the past which were worthy of hatred, why we cherish certain sorrows.

Why curse the mirror whose falsehood makes us happy? The illusion was deceitful; but was the joy to which it gave birth any the less real? What does it matter if the thing is black, if my eyes first saw it white and the memory of this false whiteness still charms and consoles me!

What matters it that she deceived me? Why search into this mystery? And moreover, did she deceive me? I do not want to know—I want the proof which would overwhelm me to remain a falsehood. Nothing will seem to have any truth save the illusion which made me live. The Esther I have in my heart is the real Esther.

Such were the arguments by whose aid I cheered my sorrow. Thus, in taking refuge in the past with a sort of obstinacy, I still deferred until the morrow the moment of leaving the surroundings which helped me to remember. And while arranging the programme of a new life and thinking of leaving Paris, I was gradually resuming my former habits.

At the time when the classes met, I mechanically looked at my watch, as I used to do when I feared to be late, and went out slinking under the shadows of the walls, avoiding every eye and trembling lest I should be recognized. Useless anxiety! I was aged, broken, my hair had grown gray, and I walked with difficulty, leaning on my cane. When, after having passed through out-of-the-way streets, I approached the college, I saw my scholars pass by. I found this one changed, the other seemed taller; I remembered their voices, their gestures, and every particular of those times. Why could I not live over my old life, return to the college from which I had driven myself? But the logical consequences of my fault must be endured to the end; it was necessary for the consummation of the justice of Providence that everything around me should be shattered; that I should be abandoned by all; that Timoléon also—

I went to his house one day, and when I asked the *concièrge* if I could go up, the good woman stopped me, saying that he was not in.

"Will he come back soon?" said I.

"I know nothing about it; Monsieur has been travelling for a fortnight."

"And where is he?"

"This is the address he wrote himself to have his letters sent to him."

The *concièrge* looked through the pigeon-holes in a desk, and handed me a piece of paper, on which were written these few words:

"Florence: to be left at the office till called for."

I sank into a chair, and dropped the paper I held upon the floor.

XVI.

Doctor Bernard, weary of waiting for us, had gone to bed when, about eleven o'clock in the evening, our coach stopped on the Place de Favras before the sign of the *Barbe d'or.* Valentine, whom I had held in my arms all the way, was sleeping soundly. We shook the nurse, my good Marianne, whose head had been resting on my shoulder for two long hours, and got out. The hostess of the inn threw a large armful of small sticks of wood on the fire—the pans in the kitchen sparkled brightly—and seating myself near the flames, I undressed my little daughter. It was the most important thing to be done.

When she was laid in a large white bed perfumed with a pleasant odor of freshly-washed linen, and I had arranged everything for the night, I withdrew

into the next room, took off my hat, which had been
torturing me ever since morning, and opened the
window. A pale gleam of moonlight dimly revealed
the church, the square, and the tops of the trees,
among which appeared the strange, vague outlines
of chimneys and tall gables. There was not a sound
except the murmur of the mill-dam, the ticking of a
clock, the distant barking of the dogs in the farm-
yards, and the stamping of the horses in the stables.
The air was pure and fresh and full of the delicious
perfumes of the fields; I fancied that I was trans-
ported into an imaginary world. How far I was
from accursed Paris, the slightest memory of which
I eagerly repelled! I gazed into the mysterious darkness with a curious glance, seeking to guess beforehand what the day would reveal of the new scenes in
which my life was to begin. I found this perfect
calmness consoling and full of promise. Is it, then,
so very difficult to efface a portion of one's life? I
went to bed, and before falling asleep re-read the
doctor's letter, in consequence of which I had undertaken this journey.

I had known Bernard at the College of Orleans,
and although several years older than I, we had been
in the same division. I had always retained a certain regard for him, and even written him a letter at
the time of my marriage. Therefore, when I had
fully determined to retire into the country, finding
myself greatly embarrassed in regard to the choice
of a place of retreat, I asked the advice of my old
fellow-student, who, I knew, was settled in le Blaisois,
where he was practising medicine with great success.
He very obligingly promised to try to find a house
suitable to my wants in his neighborhood ; and almost
immediately after, in another letter, told me he
had discovered something that would please me, and
was holding it at my disposal. Thus, after having
collected the last remnants of my fortune, which for-

tunately would secure us the necessaries of life, I
went to take up my abode in the market-town of
Favras. The next morning the doctor came for me
in his gig, and through narrow, grass-grown roads
bordered with hedges from which the birds flew out
in hundreds, took me to the estate intended for me,
and of which he confessed himself to be the owner.
The terms were settled, I accepted everything with
my eyes shut, engaged a servant belonging to the
neighborhood at once, and was installed in the house
that very evening. It was a real curé's dwelling,
cheerful, sheltered from the north winds, ancient and
plain, situated about three-quarters of a mile from
the market-town, and surrounded by a garden where
apple trees and cabbages, gilliflowers and lettuce,
grew amicably together. There were long narrow
walks edged with high borders of box, three crumbling steps which led into the dining-room, a stone
bench near a sun-dial, and below, the stream flowing
under the willow trees among the tall grasses. Then
there was the wash-house with its thatched roof, the
wharf for the boat—nothing was lacking.

I had found a frame which exactly suited me; this
was the corner where I ought always to have lived. I
eagerly thanked Bernard. It seemed as if he had
chosen this dwelling with a feeling of tenderness, as
if with touching intuition he had divined my sad moral
state and tried to alleviate it by procuring this refuge
for me. It was certainly a proof of affection, and I was
all the more touched by it because my old comrade
carried delicacy so far as to conceal his kind solicitude
under an appearance of roughness and supercilious-
ness.

He was a short fat man, with a very ruddy complexion, and as he said himself, did not know what the
word obstacle meant. Very soon after his marriage
he had lost his wife, who left him one son, named
Joseph. He was held in high esteem in the mar-

ket-town, not only on account of his talents and his cheerful way of making them conspicuous, but for the sake of his rapidly increasing wealth, his handsome house built of brick and stone which threatened the skies with its lightning-rod, his skill in foreseeing opportunities and taking advantage of them, in buying his oats, selling his wine, becoming the purchaser of large tracts of woodland, which, to the great delight of the peasants, he parcelled out after selling the timber; on account of his enterprising, resolute character, the ringing tone of his voice, when he said : " Men square at the base like myself are never taken unawares ;" his huge stomach, small eyes, and red beard.

Far from being irritated by Bernard's rough patronizing manners, I accepted them with a sort of gratitude : the trials through which I had just passed had made me even more timid than before ; I was now isolated, destitute of advice, doubting myself and overwhelmed by the responsibility of the resolutions I should be obliged to form. It was really providential that at this very moment a firm, determined friend, who did not know what obstacle meant and was square at the base, allowed me to lean on his shoulder and cling to him.

In fact I was soon overwhelmed by the numberless cares caused by my settling in the house, or rather Valentine's. Destitute of skill in household matters, and naturally prone to foresee and weigh the consequences of things, I brought to this new task the scrupulous care of a chemist who is making a delicate analysis. Two rooms seemed equally suitable for my daughter's reception ; but which of the two should I choose ? One, it is true, was warmed by the rising sun ; but the walls of the other were thicker, and a clump of trees protected it from the wind. On the other hand, this clump of trees might cause a dangerous dampness ; and this was not to be feared in the first room, which I should undoubtedly have chosen had

it not been for the thousand inconveniences I discovered every moment.   By means of reflecting I succeeded by logical deductions in increasing my uncertainty, and nothing more.   I went to the market-
town several times to get the doctor's opinion ; but
when I was in his study, filled with engravings, and
saw him, wrapped in his dressing-gown, seated before
his huge desk covered with important papers ; when,
after brushing his hand across his forehead, as if
disturbed, he said, laughing in my face : " Well, what
is it now, my poor Babolain ? " I was checked in my
desire to unbosom my troubles ; and comparing my
affairs with his, accused myself of childishness, of in-
discretion, and usually left him without having spoken of what brought me there.   I can still remember
the fit of merriment that overpowered him when
one day I asked where, in his opinion, was the best
place on my estate to put a rain-gauge, the want of
which I felt in regulating the watering.   And yet, to
a rational mind, nothing is more natural than this desire to have a rain-gauge : how can we give the earth
the proper quantity of water, if we are ignorant of
what each square yard can and ought to receive ?
But what does all this matter ?

When Valentine's room had been selected, other
cares succeeded which I would trust to no one but
myself.   I began to put down carpets, to stop up the
chinks, to nail pads under the doors, and from the
first day, my hands were bruised with blows from the
hammer.   Moreover, I devoted myself to the garden
after a fashion, and gave directions to the carpenters
and locksmiths I had summoned to make some little
changes.   This was a very great affair !   In regard
to carpentering and locksmith's work I was reduced to
the memory of my former study of mechanics, so that
these orders gave me considerable difficulty.   Perhaps I even calculated the probable consequences
of everything too scientifically, for it often happen-

ed that they were obliged to begin again the next
morning at what they had done the night before. I
apologized to the workmen and tried to make them
understand upon what principle I had based my rea-
sonings.

Unfortunately they were destitute of even the
most elementary notions.

Bernard said to me one day: " What kind of
trade are you forcing upon your unlucky workmen,
my poor Babolain ? The people in the town talk of
nothing but you."

Yet I had but one wish, that the whole world
would forget me and my little girl, and leave us at
peace in the corner where we had taken refuge.

At last quiet and calmness were restored ; we
were settled in our new home, were alone, and very
comfortable. Then a strange phenomenon took
place in me. The silence of the fields, the purity of
the vivifying air which restored my health and seemed to intoxicate me, the trees, the flowers, the blue
depths of the skies, disposed me to fits of meditation
and happiness never felt before. I allowed my
whole being to be pervaded by the fair nature I now ·
saw for the first time ; I gave myself up to her, was
perfectly confident, had no fears for the future ; and
during hours spent in lying upon the grass, lifting
the bits of moss, searching among the tiny flowers, I
listened, waited, and absorbed indefinable sensations
vague and confused, but sweet and consoling. And
these were not purely physical impressions, there
was an exchange of emotions and actual feelings between nature and myself. I perceived the presence
of a soul which was speaking to mine ; there was
tenderness in the warmth of the kindly sun which
caressed my back ; charitable hospitality in the
tree that sheltered me with its foliage. My little
garden was kind-hearted ; it was a safe, prudent confidant, always ready to hear, never weary of consoling

me. There was no more mocking, no more distrust. When I was alone I was surrounded by friends.

The annoyances and sorrows of former days produced upon me the effect of the low continuous base the rolling of a carriage causes, and which tempts one to sing. In the morning, when I opened my window-shutters into the fragrant tufts of clematis and jasmine ; when the pure air streamed in, and I saw my trees invigorated and rejoicing in their existence, my turf besprinkled with dew-drops ; when I heard the warbling of the redwings and nightingales, my soul expanded joyously.

I thought to myself: "Can it be that the horizon becomes more vast as the scenes amid which we live grow more contracted ? Can it be that infinity is within our own souls ? Is it possible that God Himself is in our hearts, and wills that we should seek Him there ?"

All my past, with its sufferings, its wild aspirations, now seemed inexplicable. People should never be allowed to run to the ends of the world to study exotic plants until they are perfectly familiar with the gilliflower that grows in their windows. We all have a strong chain that holds us prisoners : by pulling at it we hurt our feet but do not lengthen the bond. Browsing goats are strange animals ; put them in the centre of the most beautiful lawn, and they instantly rush to the end of their rope, tugging at it till it strangles them, sighing for the twigs they cannot reach, and indifferent to the nice tender grass that surrounds the stake. Had not I been like the goat ? " Eat your grass, Babolain," I said to myself, " and you will see afterwards." It seemed as if Valentine, young as she was, must feel the same emotions as I. I should have proof of it, by and by, when she knew how to speak and could tell me her childish impressions. She was certainly happy, rolling about on the greensward while Marianne was stretched in the

shade. The dear little thing could not criticize me
yet ; she did not think me either stupid or ridiculous ;
I was not disagreeable to her. I must take advantage
of the moment, secure her affection in good time ;
and I racked my brains to find means of making myself beloved. Often, vexed by my steady gaze which
she did not understand, she avoided me as we avoid
the rays of sunlight a glass casts upon us ; so I prudently waited for her to fall asleep that I might search
her face at my ease. Opportunities were not lacking.
My little girl, who spent the whole day in the open
air, fell asleep in an arm-chair almost every evening.
Then like a miser who goes down into his cellar, very·
sure of not being watched, I approached her, taking
a thousand precautions, slipped a cushion under the
little sleeper's head by no means unskilfully, upon
my honor, drew her little limbs nearer together,
raised her rounded arms, adjusted the lamp-shade,
and bending over her on my knees, feasted my longing eyes.

"Sleep, my treasure, sleep calmly, my little angel !
How happy you make me ! Shall I be able to repay
you some day for all the joy you give me ? "

And I listened to her quiet breathing, saw her
transparent, velvety nostrils rising and falling regularly, her thick long lashes stirred by almost imper-
ceptible movements. I saw the satin-like skin of her
little neck, and behind her ear, fresh and pink like
the petal of a flower, the soft curls upon the nape of
her neck, half hair, half down, sucking in with their
greedy roots the sweet juices of this living cream.

How many beauties and marvels this little body
contained ! What will it be then when I enter her
mind and heart ; when we shall be able to talk, to
think together, and share the same emotions ? What
perplexed me was the smile that sometimes, during
her slumbers, curled her lips and deepened the dimple in her cheek. I asked myself what the cause of

her amusement could be? What ideas were forming in that little head? I would have liked to know all this in order to understand her better, and thereby obtain more complete possession of her heart. One thing is certain, my presence imposed no restraint upon her, and I thanked her for being happy before me.

Marianne almost always surprised me in the very act of adoration; it was terrible. I believe the woman did it with a certain spice of malice, for where Valentine was concerned, she was almost as jealous as I.

" It's quite time for children to be put to bed," she said, entering suddenly.

" But you'll wake her. Besides, the clock is fast, very fast." And when, having carried my daughter into her room, we began to put on her night-clothes, the discussion was continued in a low tone. Marianne charged me with pulling off the buttons, making knots in the strings, committing a thousand blunders, understanding nothing about this kind of work—all of which was perfectly true, but I would not admit it, and defended myself as well as I could.

" Well, the darling will catch a cold on her lungs, if Monsieur spends half an hour in putting on her night-cap."

It is true that I did not hurry much; less, however, on account of my awkwardness than from a selfish desire to prolong my happiness. Often I have waked up in the night imagining that I heard her cough— pursued incessantly by the idea of a cold on the lungs, with which the nurse was always threatening me.

Ah! the happy moments I spent. It must be confessed that I had not wholly forgotten the past; a curl of my child's hair, a vague resemblance, a gesture, a nothing, made me start, and many wounds re-opened; but these moments were short, for the charm of my new life calmed the memories of former days by veiling them. I was forgetting myself.

On those dark, damp days when the rain falls incessantly, and one grows sulky in spite of himself, I put on my great boots and went to walk in the woods. There, on seeing the new shoots, the plants and trees revived and freshened, strengthened by the life-giving water they drank with delight, thinking of the roots which would inhale moisture and life from the wet soil, I forgot my ill-temper, my dripping garments, the mud through which I was splashing, and smiled at the ugly black clouds. All the created beings in the world cannot be happy at the same time. Each in turn has his share of joys and sorrows. There are no useless griefs, for all counterbalance certain joys. Every tear that falls is a dew-drop which will give birth to a smile. It is a great consolation, it seems to me, when we are suffering, to say to ourselves: "At this very moment I am giving happiness to somebody in the world."

And then, before cursing anyone or crying out to heaven: "Sorrow, you overwhelm me!" we should reflect a little, try different positions as the sick do, for there is always one in which the wound becomes endurable. For my part—is it an excess of egotism and pride—I don't know, but I have often found a charm in examining my pain, studying its details, observing its progress as if from a balcony, opera-glass in hand.

Months, years elapsed amid the quiet pleasures with which I had filled my life. An imaginary wall was rising between society and myself which grew higher and more impassable day by day. Since I had settled in the country, I had not been three times to the town, which inspired me with a sort of terror. Bernard himself had forgotten the way to the house, and I knew that the peasants who lived around us considered me an odd stick, *a little cracked in the upper story*. For all that, however, they treated me with respect on account of the rain-gauge that appeared

above the hedge, and which was called in the neighborhood, the machine for making rain.   Meantime
Valentine was no longer the child whom one could
cradle in one's arms and lull to sleep with a song;
she had reached that delicate and charming age
when the woman begins to appear in the little girl.
By degrees her mother's features began to reveal
themselves more clearly in her face ; she had Esther's
manners, gestures, and tones.

At first I was troubled ; not because resentment
and hatred awoke in my heart, but, on the contrary,
the memory of the illusions, the delicious raptures I
had enjoyed.   However thick the dike with which we
protect ourselves may be, a moment comes when the
water oozes through and penetrates it.   Past delights
have echoes which continue to sound.   If I had known
how to understand my wife better, how many sorrows I might have escaped !   Perhaps nature had
made her as good as she was beautiful.   Sometimes
proofs of her goodness and beauty, blending together, assailed me in throngs.   Ah ! if I could but commence life anew.

While I was thinking over all this, another source
of anxiety was gaining upon me.   Valentine had curious ideas I could not explain, little coquettish ways,
refined womanly manners that awed me ; and the possibility of exchanging our thoughts and feelings,
which had been the brightest of promises, now terrified me.   I found her too intelligent ; I felt that I
had a watchful, inquisitive, subtle judge, who would
soon allow nothing to escape notice, and I already saw
impending jeers — involuntary, inoffensive jeers —
which I should never think of imputing to her as a
crime ; poor child, could she help being lively and
witty ! From this time forth I watched myself more
scrupulously than ever, that I might not make a gesture, utter a word, that could displease her.   I knew by
experience what a piece of awkwardness or a blun-

der may cost. The point in question now was not to compromise the future—to calculate in advance the probable consequences of my slightest actions, to compel her to love me, to make her happy, to watch her tastes, to understand her nature.

Sometimes, treating her like a little woman, I asked her advice, appealed to her experience. During our walks I told her of my feelings, invited her to dream with me — then remembering her age, and trembling lest I had committed some imprudence, hastily retraced my steps and energetically began some purely imaginative story, full of the broad fun children like. Strange, she remained grave and silent, watching me with an earnestness that put me out of countenance; I sought for words, my sentences became confused, I felt that my gestures had no connection with what I wanted to say, I was conscious of being pitiably involved; and she, after having noticed all this, withdrew her hand from mine, murmuring: "Oh! dear, that's so tiresome."

This confession gave me actual pain, and yet I could not help admiring the touching cruelty of children, who, careless of consequences, always say not only what they think, but all they think. I said to myself: "Valentine has a mind beyond her years; she will be a woman of great intelligence, like her mother!" I ought to have understood all this at once. Her mind needs more solid food. The time has come to instruct while amusing her; yes, I must do it; I am responsible to society and my own conscience. This thought thoroughly delighted me, both as father and professor. I was in my element; the toilsome years of my youth, my former triumphs, returned to my mind, and I was grateful to her who had indirectly awakened these memories. I reflected deeply, and as I considered that the most precious treasure in life is the faculty of judging with accuracy, and analyzing everything, I determined to commence my daughter's education by the study of the natural sciences. Although I always sought for some ingenious excuse for instructing her, I was perhaps wrong in pursuing my course of teaching too closely.

If, for instance, I wanted to take Valentine to the bank of the river, far from imposing my will upon her, I sought by skill and gentleness to arouse in her mind a desire to go there. Then I improvised excuses to the best of my ability; now it was a butterfly to be caught, then a little farther on a huge strawberry to pluck; and by going from butterfly to strawberry, from strawberry to butterfly, we reached the bank of the river. Then by a skilful jerk, made without her notice, I threw my straw hat into the water.

" Oh ! dear, my hat has fallen into the river," I cried, trying to give the exclamation a tone of real astonishment. When she had stopped laughing, I continued, for I had my object : " There, see my hat float away, darling. Why does it float away ? " I walked on a few steps, and fished it out with a stick. Then, my premises being established, I thought myself certain of the result, and said boldly, taking her by the hand :

" I am sure you have been wondering why my hat floated away from us ? "

" No, papa, I don't care."

" Ah ! you haven't wondered about that ! But you won't be any less glad to know, for you are a little girl who wants to learn : hum-hum. The cause of this phenomenon, my dear, is the force of gravity. You are going to say : ' What ! papa, does the force of gravity make the river flow?'" By this means I tried to give my demonstration a little animation and life.

" I haven't said anything at all," murmured the little witch, pulling me towards the strawberries.

" You haven't said it, but you thought it, my love ;

and really it isn't easy to understand. You must imagine, in the first place, that there is a force in the
middle of the earth that attracts everything on its
surface : the stones, the trees, the men, the houses,
the—"

" Papa, the strawberries."

" Yes, my daughter. We say bodies are heavy
because when we want to lift them we have to struggle with the force which we call grav-i-ty. Now I
have finished my story ; isn't that very curious ? "

" No, papa."

" Now the water in the river, like all other bodies,
is subject to the action of gravity; and you will understand in an instant why my hat—"

" But, papa, what difference does it make, so long
as you've caught it again ? "

" Of course, but "— Should I persist or keep silent ? It is true that by continuing I was, thanks to
an accidental circumstance, engraving upon her memory a valuable scientific idea; but on the other hand,
should I not fatigue and annoy her by making too
prolonged a claim upon her attention ? And as Valentine pulled me nearer and nearer to the strawberries, a sudden inspiration came to me. I gathered
one, and holding it carefully between my fingers by
the fragile stalk, said : " Even this fruit is subject to
the laws of gravity; and a proof of it is, that if I drop
it, it will make every effort to go towards the centre of the earth which attracts it. In fact, you see I
open my fingers and leave the fruit to itself—what
does it do ? It falls—"

Unluckily I could not finish my sentence, for Valentine, with a bound, hastily snatched the strawberry
and ate it, laughing heartily.

" It won't do to insist," I thought to myself ; " to
insist would be to compromise the future. I have
been imprudent ; I went to work the wrong way.
It's really fortunate she stopped me by her roguish

prank, for I might perhaps have forever deprived the wonderful principles of gravity of all poetry. What can be more attractive to a young mind than to raise the veil which conceals these great laws of the universe? Another time I will prepare my exordium more carefully, and find a more roundabout way of entering upon the subject."

Meantime it became evident that my daughter was resolutely determined to avoid our instructive conversations. It was useless for me to divide my pills into the smallest possible fragments and wrap each in the most fragrant honey; the child smelt the drug and fled at full speed. In vain did I beg and entreat her; in vain did I show her glimpses of the poetic side of human knowledge—all was useless. She did not recover her usual good-humor until she was set at liberty, and could rejoin her nurse and help her pick beans, or spread the clothes upon the hedges in the kitchen garden. Yet I had a mission, a duty to fulfil; what was to be done? I followed her with a sorrowful gaze as she made her escape and ran into the sunlight; I shivered as I heard the sound of her laugh, and grew more and more jealous of the fat peasant woman with the red nose and merry eyes, who, without any effort, knew how to make herself beloved. I bore her a grudge for being merry, cheerful, faithful; for having given my child every proof of affection; I grudged her the privilege of dressing her every morning, of braiding her fair silken hair, which I would so gladly have dressed if I had been allowed; I hated her because she made the cherry tarts of which Valentine was fond—in short, I was jealous, and suffered deeply. "I have base feelings," I said to myself; "and if this Marianne, ignorant and superstitious as she was, should have a baneful influence over my child, would it not be my duty to send her away?"

And suddenly calming myself, I added: "I have

not even the courage to be frank with myself. I
slander the best of women because she is loved and
I am not."

Yet my daughter was really very much attached
to me; I knew it by the love I felt for her. My awkwardness was the sole obstacle between us. I had
never known how to go to work the right way.

Since that time I have analyzed all this, and collected many ideas which would have been useful if I
had had them before. The little women we call young
girls are assailed by a thousand capricious fancies, a
thousand indefinable whims, against which they can
struggle only by trusting themselves to a mind they
know to be destitute of weaknesses. They are grateful to the energetic person who compels them to
come out of themselves, and delivers them from the
notions that have taken possession of their minds.

How many times they pursue with their persistent caprices the man who loves them in order to
put him to the test—to feel their way. It is not
that they wish to make game of him. Their conduct
is instinctive; is it not natural to test the firmness
of a stick before one leans upon it! How well they
know that their great desires are extravagant, their
temptations inadmissible; and how humiliated and
lonely they feel when through weakness people approve of them when a frank refusal would deliver
them! They do not seek a master, but an infallible
friend to choose and cull from amid the confused
mass of their fleeting impressions.

I had never had the strength to be this friend.
Even on the unlucky days when Valentine persisted
in not understanding an explanation twenty times repeated, the tone of my voice never expressed impatience; it was my way of loving her. I had never
known how to manifest my affection except by surrounding her with an atmosphere of patience and
gentleness, making her hours equally pleasant and

happy; so that my little darling's position was like
that of a person living on the banks of those pure,
tranquil lakes which one cannot look at long without
feeling a desire to trouble their calmness by throwing
a stone into their depths.   My patience, which somewhat too nearly resembled docility, irritated her; she
felt her mischievous mood increase in proportion as
I deprived her of excuses for manifesting it.   She
was tempted to get the better of my gentleness, which
she had never seen exhausted : curiosity soon mingled with the wish, and she became very naughty; the
poor darling was aware of it, and the vexation she
felt increased her ill-humor.   She could not help it;
why did we not check it?   Why did we not assert authority over her ?   Was it her fault ?

Dissatisfied with herself, she was angry with others, which was very natural; we always seek for the
root of the ill weeds that spring up in us, in our
neighbors' homes.   She loved me, undoubtedly, but
it was with a somewhat compassionate tenderness,
for she knew too well that my fate was in her little
hands.

And then my caresses were never given at the
right moment.   Nothing is more cavalierly received
than a kiss that is not wanted; and even a guardian
angel, who conversed with his protégé every instant
in the day about his future plans and his solicitude, would become very wearisome in a short time.
I understood all this afterwards.

Both large and small children easily become intoxicated with what is arbitrary, and the difference
between the possible and impossible soon vanishes
entirely.   My Valentine set her pretty little foot in
this path.   She commanded, ordered, regulated everything in the house ; but her voice was so well modulated, she was so charming in her rôle of mistress
—it was a pleasure to bend one's neck to her yoke.
" How precocious," I thought ; " she does whatever she

chooses with us! What clearness in her ideas, what precision of sight! She has a critical judgment, and no timidity, no indecision—the two defects she might have inherited from me, and from which I had suffered so much." It was very natural that, being gifted in this exceptional manner, she should like to give orders, to have them executed promptly, to prove her evident superiority. I loved even the impatient words and little fits of temper that made my beloved daughter's eyes sparkle more brightly, and deepened the color in her cheek. Her way of making the boards in the floor creak startled me; it was no mere noise, but music whose echo charmed my ear long after it had ceased. My child's beauty so vividly recalled her mother's, that at times, when absorbed in reverie, Esther and Valentine became merged into one person; the present, the past, and the future blended together. In the depths of my heart I felt deep sorrow or extravagant joy over the merest trifles; and thus concentrating my whole existence upon a single thought, strove to render the hermit-like existence in which the whole world was contained to me, more narrow still.

One day when I was putting my grapes into bags, Marianne informed me that the curé of Favras wanted to speak to me. I was greatly surprised, for no one ever came to the house, and there must be some important reason to bring the priest to my door. I had scarcely descended the ladder when I saw Monsieur le curé himself coming down the walk towards me. He was a very affable man, with a smiling face, and, seeming touched as he perceived my embarrassment, bowed very courteously.

"Monsieur," said he, "pray excuse the step I have taken if it is intrusive, but I thought it my duty to come and request a moment's conversation with you."

Then with great caution and kindness he spoke

14

of Valentine, whom he had seen several times, praised her grace, her personal charms, and the moral qualities of which these external attractions must be merely the expression.

What was he driving at? What did it matter to him whether my child was charming or disagreeable, beautiful or pretty? He spoke of the sympathy and admiration the inhabitants of the town felt for her, and also the sorrowful surprise caused by the strange solitude to which the poor little girl seemed to be condemned: there were duties parents could not escape; the society and friendship of other children was an inevitable necessity; and religious instruction, so long withheld from Valentine, was a benefit of which she could not be deprived without positive crime. Seeing the impression his words made, the priest, while redoubling the affability of his manner, spoke to me more plainly, and I learned that the people in the neighborhood considered me a monstrous being, a detestable tyrant, and he himself had obeyed the indignation of the whole town in paying me this visit.

"But Monsieur le curé," said I with deep emotion, for I felt myself threatened with a great danger, "I have never had but one thought, to make my daughter happy—she is still a mere child; she is— dear me, I don't know her age exactly, but she is a child I assure you—we have been so happy. You can't imagine how pleasant our life is, she would tell you so herself."

"Take care that your somewhat too jealous affection does not seem blind egotism to the eyes of the malevolent. In fact, might not people believe that in imposing so unusual a life upon your dear child, you think more of gratifying your own tastes than of securing her happiness?"

I remained silent for a long time; many old sorrows awoke, a veil was suddenly torn, and the proof appeared as clear and cruel as a sword. No longer able to control myself, I took the priest's hands in mine, and said with a tone of despairing frankness:

"Yes, Monsieur, you are right: I think only of myself, I have never thought of any one else: I am a bad father as I was a bad husband. I feel, I see it."

"Calm yourself, my dear Monsieur Babolain, I have doubtless expressed my meaning badly; forgive me for causing this grief."

"Let me tell you all, I beg of you; at heart I am neither a hypocrite nor a liar. My selfishness is so deeply rooted that I am usually unaware of it; I am a wretched man; scorn me, you think me a pitiful object, do you not? And yet, in the course of my life, I have had every chance of happiness, but alas! I have ruined, withered every thing around me, and wished to condemn my child to breathe the same air, although I love her most devotedly. Oh! God, if I must always be a source of trouble to her, always bring misfortune upon her, it would perhaps be better to kill myself."

"Those are terrible words and ought not to have come from the lips of a father, a scientific man, a philosopher, even if the philosopher were not a Christian."

"It is because I know what I am, Monsieur le curé! I suffer cruelly, and I feel that my sufferings are deserved; that is all. Then the people in the town know that my daughter also seeks to fly from me, to shun me? They know she instinctively recoils from me as from a wretch who ought never to have been born."

The good curé was an excellent man. He offered me his friendship, entreated me to have confidence in him, and promised that if I would allow him to take charge of Valentine he would make her the gentlest, most affectionate of daughters, bind the ties that united me to her still more closely, and destroy

the bad opinion of me prevalent in the neighborhood. He made the acts my duty imposed perfectly
clear, and assured me that he would find means to
render them easy. In short, he possessed such per-
suasive eloquence, gentleness and goodness, that I
gratefully consented to everything.

"It's because I have never been separated from
her, Monsieur le curé," I murmured, as I took leave
of him. "She really loves me—I say it without pride
—too long an absence would be painful to her—although perhaps she would not venture to acknowledge it. And then, if the roads should be damp, if it
should rain, her little feet—her throat has always
been delicate, Monsieur le curé."

"Oh! of course, of course. Do you suppose we
would expose your daughter to a fit of sickness?
If the weather is bad, a carriage will come for her
and bring her back; ten people in the town, beginning
with myself, will be happy to do her this little service."

"Isn't the church too cold?"

"We will have a foot stove; we must take care
of both body and soul, ha! ha! ha! *mens sana*—
Good-bye, my dear Monsieur Babolain."

The first time Valentine left the house to go to
the catechism class, accompanied by Marianne, I
followed her with my eyes a long time. I had given
her careful directions early in the morning, and put
in her pocket a silk handkerchief, a piece of chocolate, and three gum balls. When I saw her merry
and talkative, selecting her prettiest ribbon to fasten
her braids, her freshest dress, her most becoming hat,
bursting into shouts of laughter and bowing to herself in the glass, I tried to be gay that I might not
damp her joy. But now that I was alone and watched her going down the path, I felt a keen pang in
my heart. "Alas! this is the beginning," I thought,
"the wings are unfolded; she is flying away, she is

leaving me, and this separation seems to her a deliverance. She does not know how to conceal her feelings, dear little thing. I wearied her, made her unhappy, everybody noticed it except myself. Who, since the hour I was born, has ever been able to endure my society without complaint? I could still see her blue dress gleaming in the sunlight as she crossed the fields, her straw hat relieved against the green hedges, and her little white legs bounding gayly along. No doubt she will turn at the corner of the path to wave her hand to me—will she turn? It would be so. little trouble."

She did not think of it. Still skipping merrily on, she continued her way and disappeared.

" It is a law of nature," I thought, " that each has his share of individuality; what right have I over her? Because I am cold, is it any reason why I should take her warmth? Ought I to strengthen my old withered body with her young red blood, stimulate my old age with her gayety, her youth, her illusions? She owes me nothing, it is I who am her debtor. In exacting a smile I take advantage of her, I rob her, I am happy at her expense, I stifle, crush her. If you can only live by clinging to this young branch, cease to be harmful and parasitical, fall to the ground and at least fertilize the soil, cease to be somebody and become something." Could I be committing the folly of complaining? Does the seed the wind bears away and places on a barren soil complain of its fate and envy the other seed which grows in the next field? Is not the law that condemns one being to die without issue, and another to leave descendants, that makes one handsome and gay, another ugly and sad, a wise and salutary one? Nothing is useless in this world ; the grain of dust that whirls through the air is no more given up to chance than the planets that revolve through space. Have I ever complained that an equation was inflexible and unyielding? Well! what are the beings who think or vegetate; what are the things that transform their shapes, blend together, and succeed each other, but the innumerable terms of the supreme equation of whose unknown quantity we are ignorant? Is it not something, after all, to feel one's self a necessary atom in the progress of the great problem, to prove that one's own sorrows are not the result of a caprice or fancy, but the inevitable and sublime consequence of the divine law that governs us all?

I looked at my watch—it was an age since Valentine had left me. If only there were no draughts of air in the church! How agitated and troubled she must be among all those strange faces! They must have overwhelmed her with intrusive questions, and she was so delicate, so sensitive. What is she doing now? Perhaps she will come home with tears in her eyes—have I not been cruel in exposing her to this trial? For my part, I should have liked to have her return with a swelling heart, cured forever of all liking for the town and its happiness. But no such thing happened. The doctor brought her back himself with a pair of horses, and when my daughter sprang to the ground, her eyes were sparkling, her cheeks flushed, and her lips bright with smiles.

"You see, my friend, I bring her back in good health," said Bernard, clapping me kindly on the shoulder. "Ah! I owed you a grudge for your shyness, but we'll say no more about it. Your Valentine is a charming creature, and has taken Favras by storm. No one could be more graceful and attractive, and besides she is as pretty as an angel. We won't say that too loud, although I fancy the revelation wouldn't surprise her very much."

"Indeed! did they really think her charming?" I forced a smile, for these praises caused me both pleasure and pain. My child's admirers were so many intruders forcing themselves between myself and her. Now she would make exertions to please these people. From this day forth Valentine was suddenly transformed. Always merry and good humored, she sang, danced, eat with an appetite she had never had before, told us the news and tittle-tattle of the town in such a comical way that Marianne, suddenly overwhelmed with mirth, broke the dishes. She drew this one's portrait, imitated the other's voice, related the attentions of which she had been the object. I thought that she had a great deal of intellect, that she was made to shine and please, and that I should perhaps witness her triumphs. While she was continuing her pranks. I watched her with a sorrowful glance, until throwing her arms around my neck she would cry: "Dance with me, papa," and there was no resisting her; I was obliged to raise my dressing gown, and shy, ridiculous, yet happy, begin to dance.

I fixed my mind upon it, but my lips murmured in a low tone, one, two, three, while she hummed the air of a waltz, bent her graceful figure, turned her head aside and smiled at the glass.

As the good curé of Favras had told me, my dear daughter's fits of impatience, disobedience and rebellion, gradually disappeared. It is true that, vanquished, overwhelmed by the unaccustomed tokens of affection she lavished upon me, I no longer dared to open my lips, asking nothing, accepting everything, allowing the last fragments of my authority to crumble away, while I enjoyed to the best of my ability the quick, constant caresses with which she seemed to pay for her independence.

I knew these threads of gold and silk with which I was surrounded were so many bonds that would paralyze and reduce me to obedience, but what did it matter? She was obliged to busy herself about me in order to hold me captive; it was necessary that her little hand should constantly draw these threads and flutter around me, and all these attentions bore so close a resemblance to affection. Besides, I said to myself: " Since I am incapable of guiding her, I ought to frankly confess my helplessness and submit to the consequences. I must keep in the background; what have I to teach her? It is ridiculous to wish to inoculate her by force with my ideas and theories, which I know are detestable. She is a woman already and I must respect her individuality in everything. So I yielded what had long since been snatched away from me. How many sovereigns, when violently expelled by their subjects, write in exile their act of abdication, and give themselves the consolation of disposing of a crown which was shattered upon their heads.

Already sure of her own power, Valentine assumed the reins of government and soon had her relations, her habits, made herself a mode of life apart from mine, and was amazed that I should remain as if overlooked, cowering in my corner. She was right, for I cut a sorry figure. She scolded me about the old-fashioned cut of my clothes, she did not want to have to blush for her father, required him to be in the present style, to wear fresh gloves, to become foppish—and when I answered smiling: " What is the use, my darling!" she had an impatient, witty, charming way of answering:

" Your opinion isn't asked, Monsieur. Oh! how unfortunate it is to have an obstinate papa."

" You are laughing at me, don't you know I do everything you wish?"

She became serious, and began to read silently in a corner like a very submissive little girl who has just borne an unjust reproof. I said to myself, looking at her out of the corner of my eye, "I have wounded her unintentionally; of course she misunderstood my words, I really seemed to be reproaching her for the influence she has over me." I tried to find some pre-

text for resuming the conversation, and soon murmured with the awkwardness of a man whose conscience is not quite clear :

" Valentine, my daughter, what are you going to
have for dinner this evening ? "

" I don't know."

" Are you vexed, my little Valentine ? "

" I have no right to judge my father's conduct.
People can suffer without complaining," she said with
the tone of a woman of thirty, " and I do not complain."

" I make you suffer, my child ! You are not speaking seriously. You didn't understand me, you misunderstood me, I assure you." I kissed her hands
and added in a low tone: " You know very well I
love you more than my life, more than everything. It
is true, my little angel, it is perfectly true. Won't
you smile upon your awkward old father, who is constantly doing foolish things without meaning it ? "

" Well, yes, I am angry, because I am always
alone like an orphan, because people never see you
in town and must think you hate me."

" Who told you that ? Who is the wretch who told
you that ? oh ! "

" Dear me, parents are generally glad to go with
their children, to witness their little triumphs—the
other day in the procession, I cried."

" You, my darling, you wept, wept in the procession."

" Of course, for I said to myself : ' If my father
loved me, he would be near me.' And then when
everybody came up to congratulate me because I sang
well—I was still more sad."

" I will go with you," I said suddenly. " Not love
you ? You an orphan ! Never say that word." It
seemed as if I heard my wife sobbing and calling me
to an account for my conduct. " No one is loved
more fondly than you, my darling. Oh ! I'll go, I'll

go with you everywhere now. An orphan! I was
afraid of being in your way. And then I am a little
—awkward you know. I see what must be done, I
know how to give myself orders, but I have great difficulty in obeying. What is very natural to others is
not always so to me. I tell you this that you may be
indulgent, my little pet. You will hear a great many
things said of me. People have judged me severely
with good reason, but don't form an opinion of your
father hastily, my love, I beg of you—I have had many
little obstacles in my life—I'll tell you all about it
some day—don't judge me until you know me. When
you don't understand me, say without fear: ' Papa,
why do you think so, why do you do that? It's an error, papa, you are mistaken, you have your old ideas
again.' It will give me so much pleasure if you will
treat me as a friend. I shall have such happiness in
confiding my thoughts to you. You will never say
again that you are—you know, the ugly word you
used just now."

" Then you will come to mass on Sunday ? "

" Yes, yes, my daughter, wherever you wish, to ves-
pers too, everywhere."

" You'll take me to the doctor's fête ? "

" What fête ? Will there be many people
there ? "

" Don't you know that Monsieur Bernard is going
to give a breakfast at the mill for his son, who has
come to spend his vacation here ? "

" True, this is August. Well, we'll go and breakfast at the mill if you wish. We won't be parted from
each other again. Will it really please you ? "

" Of course it will."

" How good you are, my child, if you only knew
what happiness you cause me ! "

" You'll go to Blois to buy some gloves ? "

" That is true, gloves. You think I neglect myself, don't you ? "

" It is God's will that we should pay a little attention to our dress when we go to His house."

" We must not offend God. I will get some nice
gloves."

" Yellow ones ; and patent leather boots ; all the
gentlemen have them. You will be able to have your
hair cut at the same time, papa—and bring me my
dress from the dress-maker's, you know, on the main
street. People generally think your daughter tolerably pretty, Monsieur papa, and you will only be doing your duty if you go to a little expense to act as
her cavalier."

" Of course; especially if I please God at the
same time. Do you want me to kiss you now ? "

" I have a great mind to refuse you for your im-
piety."

It seems that my appearance in the town produced a sensation. I have learned since that Marianne was eagerly questioned about all the particulars
of my conversion. Had I seen a spectre, had I confessed, did I keep the rogation days, how did I conduct myself at Easter ? All that time I was very far
from thinking that my actions could excite curiosity
to such a degree.

When I saw my Valentine in public, surrounded
and petted ; when I perceived the attention her beauty,
grace and wit procured ; when I even felt, so to speak,
the foam that dashed from it myself—I was agitated as
I had been during the most solemn days of my life.
I had never seen my child under such circumstances.
I was terrified, and yet at the same time experienced
a sensation of pride, wholly new to me ; I was the
father of a brilliant, charming young girl, whom
everybody admired. The ladies surrounded her,
praised her good taste, the beauty of her dress, the
graceful way in which she arranged her hair. The
gentlemen, the doctor's son at their head, little Joseph whom I had known as a child, crowded about

her, bowed to her respectfully, spoke to her with an
eagerness which clearly proved their enthusiasm;
while she, suddenly transformed, responded to everything with wonderful grace and ease, accepting the
homage as perfectly natural.

I stood before her and devoured her with my
eyes. It was my daughter, she was mine, and I could
not conquer this feeling of possession. If she smiled
I smiled too; I instinctively repeated her gestures and
thanked her with a look when people complimented
her.

When this first moment was over, it seemed as if
people were not paying me sufficient attention. So
they did not remember that we were united by the
strongest ties in the world. I should have accepted
half her triumph without either embarrassment or
timidity. My daughter, after all, was myself. True,
all these people were on terms of far closer intimacy
with her than I had ever been. This was a very surprising misunderstanding. Perhaps, from motives of
delicacy, she had wished to remain a child at home,
that familiarity might be rendered easier. She had
feared that I might be intimidated if I saw her becoming a woman. I'm such an odd stick, and she is so
observant.

A feverish restlessness took possession of me. I
too wished to make a part of this privileged public on
which she smiled; to cease to be the timid, trembling
little old man for whom she must blush. Henceforth I
must keep my place, show myself worthy of her, and
forgetting the obstacles against which I had so often
jostled, driving away all fear, I threw myself head
foremost into the pleasures of the town as a gay man
plunges into the infernal whirlpool of worldly dissi-
pation. From that time, I mingled in every conversation with my little rasping voice, bustled about,
elbowed my way, interrupted everybody, and the constraint I imposed upon myself in order to play a part

so far beyond my powers, increased my excitement. By degrees I persuaded myself that in this desperate contest I was fighting for my daughter, for her happiness, defending her from the attacks of those who surrounded her. I was no longer conscious of my own absurdity; the opinions of other people made very little difference, and I would have intentionally committed the wildest extravagance to make Valentine turn her eyes towards me, and notice my presence.

"You are talking a great deal, father," she murmured as she passed, "are you not afraid of getting tired ?"

I made every effort to resume the character of a discreet and silent father, but if Joseph (I cordially hated him) approached my daughter and made the simplest remark, I forgot all caution, sprang towards my child, drew myself up in fighting trim, clung to her despairingly. "What fly is stinging you now, my good fellow," cried Doctor Bernard, laughing. "Devil take it, we must give way to the young people ; let your daughter alone and come and play a game of billiards."

I obeyed, but I confounded the red with the white, took the cue by the small end, looked out of the window every moment, and, at last, pleading a headache, made my escape.

In the midst of my foolishness I tried to analyze my feelings, but it was impossible for me to fix my attention ; Valentine filled my horizon, and while wishing to study myself, I drowned all personality in watching my child. My affection was strangely changed ; it was now mingled with a shade of bitterness that intoxicated me. Several times I resolved to leave the country suddenly, and undoubtedly should have done so if it had not been for the fear of Valentine's accusing me of despotism or tyranny.

Fortunately, winter was approaching ; Joseph had just returned to Paris to pursue his medical studies ;

many people who merely lived in Favras, or its suburbs, during the summer, had also disappeared; and the town, being thus reduced to its own resources, resumed its ordinary aspect and little every-day customs.

I breathed freely again; my daughter was re-stored; the storm was retreating; I no longer had any rivals. I smiled as I looked at the huge supply of wood which was to render our retreat warmer, our intercourse pleasanter. My great care was to make the house attractive to her. I had a little hollow dug in the garden, which was to be filled with aquatic plants; I surprised her with a new set of furniture for her room—a piece of extravagance, for my income was very small, but what sacrifice of money would I not have made to recall the smile to her lips! Alas! all my efforts were vain; it seemed as if she was exiled. Often while we were talking together in the chimney corner, she suddenly left the room, wrapped herself in her shawl, and, in spite of the wind and cold, went to the upper part of the garden, from whence one could see the plain, bordered in the distance by the forest, and remained there motionless with her eyes fixed on the large clouds the wind drove across the sky.

She had taken a dislike to the rest of the garden, the rain-gauge, and the weathercock, the little groves, the sun-dial, the rustic kiosk I had built myself, a charming little affair; everything irritated her nerves, I know not why; yet this was the part of the grounds where she had played and laughed during her whole childhood.

"I want room," she said in a choked voice, "the mind needs it as well as the eyes, and I hate common-place things."

On the days when the owners of the neighboring chateau hunted in the forest I was sure to find her at her post about sunset.

She started at my approach, and we watched the horsemen, the whippers-in, and the pack pass by. When the horns sounded the call to the dogs, her face brightened. "They are happy people," said she, "to be able to gallop all day long upon a horse that goes like the wind, and never gets tired."

"There are pleasures for every purse, my child, and little nobodies, like ourselves—"

"Oh! I know what we are very well," she murmured with an expression of repressed suffering.

One day I surprised her standing in my room before the little portrait of my wife, which I had hung near the glass some time before.

When I entered she went hastily away, but it seemed to me that her eyes were wet. So she had guessed that past which I had never dared to confide to her. She must be informed of it some day, but when should I have the courage to tell her all? From the hour I supposed she knew the whole I avoided her glance as I would have that of a judge; I scarcely dared to speak to her, and her coldness towards me visibly increased. I was very unhappy, but she suffered too. By the expression of her face, her step, the few words that fell from her lips, a thousand trifles, I saw that she considered herself the victim of a fatality which I could not understand. Suddenly religious observances assumed a marked importance in Valentine's life; and I rejoiced, for I thought she would find consolation.

Under her influence the social gatherings in the town assumed a graver character; cards were usually excluded and replaced by the performance of sacred music or the reading of some classical masterpiece. The evening seemed particularly long at the notary's, who, being gouty, liked to preside in his arm-chair, with his leg resting on a support. People sat around him in a circle, each with a small rug under his feet. The master of the house maintained the arrangement

by a smile or a polite wave of the hand, and I caught
Valentine steadily watching the candles which persisted in not burning down.

Sometimes Doctor Bernard, who continued to be
the busiest man in the neighborhood, suddenly
arrived. We heard the noise of his carriage rolling
over the pointed stones, and then his loud, sonorous
voice. The gouty notary smilingly pointed out the
place where the circle should be enlarged to make
room for the new arrival, the doctor entered with a
smile, and gayety kindled afresh as the flame bursts
forth from smouldering brands when a door is
opened.

"Good-evening, doctor, have you heard from
Joseph?"

"Yes, yes; excellent news. My boy's a wonderful fellow."

And rummaging in his pocket he drew out a letter
from the medical student and read the principal
passages. The writing was clear, close, and regular.
Joseph spoke only of himself, his studies and his
future prospects. "I have arranged my time," said
he, "in such a way that I gain an hour's work without shortening the two evenings I devote to society
every week. From nine to eleven o'clock I can
make three calls, certainly two, which is sufficient if
one knows how to select properly. I want to obtain
the gold medal on completing my term as house sur-
geon, and at the same time pass the examination and
the central office. It is possible, and I will do it. I
have strength for a great deal of work, and an excellent method of arranging my time into the bargain.
As to old Brillette, in whose favor you ask me to
make an application to my chief, I will answer you
very frankly, my dear father, by a flat refusal. The
situation is certainly very touching, but mine is still
more interesting, and I don't wish to fritter away my
credit. Besides, you can help the man with money.

Give him the five hundred francs you were going to send me, I need nothing; nay, I have a thousand excellent reasons for remaining poor. My religious principles continue to excite the jeers of certain persons ; I fully expected and rejoice over it."

General enthusiasm was excited by the reading of that letter, whose salient passages were commented upon by the doctor. "How much resolution, what energy, what admirable courage this young man's conduct displays," they said. "Square at the base," added Bernard, fondly.

I confess that I had not shared the general excitement. The unbending will of this Joseph, who seemed ready to sacrifice everything to attain his object, made me shudder. I remembered his stiff manners, his cold glance, and the aversion I had felt towards him increased. Valentine, moreover, seemed to feel the same impression as myself, for she had remained silent all the evening.

When we were alone on the way home, lantern in hand, she began to walk very rapidly, clinging closely to my arm ; one would have thought that she wanted to fly from the town.

"You are frightened, my dear," I said, smiling.

"No, no, I'm not afraid."

"Why, you seem very much agitated," and to divert her thoughts I spoke of the famous letter. "This Joseph is a bar of steel," I said, "or at least he isn't sorry to pass for one ; don't you think so ? Under the words of this ascetic worker, perhaps it might not be necessary to seek far to discover an— ambitious, intriguing man. I don't like—"

"You don't like conflict, struggle," she said suddenly in a ringing voice, quickening her pace. "Yet these eager workers whom difficulty excites and arouses, who rush head-foremost towards a noble aim, these superb lunatics, born for the intoxication of a great career, are needed."

15

" But, my darling, that's not what I meant."

" Walk faster, faster, I don't feel well this evening."

" I understand all ambitions, although calmness has now returned to my heart. I, too, have had my dreams, and have worked—perhaps as much as Bernard's son. I have never told you about all that. Ha! ha! ha! I know what constant toil is."

" Well, you must rest now—here we are at last."

" When I was about to enter the normal school— and afterwards, at the examination—I have spent many a night, and it wasn't very warm that winter, in my little room. I remember now—wait till I push the gate open—I remember that I had a rabbit skin to protect myself from the cold—Ha! ha! ha! yes, I've worked as hard as Bernard's son."

" Indeed! Good-night, father."

" Yes, and perhaps harder. I don't dispute his merit, you know, my dear. I really think him an uncommon lad, and one well calculated to steer his own ship; I fear only one thing, and that is that he'll steer her too well. You'll see what a daughter of Crœsus this fine fellow will hunt up."

My daughter suddenly disappeared, and I heard her chamber door slam violently.

Joseph seemed to have said good-bye to the town of Favras forever. Two or three times a year my friend Bernard went to Paris to spend a day with his son, and always returned in a very enthusiastic mood. The student's triumphs really did seem marvellous. He would be one of the bright particular stars of medicine, one of the most remarkable men of his age if his health could endure the severe labor he imposed upon himself. Several very remarkable works had already raised him above all his companions in the school, and his teachers had asked his advice in certain difficult cases. Gifted with medical

tact in an unusual degree, highly educated, energetic, patient, indomitable, in spite of the most angelic modesty, to what height must he not attain?
Having become a constant visitor at the hotel de
Vélizy, where he was received on the footing of an
intimate friend by the old Marquise, who could not
do without him, the most desirable practice awaited
him.

Such were the reports the doctor brought on his
return from Paris. The impression produced upon
the population of the young hero's native town was
immense. For whole evenings people discussed
Joseph's future, recalled the wonderful things he had
done in his childhood, and certain persons even declared that the tokens of genius were plainly visible
upon his brow at that period.

One evening, when we went to Bernard's, we
were astonished to find the large gate wide open.
The kitchen was brightly lighted, and baggage was
piled in the ante-chamber; a door suddenly opened
and the doctor appeared with a flushed, beaming
countenance.

" Ah ! it's you," said he, " come in, my son is here,
I was going to tell you. I only received his letter
this evening."

Joseph was very much altered. He was now a
grave, dignified man, who inspired respect at once.
His pale, smoothly shaven face, furrowed with deep
wrinkles, had an aspect of manly beauty ; and his
bright, steady glance pierced you through and
through. His mouth was small and clearly cut, and
his high forehead, rendered still higher by a mass of
long hair pushed backward, really seemed to be the
brow of a man of genius. His gestures were made
at rare intervals, slow and very simple ; he said little,
in a voice that was weak though well modulated, de-
laying his answers like a man constantly pursued by
pressing cares. Although very young, one could per-

ceive that he was matured by experience, knew his own value, and was accustomed to the respect and esteem of others.

When everybody was seated, Valentine, whose manner was more cold and indifferent than usual, approached the lamp, drew from her pocket the piece of embroidery she had commenced, and began to work as usual. It gave me pleasure to see how little impression the sight of the young conqueror made upon her.

We talked a great deal that evening; reassured by Joseph's really surprising modesty, and stimulated by the presence of a distinguished person, Bernard, the curé and I were a little too loquacious.

Scarcely had the hero uttered a word when all three, hastily rummaging in the bag of memories, ventured our little stories. We too had had our triumphs, our moments of brilliancy. Even the good priest had had intimate relations with the aristocracy; he had converted the young Marquis de P., been the confidant of the Comtesse de C., and in his heart the Duchesse de K. placed her last hopes.

As for me I should never have ceased recalling my doughty deeds at the normal school, had it not been for the imploring looks of my daughter, whom I was evidently torturing by my absurd vanity.

It was not until nearly ten o'clock that we thought of taking leave. When everybody was in the antechamber, Joseph, addressing the priest with every token of respectful consideration, said :

" To-morrow will be Sunday, Monsieur le curé ; does the service still begin at nine o'clock ? "

" At nine o'clock, yes, my dear doctor, high mass is always at nine o'clock. Our church will seem strangely plain to you who have been accustomed to the pomp of religious worship in Paris."

" God is everywhere, Monsieur le curé ; God is everywhere."

"I hope at least you will take your seat in the church-warden's pew beside your father."

"I am deeply touched by the favor, and will gratefully accept it."

"We are the favored ones, Monsieur Joseph—excuse me while I light my lantern—the house of God—thank you, I have some matches—it is an honor to us, I assure you. I wish you a very good evening."

Valentine's conduct completely effaced from my mind a thousand little anxieties which had haunted me. Not a word was exchanged between her and myself on the subject of Bernard's son, or, at least, if I spoke of him, it was in a very indirect way.

"Nothing is so alarming," I said to her, "as exceptional good fortune. To enter upon life in a chariot and four and pass under a triumphal arch is the greatest of calamities. How is all this to be paid for afterwards? You perceive, my darling, it is giving destiny terrible pledges. There are certain laws fixed by fate: a sun high in the heavens attracts great clouds; inordinate ambitions cause terrible downfalls. When our eyes are fixed on the horizon, we plunge violently into the first ditch that crosses the path, and life, my child, is furrowed with ditches and old roads. The wise man imitates the prudence of the blind: he goes step by step, and feels the way with his stick. He does not leap over the ditches, but quietly descends and goes up according to the whims of the ground. Then when he finds some little spot sheltered from the sun and wind, he puts down his wallet and pauses to see others pass by. It is for this purpose that critical judgment is so precious a gift."

Valentine did not seem to hear me, but by her silence I guessed that she understood me and shared my ideas. One particular of her conduct afforded me great pleasure: not content with the somewhat

austere manners she had adopted since Joseph's arrival at Favras, she suddenly changed her style of
dress, and wore nothing but black or very dark garments, entirely destitute of ornament. Even her
mode of arranging her hair was excessively plain,
and I said to myself : " It is very evident that she has
no desire to please him." What strange fancies I had
got into my head. I have misunderstood her simple
heart, her lofty character. Then, of what avail has
this faculty of analysis I possess been to me, except
to strip the bloom from all good things and render
evil ones still harder to bear ?

I frankly confess I was not sorry that she should
be marble to every one, but what I could not understand was that she should retain her melancholy, resigned expression when in my society, and again
keep me at a distance by her repellant manners.
For a long time she had avoided my caresses, doubtless that she might not be compelled to respond to
them. True, it was only natural that her fresh, rosy
lips should feel a repugnance to pressing my old,
withered cheeks, but why did she show these tokens
of apparent hostility ? How many times I have hurried away from her, swallowing down my tears. I
went into the darkest corner of the garden, cut and
hacked away furiously with my pruning knife hap-
hazard, and if my dog surprised me in the midst of
my sorrow, I took him between my knees, looked
into his eyes, and overwhelmed him with questions. " Why is she unhappy, tell me, Sultan ?
What does she want ? She no longer pets you ; you
are troublesome, too ! " And I consoled the poor
animal which wagged his tail and thrust his nose in
my face.

A horrible thought occurred to me. " Suppose
my daughter's conduct should be logical," I said to
myself ; " suppose I am merely gathering the fruit of
the germs I have sown ! " I remembered the succes-

sive transformations my affection had undergone as
my child became a woman and the symptoms of her
unfolding beauty appeared. I examined my heart
and was terrified. Is it with a father's eye that I
watched with so much intentness her graceful bearing, the undulations of the pliant figure while she
was running about in the garden; that I studied her
features, analyzed her smile, took pleasure in her
very faults without having courage to call her attention to them? And afterwards when I suddenly saw
her admired by everybody, did I not feel an emotion
of monstrous jealousy? Was not I, her father, the
first to encourage her taste for finery, the first to tell
her that she was pretty, bewitching? Have I not
implanted the germ of a love of admiration which
might destroy her, but whose charm was irresistible
to me? How many times, in giving her a good-night
kiss, I had noticed how much she resembled her
mother, and embraced her a second time as if to envelop both in the same caress. There had been the
echo of another feeling in my paternal love—the
memory of a past I could not forget, the light of a
fire which could not be extinguished. How many
base, shameful feelings there are in the human soul!
Was it surprising that she should have neither respect
nor esteem for me? I dared not speak to her, look
her in the face. It was a positive torture. Although
her habits were still the same, it soon became evident
to me that her health was affected. She fell into a
state of languor and weakness, whose every shade I
secretly watched.

This painful situation had lasted about three
months, when one day, in passing near the house, I
heard the sound of stifled sobs proceeding from Valentine's room, whose shutters were tightly closed. I
was the more surprised because I supposed that my
daughter was detained in town that portion of the
day by her tasks of benevolence and piety. My first

thought was that some accident had befallen her, and I was beside her in an instant.

The poor child, with her hat still on her head, was stretched on her bed, a prey to a most violent fit of hysterics. Her hands were clenched, her face was deadly pale and wet with tears, and her half-closed eyes had an expression of insanity. I bent over her and clasped her in my arms. Was she going to die? "What is the matter, my child, tell me, what is the matter?" I asked, trying to maintain my calmness; she burst into a convulsive laugh, and pressing my arm with wild violence, murmured:

"Yes—forever—you have guessed right—I love you—"

"And I love you in return," I answered, "I love you with all my heart, my child, my Valentine."

"In life and death—forever."

"Calm yourself, my darling. Yes, we will be happy. I will do all in my power."

The fit of hysterics gradually passed away; her eyes opened wider; she turned towards me, and recognizing me, uttered a cry of terror.

"The letter," she screamed in a tone of anguish, "the letter!"

"What letter, darling? It is I, your father, don't you know me?"

"Well, why are you here? Where is the letter?"

I saw a scrap of paper which happened to be lying on the floor, and holding it out to her with a trembling hand, said: "Is this what you want?"

She seized the fragment I offered, and kissed it with passionate tenderness.

Doubt was no longer possible, my daughter was insane.

I shouted to Marianne; and when the good woman came, rushed like a madman towards the town, where Doctor Bernard would certainly be at this hour.

I should not be able to tell the wild thoughts that pursued me as I hurried on. I unconsciously took the Rochemont road, and was obliged to retrace my steps in a run. Perhaps the delay was irreparable.

On entering the doctor's house I saw him in the ante-chamber, pacing to and fro, with every token of the greatest excitement.

" Bernard," I said, throwing myself into his arms, " I am very unhappy. My daughter, my poor daughter ! " The speed with which I had come deprived me of all power to speak, and I embraced my old friend with increasing agitation.

" In the first place," said he, indignantly releasing himself, " do me the favor to be quiet and come into my study, there's no need of crying all this on the housetops."

When we were seated and the door was carefully closed, the doctor took his snuff box, plunged his huge finger and thumb violently into it, and shut the box by a resounding rap on the cover.

" Make haste, I beg of you. My Valentine is ill."

" Don't make any sentimental demonstrations, I hate them. Let me alone. I want to have my say. Confound it, there's no doubt about my views. I've always been square at the base, and I tell you frankly, I consider this affair deplorable, absurd, mad ; I disapprove of it, I am heart-broken."

" All the reproaches you can make I have already heaped upon myself," I answered. " But let us go, let us go at once. Do you consider her condition hopeless ? Oh God ! what a terrible misfortune ! "

Bernard impatiently drew his dressing-gown closer around him, looking me steadily in the face.

" 'Terrible misfortune ! Devil take it, I consider that joke out of place, and you are strangely mistaken in the situation of affairs. Do you suppose I am the dupe of this clumsy comedy ? Do you take me for a

simpleton, a fool? Do you think me stupid enough
to keep quiet while my son makes a marriage like
this? He who could aspire to the most brilliant
matches. Valentine is pretty, I don't dispute it, she
is undoubtedly accomplished, but—"

"What! What do you mean? Explain yourself,"
I cried, growing furious in my turn. "Valentine
marry! At a time when her life is in danger. Marry Joseph! Never. Who has said this? It's a
slander, a horrible falsehood, I will not allow my
daughter's inclinations to be forced. Marry Joseph!
I won't have it, it shall never be. I too have rights.
I am her father. I will defend her, and if any one
has the baseness to disturb her mind with such in-
sinuations I swear he shall have to deal with me.
To seek to ensnare a poor child who is living quietly
and happily, tear her from her father's arms! Well,
let them come on. If necessary I will commit a
crime, yes a crime."

"Don't gesticulate so, that's all stuff and nonsense. Who will believe that a man of Joseph's importance would have formed such a resolution if he
hadn't been beset, overreached? What means were
employed? I don't know, but it's certain that my
son is a victim of a plot, that he has fallen into a
snare which has doubtless been spread for a long
time."

At such an accusation my fury knew no bounds,
and seizing a carafe, which stood near, I cried, trembling with rage: "If you continue to insult my
daughter I will kill you, break your head this instant.
I want a disgraceful marriage with an ambitious,
intriguing man whom she detests, whom we both detest! A likely thing! I will protect her. I am
strong, they shall see I am strong."

I was fairly beside myself. Bernard put his great
hand on my shoulder and looked at me compassion-
ately. "Go home, poor fellow. Put down that

carafe, you will wet my carpet. I will speak to you to-morrow. Come, go. Confound it, don't you see that if you stayed I should be unable to control myself any longer ? "

I was pushed out of the house, and walked away staggering like a drunken man.

It was autumn, night had fallen and the wind was blowing violently. The trees bent towards each oth er with a grinding sound, the dry leaves whirled around me with a diabolical laugh, and my thoughts also whirled through my brain. I sat down on the edge of a ditch, fairly terrified at my own condition. Amid the nightmare which had taken possession of me, I felt the presence of some mystery and said, mechanically, "What does it mean, oh ! God, what does this mean ! " Suddenly I remembered the position in which I had left my daughter. Perhaps she is no longer alive, I thought with terror, and continued my way as fast as I could.

At last I arrived at my destination, pushed open the garden gate and entered the garden. I was only a few paces from the house when the door opened and I saw Joseph, accompanied by my daughter who was lighting the way with a lantern. I instinctively slipped behind a clump of lilacs that grew by the walk. Valentine's face wore an unusual expression, which it was impossible for me to define ; every trace of suffering had disappeared. The two young people came down the path talking together in so low a tone that it was impossible for me to understand anything ; but when they had almost reached the spot where I was hidden I could distinguish the meaning of their words.

" Yes, yes," said my daughter, " if people could die of joy, I should have died to-day, my dear one." She held out her hand to him and added : " You will probably meet my father on the way, I am sur-prised that he has not returned."

" I regret it.   He doesn't suspect anything ? "

" Of course not, poor man."

" How your ardent, noble nature must have suffered under the deadly pressure of this old man with
his strange manias."

" I was somewhat stifled indeed. I was particularly
ashamed of his half-dead manner, his pitiable idleness, when others were struggling so nobly, entering
upon the battle of life with so much courage. Oh !
I assure you, I feel I have the strength to understand
and aid you.   But let us say no more about it."

" Do you love me ? " asked the scoundrel, lower-
ing his voice.

" Yes, I love you, Joseph, and I admire you.   Go
now, go."

" God has approved of our betrothal."

When I regained my consciousness, I found myself in bed. On opening my eyes, the first person
I saw was Marianne, who was putting a bandage upon my forehead.

"Oh ! Monsieur," she said in an accent of real
delight, " so you have revived again.   You frightened
us terribly ; but it's nothing serious. It's only a fainting fit—your color is coming back a little. I'm not
binding your head too tight, it's because you rubbed
the skin off your forehead when you fell. I almost
tumbled down myself, tripping over your legs which
came out beyond the lilac bushes."

" Well, my poor father, are you better ? " said
Valentine approaching and holding out her hand to
me.

" I have had an attack of giddiness, it is nothing.
You have not been anxious, I should be sorry to
have troubled you."   My heart was swelling, for I
now remembered all that had passed, and said to myself: "She gives me her hand, but withholds her
heart—I thank you and Marianne for having nursed
me, I am ever grateful to you."   Then I added in a

lower tone : " You know perfectly well, my dear daughter, that I place your happiness above every-thing, don't you ?   I most solemnly assure you that it is so—if you had—a wish—a plan, it would only be necessary to tell me, my love.   Oh ! have no fear, I shall make no comments—not one remark, you must be happy, it is natural."

" But, father, I—"

" Don't tell me anything now, I beg of you.   Some other time.   Go, go, my darling, you shall be happy, my daughter."

And I pushed her gently away, for I feared she might not dare to confess the whole truth, and wish-ed to avoid even the semblance of a falsehood from her lips.

When Doctor Bernard saw me come in the next day he frowned and said rudely enough : " Oh ! there you are, you have come to talk the matter over."

" I have come—you will let me sit down—I have come to apologize for my conduct yesterday."   I fairly dragged the words from my lips, so to speak, for in my heart I felt an aversion to Joseph which now re-sembled hatred.   " I was not in my right mind, I am shocked that I allowed myself to go so far—I believe I threatened you—I beg your pardon, Bernard."   I was seeking for the best way of expressing my re-pentance, for it was necessary to disarm and soften him ; his consent to the marriage upon which my daughter's future depended was to be secured at this cost.   " I think," I continued, " you will forget the angry words that escaped me.   The idea of being separated from Valentine was making me so wretch-ed—and therefore you will not bear me a grudge.   If I had known our two children had so much affection for each other, I should have said nothing, my dear Bernard, for it is a father's duty to do everything for his child, literally everything."

" If I were not convinced of that, I shouldn't have

admitted the possibility of a union like this, or allowed the violence to which you permitted yourself to give way to pass." He took out his snuff-box and shook it angrily. "But not a word more upon the subject, since my son desires it I accept—in short, I accept your apologies, but under any other circumstances I swear I should have—"

"Once more, Bernard, I entreat you to pardon me."

"I should have crushed the insolent fellow, the audacious knave, who could have forgotten himself as you have done. Haven't I given you every possible proof of friendship? Come, speak! haven't I?"

"Undoubtedly my friend, undoubtedly."

"And when I am on the point of consenting—once more, I have no wish to recur to that scene, which I attribute to a momentary fit of insanity."

"Yes, that's it: I didn't know what I was saying."

"Good, very good: people trample under foot every feeling of gratitude and friendship, insult others—and all this is of very little consequence if they add: 'I am sorry, I wasn't aware of what I was saying!' Oh! you should have merely said, 'Bernard, the prospect of entering your family confuses me. I was so far from expecting that my daughter could ever marry a man of Joseph's merit, I don't know how to express the emotion, the bewilderment'—that's what you should have said to me. Do you know that my son, besides the profession which will secure him a brilliant fortune in the immediate future, possesses at the present time, in right of his mother, a property of one hundred and ten thousand francs, besides what I shall leave him? What dowry do you intend to give your daughter?"

I started. My first thought was that my small means would prevent this accursed marriage, which however I desired with all my heart.

"I will do all I can," I stammered, "but I am not rich."

" We are not here to joke." He shook his snuff-box again. " Confound it. Do you suppose my memory is short enough for me to have forgotten the large property you formerly inherited ? Joseph's inexplicable folly gives you considerable advantage over me, it is true, but I don't advise you to presume upon your situation. Mine isn't the nature of a dupe, I warn you. Let us speak seriously. What do you give your daughter ? "

" Why, everything, my friend. Everything I have."

" State what you have exactly, exactly.".

" Good Heavens ! I haven't thought of it yet ; in the first place, the house we live in, with the garden. She must have her home, of course—with the furniture, I don't wish to change her habits in any way. Besides, she has associations with it—you know, Bernard, we have lived there so long ! She was very happy in her little blue room with the clump of rose bushes under the window. Perhaps you have not noticed the rose bushes—I planted them all—"

" The property has increased in value since the rail road has been planned; I estimate it at the present time to be worth about fifty thousand francs. You see I set it at a high valuation. So you will give your daughter this house and estate, valued at fifty thousand francs: Well, and then ? Make haste, Joseph will soon come back."

I concentrated all my energies to make an exact inventory of the fragments of my fortune. " Oh ! " said I, " I have an income of two thousand and some odd francs from property invested in stock: if you want that—"

" Of course, and then ? "

" Then, why I have nothing more—I beg your pardon, my friend, I forgot—"

" I suspected you would forget something."

" I have my dictionary, which brings me in six or eight hundred francs a year. Can I make over my copyright to Valentine? I would bind myself to do it in writing."

"Certainly, that's a matter of course. Now listen to me, Babolain, let me tell you just what I think: your conduct is that of a contemptible wretch. Never, no never, did any one see a father in your position haggling in this way when the matter in question concerned the future and happiness of his child."

"I solemnly assure you I am giving all I have left, literally all, my dear Bernard; I have kept nothing for myself except the five hundred francs the ministry gives me as an old professor. Oh! it is quite enough. People don't want much at my age. Besides, Valentine and—her husband will let me live near them, close by them—a little room will be enough—I shan't be in their way, they will see me very little, I have always lived near her, you know." Bernard began to drum on the lid of his snuff-box. "If it is necessary, absolutely necessary—I'll go away, but I could do many little things for them, save them trouble. Valentine is accustomed to have me near her. She has more affection for me than she thinks. When a child not very long ago, she called upon me to help her in the smallest things. Oh! she is a good daughter who loves her father I am sure—"

"What is most evident in all this," said the doctor, "is that my son's future wife will have a dowry of fifty thousand francs, with an income of two thousand, and a somewhat doubtful revenue of a few hundred more. You're a clever man, but we shall see. Joseph will open his eyes. Devil take it! People don't throw themselves into ditches in this fashion."

"I should like to have more to give her, but—"

"Where is your fortune then?"

"I have met with heavy losses."

"That is, you are utterly ruined, and hope to repair the misfortune by marrying your daughter. I'm sorry to say so, but it is the act of an adventurer.

You've had your eye on my son for ten, perhaps fifteen years."

"Oh! Bernard, don't say that, I beg of you, it would be horrible."

"I've been deceived by your manner, I've been ridiculously trustful. Why should you have taken refuge here, if you had had nothing to conceal? What do I know of your past? What are the follies that have ruined you? Why should your wife have left you? You have carefully avoided confiding all this to me. What has become of your child's mother, Babolain? Undoubtedly the poor woman, driven to despair, was compelled to abandon her fireside. Come, speak, what reason have you to reproach your wife?"

"I accuse no one," I murmured. I was suffering deeply, for I saw the phantom I supposed had vanished, once more appear before me. As if the future were not a fatal consequence of the past, as if one could escape from the logical connection of events! I had been foolish, proud, and the burden of my faults was now falling upon the head of my beloved daughter. Perhaps my past would prevent her from being happy. I continued: "I have committed great errors, it is true. Undoubtedly I was not formed for married life, the ladies were artists, and lived only for their art; I was very different—consequently, they suffered, and I suffered too. My wife and her mother are in Italy. At least, I think so, for I have rarely received news of them. I must even say that—they have never written to me since our separation."

"Poor wife," said Bernard. "And for twenty years the thought of repairing your wrongs has not once entered your mind."

"They committed equally great ones."

"What! speak frankly. With what do you reproach them?"

"Little things," I hastily replied; for I trembled
16

lest I should injure Valentine by accusing her moth
er. "A great many little things. But I've forgotten
them all."

" 'Then why not recall your wife, why not live
honorably with her? do you think my son will accept
a situation like yours in his family? Never, no, never.
For my part, I cannot consent to it."

" Bernard, you know very well that if this marriage did not take place, my daughter would die.
She loves Joseph, my friend. You cannot imagine
the ardor and purity of her heart. You won't oppose
this marriage, I beg of you—it would be a sort of
murder, with which you wouldn't wish to have cause
to reproach yourself."

"'That's something like, I prefer you so. You
show the full extent of your ambition at last."

" I have no other ambition than that of saving my
daughter from dying of grief. I will do what I can
to bring the ladies back; I bear them no ill will, I
have no hatred towards them. If it is necessary to
entreat my wife and her mother to return that Valentine may be happy, I will do so. But they will not
wish to come back. I'll write to them; I'll tell them
I am the sole cause of all that has happened. What
does it matter if I do humiliate myself, I have always
meant to do everything for the best, my friend; Valentine is not responsible for her father's faults."

We talked together a long time, and I went away
feeling very sorrowful. The more I tried to soothe
him, the more irritable he seemed. Yet it is hard to
be compelled to wish for a thing one hates.

Meantime, in spite of the protestations of
Bernard, who said he was decidedly opposed to the
marriage, affairs seemed to progress rapidly. I dared
not speak of it to any one, but I saw seamstresses
from Blois installed in the house, making up pieces of
linen, cutting and sewing from morning till night. One
could hear their bursts of laughter and their songs.

Valentine, who superintended everything with the greatest energy, seemed to find all this gayety very natural. I understood that the trousseau was the point in question.

The saddest part of the whole affair to me was the strange transformation that had taken place in my daughter; she was now unrecognizable; her whole person was instinct with health and happiness, and the smallest details of this development were obvious to me; nay, she even lavished upon me attentions and cares to which I had long been unaccustomed. Could I tell her that her affection tortured me? Our house, which I loved with all my heart, had become intolerable to me. Early in the morning I made my escape through the little garden door, but avoided the highway and travelled roads that I might not be compelled to submit to the compliments with which the neighbors overwhelmed me on the subject of the marriage, which was already known throughout the country. All the people who smiled upon me seemed to be saying : "It's none the less true that père Babolain, for all his innocent air, knows how to feather his nest, and has snared the young doctor from Paris very cleverly."

I instinctively returned to the places we had frequented when she was a child. In the forest, by the bank of the river, I found her everywhere. Here she had paused, yonder she had smiled as she turned towards me. It was like so many apparitions, whose reality plunged me again into the scenes of the past. I saw her, I talked with her. There was something of my daughter in these scenes ; she had left traces of her presence as she passed, and I collected them all step by step, followed by my dog, which, seeing me sad, became more gentle and watched me with a drooping head.

If instead of being petted, beloved by every one, she had been repulsive from her plainness and hated

for her faults, I, her father, would have loved her just
as much, and she would never have left me.   In my
selfishness I fancied her sickly and repulsive, and
thus had her entirely to myself.

The hardest moment of all was that in which I
was obliged to smile upon Joseph and consider him
openly as my son-in-law.   I really believed I should
never be able to do it.   In vain I said to myself,
"Hatred and jealousy blind me; Valentine would not
love him if he was not worthy of it.   I detest him because he is superior to me, because he possesses
qualities which I have not, it is shocking."   I said all
these things to myself, but did not succeed in diminishing my antipathy to Joseph, so I took an extreme
course, embraced him, overwhelmed him with protestations, pressed his hands, stopped people to sing his
praises.   I was a liar, a false wretch, a scoundrel;
but thanks to the violence I did my feelings, I succeeded in concealing my aversion from him.

Two days before the contract was signed, Doctor
Bernard, who under his son's influence had become
strangely softened, drew me into a window corner
and said, "I'm sure you haven't thought of getting
your wife's consent."

"Good heavens!" said I, despairingly, "is that
necessary?   Then the marriage can't possibly take
place."

"Fortunately Joseph, who foresaw your negli-
gence, anticipated the difficulty, and—"

"What!   He has seen my wife?"

"No; but Monseigneur de Pansol, brother of the
Marquise de Vélizy, was kind enough to undertake
the duty of making the application.   He addressed
himself to the Comtesse de Monte Revilla, who is a
very influential person in Rome.   This Comtesse, it
seems, is very intimate with your wife, for Monseigneur de Pansol received Madame Babolain's consent
to Valentine's marriage by return mail.   The docu-

ment was accompanied by a letter from the Comtesse
de Monte Revilla, couched, it seems, in the most exquisite language. In it she states that Madame Babolain, who has been detained in Rome a long time by
ill-health, cannot be present at her daughter's marriage, but that from afar the poor mother will pray
for the happiness of her child, and God will hear the
supplications of a heart purified by affliction. Monseigneur de Pansol's eyes were full of tears as he read
the letter. 'I clearly recognize there,' said he, 'the
generous soul of the Comtesse de Monte Revilla, who
is well fitted to be the interpreter and consoler of all
who mourn.'"

"You will excuse me for repeating these words,"
added Bernard with great dignity. "I have no power
to judge between your wife and yourself, as you must
perceive, and your conscience will be more eloquent
than I."

Was it then true that my wife was unhappy and
penitent? And for twenty years I had made no effort
to lessen the distance between us. If Esther had not
effaced the past by twenty years of virtue ; if she had
not been in every way worthy of respect, would this
great Roman lady, this Comtesse de Monte Revilla,
have taken up her defense so warmly?

I still imagine I am in a dream when I think of
the tumult of feeling in my heart during that cruel
week. The day of the wedding, in particular. I am
conscious of having behaved like a lunatic. My head
was empty, my brain withered, I had lost all control
over myself, there was no longer any one at the
helm ; and yet I remember every detail of this nightmare with the greatest precision. After having signed
the register in the vestry, instead of carefully laying
down the pen, I let it fall, still full of ink, and threw
myself into the curé's arms, calling him my dear
friend. A loud murmur made me turn my head, and
I saw all the bystanders looking at me indignantly.

My pen had dropped upon the dress of the mayor's wife and made a huge spot. I was not surprised, the accident seemed perfectly natural; but the mayor approached me, saying in an authoritative tone, "I expect an apology, at least, Monsieur Babolain. It would be behaving like a gentleman not to delay it."

I took his hands, clasped them in my own, and smiling affectionately at him, said, "It's of no consequence; thank you, thank you, yes, it's a very fine day.".

The doctor and Monsieur le curé were compelled to interpose to calm the mayor, who was positively furious. To cut short any explanations, they made all the guests enter the carriages stationed upon the square. I then perceived I had left my overcoat and hat in the vestry, but on entering the church thought no more about them; and after wandering around a few moments, paused before the wax-tapers the sexton had just extinguished. I could not turn my eyes from the bluish smoke that circled into the air, leaving a most unpleasant odor. How could this ascensional force be utilized, I thought to myself—and suddenly the recollection occurred to me that I had given the tinman my bellows to put on a new handle. I hastily went out and crossed the square, now perfectly empty. When the tinman saw me, he cried out, "Good gracious, what's the matter, Monsieur Babolain?"

"I've come to ask for my bellows, my friend."

"Why, I sent them home to you a fortnight ago. Come in, Monsieur Babolain, you have no coat, and it's very cold."

"No, thank you, you are too kind. I did not remember that my bellows had been mended. I beg your pardon. My son-in-law is the best of men. Let me shake hands with you."

It was not until about seven o'clock that I returned home; I was covered with mud and horribly tired, for I had been walking about the country a long time, hap-hazard, but very eagerly. On entering the ante-chamber, where servants in full dress, probably hired at Blois, were rushing about, I found myself face to face with Bernard, who was giving orders.

"Are you crazy, to arrive at this hour and in such a condition?" said he.

"I've just taken a long walk,—you ought to have gone to the table without me, I'm very sorry to have kept you waiting."

This was not true; I felt no regret, for everything was a matter of indifference to me except the anguish ever ready to burst forth from the depths of my heart; and my sole care was so to concentrate my efforts that I might not lose my mastery over it. During dinner I talked excessively, attaching no importance to my words, and not even trying to give them a definite meaning. I interrupted everybody and broke in upon the conversation. Just at the moment when the mayor was saying that Monsieur le Sous-préfet had been unable to attend the wedding breakfast on account of his recent mourning for the loss of his wife, I remember that, amid the general silence, I turned towards the steward, who was putting a plate under my nose, and said in a very loud voice:

"No, I never eat asparagus; it doesn't agree with me, and besides, you have been bothering me for the last hour."

The mayor, supposing the words were addressed to him, grew extremely red, and cast an astonished glance around the table.

In vain Dr. Bernard and Monsieur le curé, who were in a very lively mood, strove to diminish the lamentable effect produced by my conduct; one would have said that everybody had an icy mantle thrown over his shoulders. After the dinner was over, the ladies all surrounded my child. I fancied I heard the condoling speeches they made to her, and even saw amid the group my beloved Valentine raise her little embroidered handkerchief to her eyes. This was more than I could bear. I made my escape, went up to my room, and, once in bed, poured forth the tears that were stifling me.

Unfortunately I had forgotten to lock myself in ; for I soon heard steps upon the staircase, the door of my room opened noisily, and by the light of the candle I saw Bernard, whose face wore a terrible expression. "What does all this mean," he said, entering. He was undoubtedly about to continue his speech when he heard the regular sonorous sound of my breathing. I feigned the deepest slumber, and even believe that I somewhat overdid my part. He thrust both hands into his pockets, rattled his keys, then folded his arms over his breast without taking his eyes from me, murmured a succession of adjectives which left no doubt as to his opinion of me, and left the room muttering : " Let him sleep then, it's better that he should."

He is undoubtedly going to tell Valentine he has found me lying in bed, I thought, and she will perhaps imagine that I don't love her, that I am indifferent to what concerns her. I will go down in a moment, it is absolutely necessary for me to go down—a father cannot stay in bed at such a moment. During this time I heard the carriages rolling over the avenue and stopping before the steps, the noise of dishes coming from the kitchen, and the confused sounds of the piano which floated up from the drawing room. How many years had elapsed since the day when I had undressed her by the fire. I sat in yonder little chair when I took her on my lap to rock her to sleep. She broke that piece of furniture ; in this corner she used to play with her doll ; and in thus re-ascending the stream of my life, I almost entirely lost my consciousness of what was passing around me.

Suddenly I heard in the passage the rustling of dresses and the murmur of women's voices. It roused me from my reverie. I rose, went to the door, listened, and soon perceived that the ladies were going to disrobe the bride.

So all was over between my daughter and myself. The edifice of my life was crumbling into a heap of ruins. Are the hopes of some men made to be crushed like glass under the foot of the passer-by. And I had not even embraced my daughter before being separated from her! I cautiously left my room, and pausing at every step to listen, went down the staircase and soon found myself seated in the garden on the little bench near the wash-house, where in her childhood she used to beat the clothes with a large beetle she could scarcely lift—the washerwomen stopped and looked at her with a laugh. I was called from the other end of the garden to see her—she was so pretty with her little bare arms, and the face she made as she lifted her burden. Those washing days were happy times! And now the sun of former years had disappeared; a wintry wind moaned through the leafless trees, and the stream flowed on beneath the melancholy moonlight; all nature was illumined with bluish rays as mournful as the reflections from steel. In the distance the clock at Favras slowly struck the hour, one by one, like the tolling of a passing bell; the house soon became silent, and the only light was in the large room on the ground floor which was allotted to the young couple.

I suddenly rose with a feeling of fury. It seemed as if that apartment was the scene of a most monstrous crime. I would have liked to destroy the scoundrel who had come among us like a robber, pillaged me, and trampled my dearest treasures under foot—she loved him.

I perceived that this light would drive me mad if

I watched it any longer. I noiselessly re-entered the house, went up to my room, and having wrapped a few articles of underclothing in a handkerchief, walked without even turning my head, towards the highway, where the mail coach would pass at dawn.

"Why, bless my heart, Monsieur Babolain, I had no idea I should take you to the city this morning," said the driver, taking my little bundle from my hand. "Make haste; I'm fifteen minutes behind time."

The mail coach, which we always called the patache, I don't know why, was hung very high above the wheels and had but one narrow seat, the left hand side of which was occupied by the driver. "You can't get up, wait till I help you." And the honest man, who, spite of the early hour, had already been drinking too much, pulled me roughly towards him. "You are frozen and you've nothing to cover you; wrap yourself in the blanket and let's be off. Where the devil are you going in this plight, Monsieur Babolain?"

"I don't know—I am going to Blois—it is very cold to-night. Oh! how cold it is," and in fact my teeth were chattering.

"It is cold, ha! ha! Monsieur Babolain, ha! ha!" said the driver, bursting into a loud laugh. Then speaking to his mare which was trotting bravely along, "Get up, get up, Grisette! It's cold to-night, but not to everybody, and it's my opinion that there are some people at your house who are not cold. Get up, get up. If she doesn't trot up hill we shall never make up our fifteen minutes." He cracked his whip. "It's not strange, Mademoiselle Babolain is a fine slip of a girl and Monsieur Joseph's a handsome man. Ah! you're going to laugh; for my part I like these things; though my hair is grey, I like 'em all the same. When my daughter was married, ha! ha! ha!" He drew his huge fur glove across his nose. "When my daughter was married, ah! that was a

time. Get up, get up—I wasn't sober for three days,
ha! ha! on account of the civilities people showed
me. It's no lie; for three days! There's nothing
more jolly than to have a daughter married; people
hug each other in the corners, push, elbow, get red,
break the dishes—oh! it's a fine thing. Yes, Monsieur Babolain, I wasn't sober—If this mare don't
get over the ground fast, I don't know where you'll
find one that does. I'll astonish you presently; why,
this beast knows what time it is and is trying to
make up the fifteen minutes. You'll see that she'll
trot up hill without my saying a word to her. It
makes no difference, but it's a queer idea to travel
at this hour—still everybody must attend to his own
affairs, of course." He continued to chatter on in
this way for a long time. On reaching the Faubourg
de Vienne he said, "Where will you get down? Eh!
Monsieur Babolain, why don't you answer me? Are
you asleep?" He took the reins in one hand and
shook me with the other. "Come, are you dead?
Here's a pretty piece of business. And fifteen minutes behind time to boot."

I heard him perfectly well, but I could not speak.
I seemed paralyzed by the cold, and my sobs almost
suffocated me. He stopped before the door of an
inn, got down, and rattled the knocker violently.
After an instant's delay a half dressed waiter, in a
cotton night-cap, appeared. Both took me out of
the carriage and laid me on a billiard table. "It's
Monsieur Babolain of Favras, who has been taken ill
in my carriage," said the driver, "wake the people
up and nurse him carefully. I can't wait, I'm twenty-
five minutes behind time." He mounted nimbly to
his seat. "Get up, get up," and he went noisily away.

Again I hovered between life and death for several months, and when the danger was over, Bernard,
who had nursed me with great devotion, said that
my recovery would be extremely slow. I was com-

pletely exhausted, my hair had become perfectly white, and I could scarcely recognize myself in the glass.

My daughter had been compelled to leave Favras almost at the commencement of my sickness, to follow her husband, who could not consent to a long stay in the country. I had a vague recollection of this departure—it was one evening just after I had had a violent attack; she entered the room in her travelling dress. I fancied she was going to town, and for weeks, it seems, asked if she had returned. Afterwards when old Marianne, who had remained with me, told me that my children were permanently settled in Paris, when I saw the unfurnished house, the empty rooms, the deserted garden, the clumps of trees choked with brambles, I was astonished not to find myself reduced to despair. One would have said that the power of being moved was utterly destroyed within me. Had Providence broken, one by one, all the ties that bound me to this world to render the death I had just miraculously escaped easier for me? Is there a sort of moral toilette which renders the great passage from life to death less difficult? Thoughts could no longer be formed within my exhausted brain; my weakness was like a shield which prevented outside impressions from reaching me; insensible alike to regrets and hopes, without past or future, the hours and days glided by empty and colorless; I looked without seeing, existed without living.

One day when they had rolled my arm chair to the threshold of the door, I saw a stranger who, accompanied by Marianne, was examining everything with great care. He soon came towards me, and very politely told me that this little property suited him very well. It did not occur to me to think these words strange, and in the evening when told that my son-in-law had offered our house for sale, I was not disturbed. What did I care for the dwelling, now Valentine had left it?

I, too, left this refuge where our lives were to have ended.

A covered cart came for us at daybreak; they put in the two boxes which contained all my worldly possessions; I took in my lap the flowerpot in which was a twig from my daughter's tree, planted before the house with my own hands the morning after we entered it, and we set out.

A moment comes when we tear a whole chapter from our lives without any very great sorrow. For a long time I could see amid the trees the red roof of the house, the rain gauge, and the poplar by the wash house, and—at a turn in the road all disappeared.

The old mansion my daughter occupied was very stately in its appearance. It was situated on the Rue du Regard, between two silent convents. The principal courtyard, which one entered first, was surrounded by old stone posts, bound with iron, and connected by heavy chains. A footman, who looked like the beadle of the church at Favras, helped me out of the carriage, supported me, and took me to a room on the first floor. The apartment was somewhat dull and gloomy; my first thought on entering the ante-chamber was that my beloved daughter must be heartily tired amid such surroundings. The walls were bare, the furniture was old, faded, and by no means attractive in shape. A door opened, Valentine came to meet me, and bending her forehead to my lips with a manner in which there was a shade of fear, murmured:

"God has not been deaf to our prayers, father. You have at last recovered your health, let me take you to the room that has been prepared for you."

It was nearly a year since we had seen each other, a very long time for a first separation, and I had often

thought of the first kiss I would give her when I saw her
again ; but her manners instantly checked all demonstrations of feeling. I don't think any woman could be
more stately than she was then. In addition to the
fact that her lovely face had assumed a very grave
expression, she was clad in a dark dress, cut high in
the throat, and entirely destitute of trimming. Her
hair, which formerly curled according to its own will,
was now smooth, flat, and covered with a cap whose
ruches framed her face in a melancholy way. How
different she was from the little girl of former days
who compelled me to dance, laughing so heartily at
my awkwardness! Alas, if she could no longer
laugh, neither could I dance. Everything changes in
life.

Valentine soon left me with an apology. She had
a great many people to receive, she said, and in fact
I had heard the bell ring several times with a sound
like an ancient bell from a monastery. I remained
alone in the dining-room, sitting near the window.
Suddenly I saw a heavy, shabby carriage, drawn by a
stout horse, enter the courtyard, turn, and stop before
the steps of the house. The coachman, who looked
like a retired merchant, got down from his seat,
opened the door with great difficulty, and a man
alighted who, though still young, had a weary expression, a dull, yellowish complexion, stooping shoulders, a face smoothly shaven as a deacon's, and long
hair floating over the collar of his coat. His crushed
hat rested on the back of his head ; he carried in one
hand a quantity of pamphlets and papers, and with
the other drew round him an overcoat, which, drag-
ing on the ground, seemed to follow him reluctantly.
He wore a black coat, with square-cut skirts, much
too large for him, and buttoned awry. The retired
merchant took out a black box with a handle, and a
foot muff, and followed his master, who had already
entered the vestibule.

It was some instants before I recognized Valentine's husband in the personage with the coat so much too large for him. I greatly dreaded meeting him, for I always felt an emotion of mingled antipathy and terror. Fortunately his cold, polite welcome greatly simplified matters. He spoke to me as if he had parted from me that very morning.

"How do you do, father," said he, in a faint voice, "the journey must have fatigued you."

"Good-morning, I really have very little strength."

"Let me see your tongue. It is terrible."

He drew a large silver watch from his pocket and looked sternly at the face while he felt my pulse, then listened at my back, looked steadily at me, and went away without saying anything. I was very glad of it.

One might have thought, and at first I myself believed, that in her husband's company Valentine was the most wretched of women; but I was soon undeceived: my daughter loved Joseph with all her heart, and wished for nothing beyond the life she was leading. She rose early in the morning, wrote until a very late hour at night, and during the whole day either received company or went out; but whenever one met her she was preoccupied and seemed to be late for some appointment. Often, in the midst of the meals, which were quickly despatched though very abundant, especially on fast days—my son-in-law being fond of good living—I saw them exchange glances which were like mute confidences. Then I hastily looked at my plate and dared not raise my eyes. At other times they uttered fragments of sentences whose meaning I could not understand. Valentine drew a little memorandum book from her pocket and hastily took a note. By a thousand incidents I perceived that there was a perfect understanding between them. At times they had the appearance of partners settling some business matter. I thought I understood that they went into society in the Faubourg Saint Germain, and in some way or other were playing an important part. My daughter, who had connections with a great many persons, also maintained an extensive correspondence. She was treasurer of a charitable society, which was also pervaded with some flavor of politics I could never exactly define.

My children's seriousness was, moreover, more apparent than real : they were joyous at certain periods ; twenty times I surprised Valentine passing her white hand over her old young husband's pale forehead, and looking at him with an expression of mingled tenderness and admiration. By what moral malady could she be attacked to love this fellow. Doubtless she was attracted by his energy, his ambitious projects, with which she was associated! She must consider him a hero ! And then this new life was so different from her former existence. All this charmed her ; she was grateful to him for his relations, his influence, his mansion, his establishment—the sight of me, which recalled constraint and obscurity, could not be agreeable to her. I did everything in the world that I might not be in their way : I tried to pass unobserved ; I entered the dining-room just in time to sit down to the table, and went away as soon as I had swallowed the last mouthful, clearly understanding that they took pleasure in being together and talking freely. I have spent very sorrowful hours in that little room, which I dared not leave, lest I might be intrusive. If I had been able to unpack my boxes— but there was not room. They were in a corner, piled one above another ; I looked at them, saying to myself : " There are my books, my papers, and a thousand little keepsakes whose possession would change my whole life." I was like a shipwrecked man, who sees the land and cannot reach it. To open those boxes and spread out my treasures had become an ideal vision to me.

One day as I came in to breakfast, my son-in-law, who was looking over some letters, said to his wife, " Why, here is some news from Favras ! " I could not help starting. " The business is settled," he added.

" Hum ! hum ! " said Valentine.

He threw down the letter and turned to the servant. " Are there many people in the drawing-room, François ? "

" They're beginning to come in to, wait for Monsieur's office hours ; there are ten people already, and five are monks."

" Ah ! five holy Fathers already ! You are very attentive to them, François, are you not ? I particularly insist upon it."

" Day before yesterday," observed Valentine, " I saw all their dripping cloaks piled upon the table in the ante-room."

" Poor Fathers, they had been out in the rain."

" And the floor was drenched. You must attend to this matter, François."

" Madame may be sure that I do my best. I've washed up the ante-chamber and laid a carpet on the room where they walk up and down to wait for the office hours."

" It's provoking that the holy Fathers should be kept waiting," murmured my son-in-law. " their time is precious. It's absolutely indispensable to have a private waiting-room near my office. I've said so a hundred times."

" Hum ! hum ! " said Valentine.

" Hum ! hum ! " replied her husband.

The evening of that very day I was in my room, watering the slip I had brought from Favras, when I heard a loud knock at the door. Valentine entered. She must have some important reason for coming to pay me a visit, and I feared that I might read traces of annoyance in her face. I set down the carafe and hastily pushed the slip into a corner.

17

Far from being angry, she said smiling: "What is the bit of wood in that little flower pot?"

"Oh, nothing, my dear—a little tree."

"That withered twig!"

"Yes, it's a slip. I was watering it a little, it isn't dead; one might think so, but it isn't."

I was reassured by the pleasant expression of her face, even thought for a moment that my daughter was restored to me, and the idea of clasping her in my arms suddenly entered my head, but from motives of prudence I succeeded in controlling myself and continued: "It's a little branch from your tree; I brought it from Favras." It seemed as if I was breathing a whiff of its invigorating air. "I wanted to take something before I came away, you know."

"Poor father," murmured Valentine, smiling at me as we soothe a child. "My poor papa, you have been deeply grieved. Such a leave-taking is always painful at first."

"The grass was full of violets."

"Of course, it's the season for them."

"There were beautiful little fresh leaves everywhere and—so many memories. You remember the new ivy? Well, I measured it before I came away, it reaches to the study window. Oh! Favras is a pretty estate. Yes, of course I was a little sorry to leave our trees; at my age we don't always have time to make new friends. They tossed their boughs when they saw me go away. Perhaps it was the wind, perhaps it was also emotion. Who knows? These beings have more feeling than people think. They all spoke of you. 'You'll tell Valentine not to forget us entirely, won't you, my friend? She played under our branches; we have sheltered, protected, possessed her—' that's what they said, and many other things too. It's a certain fact that they have retained the invisible trace of your passage, and everything, the walls of the house, the very sand on the walks was pervaded with your image—"

I did not look at her while saying all this, I was scraping the wood of the arm-chair with my nail, hunting a grain of dust, that I might not allow her to perceive my emotion; but I felt her eyes fixed upon me with a glance of mingled tenderness and compassion. She was doubtless thinking: " Poor father, how old and broken he is!" And at the same time she thought me very silly to talk to the trees and plant half-dead twigs in little flower-pots. Yet I could not help adding: " Before I came away I sat down on your bench near the willows and the river began to prattle. If you knew what a memory it has? When you went there you fancied yourself alone, you were in the shade, in the open air, you thought without restraint; well, the river heard you think, and wrote all this on its tablets; on the stems of the tall grasses, under the leaves of the water-lilies, in the nooks of the bank—I have found the treasure again. It has kept portraits of you, all of which I have seen. There are some when you were very small, in your little hat and blue plaid dress—do you remember your blue plaid dress?—and others when you were a large girl, and still others— There were thousands . of them, for the river has never reflected the smallest fragment of you without tenderly preserving the image. Thus, my darling, affection surrounds you unconsciously to yourself, and one is beloved without desiring it. There are spots on the lawn where you planted your little heel, and the grass has withered."

"Ha! ha! ha! why, that is very poetical, my poor father, let us be sensible."

"Yes, the grass didn't grow again, and it was right; why not die under a pleasant impression, bearing away a memory, a caress. Plants have hearts. Who will ever know what your tree felt when I bade it farewell and cut off a little branch?"

"Come, come my poor papa. You must calm yourself. Is that clock right?"

"I don't know, my dear. The clock yonder struck the hours exactly, whether they were sad or happy. It always struck, and it is natural, clocks are made to strike ; one might suppose them indifferent, but to a delicate ear how many variations there are in the sound."

" No doubt, but one ought not to let one's imagination run riot in this way. Besides I'm in a hurry, and I believe this clock is slow, and then it is bad to consume one's life in useless regrets. You know very well, and have confessed yourself, that my husband, being detained in Paris by his profession, could not keep the little hermitage at Favras."

" Oh ! of course, my dear, you couldn't keep the little place, and besides it wasn't handsome enough for you."

" Poor papa ! You see my husband has left you to enjoy it as long as possible. During your long illness and convalescence you were left there perfectly quiet, perfectly at home, and to all the offers that were made him my husband invariably replied, ' Favras won't be sold until my father-in-law's health is entirely restored, and he is settled in Paris.' "

" I am very grateful to you, my child ; I delayed the sale most unintentionally, but ten opportunities will occur in place of one, it is so pretty, oh ! you will easily find a purchaser."

" That is done already ; my husband learned it this morning from a letter. Favras is sold."

" Sold ! " I cried in spite of myself, but instantly regained my self-command and added : " So much the better, so much the better, since you want to get rid of it."

" You have everything you need, haven't you, my poor father ? "

" Yes, my child, thank you."

" You are at home in this house, you must not be under any restraint, I should be distressed if you hesitated to ask for what you want. But it isn't good for you to occupy this room. It faces the north, and is exposed to the wind."

" I have not noticed it."

" 'The wind is terrible on this side, and then these windows look out upon the gardens; it's very dull for you here. Fortunately I have a better one to offer you : at the other end of the suite of apartments there is a very cheerful chamber, looking out upon the court-yard and facing the south. You will see the people passing in and out, and have a Prussian fire-place, which is excellent. My husband says that merely on account of your health, you must—"

"As you choose, my children, I shall be comfortable anywhere."

" 'Then it's all settled ; good-bye father. I'm very late."

One cannot form an idea of the grace and charm of her whole manner; she went away smiling at me. I would willingly have lived in a cellar to be sometimes cheered by one of those smiles.

An hour after, the footman entered ; he came by my daughter's orders to assist in removing my baggage to another room, and began to rummage through the drawers in the bureau. I should have greatly preferred to have him let me do it, for my linen I knew had been neglected a long time, and the cloth I had bought of a weaver in Favras was very coarse and rough. I trembled lest the footman should notice all this, not for myself, but my daughter, who might be affected by her servant's opinion.

" I'm really very sorry to give you this trouble," I said to the man.

" Madame told me to do it," he answered, continuing his work.

" My daughter is too kind—she thinks of everything—I am sure you must feel great affection for her, don't you ? "

" Everybody does Madame justice."

I knew very well that it was not proper to talk so,
but I had so little opportunity to speak of her, and
besides the man's coldness excited me.   " My daughter is a superior woman.   When she was a child her
reflections astonished—"

" Does Monsieur want me to move the boxes
too ? "

" I don't care.   My daughter is hasty, I confess,
but when she is angry or impatient for a moment, you
must not be vexed.   A cross word scarcely escapes
her lips before she is sorry for it—you see I know my
daughter thoroughly.   Stop, my friend, let me help
you, you are too much loaded to open the door.   Is
the room where we are going at the end of this passage ? "   It was a closet rather than a bed-room, but
by means of pushing the bed a little farther back,
and giving up a wardrobe, which, moreover, was of
no great use to me, I succeeded in making room for
an arm chair and a small table near the window.
After all, I did not need a larger room.   This reminded me of the little chamber at the normal school,
where I had had so many dreams, so many plans for the
future.   Did not Providence, in perpetually pushing
me into a little corner, act the part of a good mother,
seek to prove the folly of my ambition, and recall me
to reason ?

Thanks to the footman, who was very willing to
help me, I removed the lid of one of my boxes and
set about adorning my cell.   The first object which
came to hand was the very one that was dearest to
me, a plan of Favras I had made myself, and in
which the smallest corners of the estate had been
carefully marked — the bench by the wash-house,
the rain-gauge, Valentine's tree, the sun-dial, and the
different places where I had let my daughter play.
Everywhere there were dots, signs, numbers, which
recalled a happy or sorrowful memory.   It was like

a library, where I found all the chapters of twenty
years of my life ; a cemetery too, where the emotions
of former days rested peacefully under their little
black crosses.

I hung this drawing by the side of a portrait of
my Valentine, and a sketch in ink and red pencil my
wife had made for her great picture of Cain and
Abel.

I had been on the point of burning this sketch a
hundred times, but could never resolve to do so. Sorrows and joys are the black and white stones of the
same edifice ; the former support the latter. Not an
hour of existence can be effaced or cursed, the most
miserable have been necessary, and were sometimes
the keystones of the arches which have prevented
the whole building from falling.

I was soon settled in my cabin. I seemed to myself like a passenger on a ship—true, I had not all
my comforts, but I improved my situation every day,
and then I was only separated by a partition from the
room where my daughter worked, so I could hear her
move, knew that she was near me. She came to see
me once, but by some inconceivable fatality the bottom of her dress caught on one of the nails of a box,
and a large rent was torn which put her in an ill-
temper. She reproached me sharply for my want of
neatness, assuring me that she should be humiliated
in her servants' eyes—but what is the use of recalling
all this? She had torn her dress, that fully explained
her irritation, besides it is true that my chamber was
very untidy, I had so little room.

One evening, when there had been company at
dinner, my daughter said somewhat tartly: "I know
people are not foppish at your age, my poor father,
but really, neglect of one's person has some limits,
and we ought to avoid certain styles of dress from respect to others."

Yet I had worn my chestnut coat, as I always did

to dine with my children. "I thought I was suitably dressed," I said, in an embarrassed tone. "It is because—I have no other coat, my dear, or at least the others are far less presentable than, this."

"Well, buy some, what shall I say to you? I can't write to your tailor myself. You'll go so far that my husband's patience will be exhausted. For my part, I haven't the strength to be a shield between you perpetually, to be constantly soothing, excusing, palliating. At least make some exertion to render the task less difficult."

How could I have displeased my son-in-law? We did not exchange ten words a week. I entered my room and carefully examined my coat. Its condition, I must say, was much worse than I had supposed; several buttons were missing, the seams were white, and the elbow was even— My children must certainly be ashamed of me, and the idea had never entered my head. In a moment of despair, I snatched off my cravat and collar; I already saw my son-in-law driving me from the house like a beggar. The important point was to secure some clothes as soon as possible; but when I had taken the little canvas bag in which I kept my money out of my trunk, and spread the copper and silver coins on the table, I perceived with terror that my whole fortune did not exceed thirty-two francs.

It was a most depressing feeling. I did not reproach myself for having given my daughter what I possessed; if I had had it to do over again, I should have taken the same course, but I realized for the first time that I should always be dependent upon my son-in-law. Fortunately I remembered the publisher of my dictionary, of which I had heard nothing for two years. I went there early the next morning, not without difficulty, for my limbs were still very weak. On finding myself again in the book store which I had once entered with so much confidence, I almost lost

courage, I felt so aged, so changed, so humiliated, in
my chestnut coat. Ah! I should have gone away
immediately if the point in question had not been to
buy new clothes. When I said that I came in behalf of Monsieur Babolain, the publisher looked earnestly at me, no doubt he had some vague idea that
he knew me. "The dictionary is sold very little
now," said he; "it was a good book, but is now
strangely out of fashion. It's possible there may be
a balance due on the account, I'll see about it."

He approached a green tube that hung over his
table, and put the opening to his mouth.

"It's possible there may be a balance due on the
account," I thought—"but suppose they owe me nothing—what is to be done then?"

"What has become of Monsieur Babolain?" said
he, looking at me again with an expression of mingled
curiosity and compassion.

"He has met with—reverses," I replied, "many
little troubles, and therefore sees very few people."

"But he hasn't given up work on that account?"

"Ah! no, and even in his—peculiar position, I
think he would be glad to have some occupation."

"I'll willingly afford him an opportunity from time
to time, if Monsieur Babolain would revise certain
books we publish, whose proof-sheets require the experience of a professional man. This sort of work is
poorly paid, it is true, but—"

It seemed as if heaven was opening before me.
So I had the means of being a burden to no one, I
was going to work again, as in former days, and recover
my self-respect. Into what a gulf I should have
fallen but for this unexpected offer.

A clerk entered and placed a paper upon the
desk.

"According to this account, we owe Monsieur
Babolain three hundred and ninety-five francs for his
copyright." The clerk retired and the publisher took

a five-hundred-franc note from a drawer and handed it to me. " Will you give me a receipt ? " said he.

My eyes were dim with grateful tears, while a feeling of shame for having concealed my· name made me blush.

" Excuse me, Monsieur," I murmured, " I did not dare to tell you the truth : I am Babolain, the author of the dictionary."

" You're not so much changed that one wouldn't recognize you," he said smiling; "good-bye, Monsieur Babolain, good-bye."

Once in the street, I was surprised to find myself inspired with a strength and energy I had not possessed before. The five hundred francs in my pocket, and the publisher's words gave me fresh courage. "No, I'm not worn out," I said to myself. " If people offer me work after twenty years of forgetfulness, my scientific value must have been real. Wasn't I professor of mathematics at twenty eight ? My dear old class room ! How could I have forgotten mathematics so long ? " I now felt all the shame of this desertion, but there was still time to make amends, to compel my son-in-law to consider me his equal, to be really the head of the family. I entered a ready-made clothing shop without the slightest embarrassment, and in a very short time selected a black suit which they assured me was the best article they had. I even allowed myself to be persuaded to take a velvet vest with small blue and white flowers, a vest in which it seems a man of my age could attend either a dinner or ball, it suited me exactly ; but I must add that I never had occasion to put it on, in consequence of a very important event which made a great change in my life.

Valentine's health was not good ; I had been in the habit of observing closely for too long a time not to perceive a thousand alarming symptoms. She had had several attacks of indisposition, one after

another, which disturbed me all the more because
her husband treated the whole affair with inconceivable nonchalance. He would not even hear the very
moderate, though firm representations, I thought it
my dúty to make on this subject. Meantime I was
about to urge the matter, as my title of father authorized me to do, when I was roused one night by
strange sounds, amid which I clearly distinguished
stifled moans. I was out of bed in an instant, and
rushing into the passage, ran into the arms of the
footman who was hurrying by.

"Bless my soul and body," he cried.

"What's the matter, my friend, what's the matter?"

"Monsieur bumped my head, I beg Monsieur's
pardon."

And he disappeared. I followed him and crossed
the drawing-room, where a candle was burning; I
was suffering torture, but it never entered my brain
that my Valentine was about to become a mother.
Yet this was the fact: my son in-law told me so,
while shutting the door in my face. I know very well
that my presence might be troublesome at such a
time, but it would have been sufficient to say: "Go
away, father," and I should have retired. Yet it was
impossible for me to stay in one place. I went down
to the kitchen to find some one who could tell me
about my daughter. The nurse, who had been hastily
summoned and was eating some soup with the cook,
burst into a loud laugh as she caught sight of me:
indeed I was in the lightest possible dress. Propriety
commanding me not to remain longer in the presence
of two women in such a condition, I went up to the
entry where I paced up and down until dawn, in the
greatest agitation. I dare not say that I shared my
daughter's sufferings, but with what joy I would have
taken the larger share of them, had it been possible !
To say to myself: "My darling Valentine is terribly

ill, perhaps her life is in danger, her moans pierce my heart "—and be obliged to pace silently up and down the corridor. I stopped everybody who passed.

" How is she ? " I said anxiously.

" Very well," was the reply, " very well, very well."

They were evidently deceiving me, for the moans grew louder and louder.

" It's a boy," cried the maid, rushing out of the room.

A few minutes after, my son-in-law and the physician came out of the chamber.

I rushed to meet them. " It's a boy," I exclaimed, " how is my daughter ? "

" My father-in-law," said Joseph, shrugging his shoulders as he turned to the doctor, and then added : " but Monsieur, for God's sake, go and dress yourself. What are you doing here in this condition ? Mother and child are doing admirably well. Go, Monsieur, go."

It was not until two or three hours after that I was allowed to enter my daughter's room, yet I remained only an instant. The nurse, who seemed like a veritable dragon, had positive orders, and would not let me say a word ; my heart was full. Scarcely had I kissed Valentine's hand—for she summoned up strength to hold out her hand to me—when I was pushed towards the cradle where my grandson was sleeping, and put outside the door almost immediately. I dared not say anything lest they should be still more strict another time, but when I returned to my room I began to weep. They were foolish tears, but I had never entirely recovered from my severe illness, and had moments of extreme moral and physical weakness. I dressed myself, took the hundred and fifty francs I had left, and went out ; my plan was formed, I wanted to give my daughter some little trinket for a remembrance of her son's birth.

After hesitating a long time I decided upon a locket which would hold hair; and as this purchase reduced my resources to almost nothing, I went to my publisher to remind him of his promise, and ask for some work. He gave me a tolerably large number of proof-sheets which I was to revise with great care, and pointed out very minutely the spirit in which I was to make the corrections and annotations. In short, all this occupied a long time, and I returned to the house at a very late hour. On seeing me pass through the courtyard, the footman came out of the kitchen and coming up to me, said : " You needn't go up the main staircase, Monsieur, I've moved all your things to your new room."

I dared not ask for any explanations, and without saying a word, allowed myself to be conducted to a small door near the stable, which opened upon a narrow staircase that led to the attic. François was doubtless a little spiteful in making me go up this way, for at the end of the wide hall where I had wandered up and down all night, was a door that opened upon the back stairs ; in fact, I usually went up to my chamber through it.

" Monsieur will have more room here," said the servant, ushering me into an apartment with a tiled floor and sloping roof, it is true, but very large; " there's another one adjoining it, where we have put Monsieur's bed."

" It is very comfortable, thank you ; dinner will soon be ready, won't it ? "

" The doctor can't come home until very late, so he has given orders that you should have your dinner in your own room."

" My son-in-law has done right."

A quarter of an hour after, the cook, panting violently, set upon the table the dish that contained my dinner. This woman, who never lost an opportunity of being disagreeable, gave me to understand that if my dinner was to be served in my room every day, she should soon be obliged to give up her place. She said many other things that were somewhat harsh, but I excused her without difficulty and even tried to soothe her, for the heat of the stove and the continual inhalation of carbonic acid makes cooks irritable. It was a fact that my change of lodgings would give the servants increased work, and I saw clearly that I should be obliged to use great care in future to keep the peace with them.

That evening I entered my children's room through the door that opened upon the corridor. My daughter was asleep, my son-in-law had not returned, and I heard my little grandson in my old room crying in a sweet, clear voice, accompanied by a song from his nurse.

Thus I at last discovered the reason of my removal, and was perfectly satisfied. They had not made me go up stairs from caprice, but as a matter of necessity to make room for the little man. I returned to my chamber. Unfortunately they had forgotten to put candles in the candlesticks, and a terrible draught came through the window. I replaced the missing curtain with my chestnut colored coat, which was not risking much, and groped my way to bed. I should have been very comfortable, but for the disagreeable smell of a pipe which penetrated into my room about eleven o'clock. One of my neighbors, the coachman, footman, or cook undoubtedly smoked to excess.

During my daughter's convalescence, I must say that I was very happy. Scarcely had my son-in-law gone out when I went down to her room, and it did not seem to annoy her. Finding herself still too weak to receive visits or employ herself in any way, she was not displeased to have her old papa to keep her company, read the paper to her, bring her her child, or pass her her chaplet. She listened without

vexation, and often with smiles to the little allusions
I made to our house in Favras, and was more unre-
served about her own affairs than she had ever been
before. She showed me a prayer book she had received from Monseigneur de Pansol, and a little gold
cross the Marquise de Vélizy had given her. Then
as secretary and treasurer of that charitable society,
whose object I never clearly understood, but whose
head-quarters were at Rome, she had obtained several precious relics from a cardinal, thanks to the in-
tercession of that great Roman lady, the Comtesse
de Monte Revilla, who at the time of the marriage
had shown herself a most devoted friend of my
wife's—it needed these little enjoyments of self-love
to make my dear daughter undertake the labor to
which she submitted. Twice a month she forwarded
to Rome a most minute report of the progress of the
charitable society and its various members. She
performed this task from verbal directions given her
every day by her husband, of whose genius she was
never weary of talking. I listened to her gladly, approved, admired everything—these confidential conversations gave me so much pleasure. Then George
grew restless—my little grandson's name was George
—got angry, and screamed furiously. I took him in
my arms, and he stopped at once, often even smiled
through his tears. The nurse, with whom I was on
excellent terms—I always got along with nurses—declared she had never seen anything like it, and it was
a new thing to me also : some one who instinctively
held out his arms and was happy in my caresses. So
whenever the little fellow was fractious, Valentine
said : " Go for his grandpapa."

Often amid these joys we heard the roll of a
carriage.

" It is my husband," murmured Valentine, and I escaped to my room as fast as possible. I now saw that
my heart had not deceived me : my daughter loved me

sincerely. Apparently undemonstrative, as is often
the case in the most affectionate natures, engrossed
in her own occupations, and controlled by her husband's influence, she had seemed cold and indifferent to me, but a week's seclusion was sufficient to restore her to her former self.   She was a mother now ;
she understood how ardent and profound is the affection we feel for our children, and my grandson, by
his mere presence, was to change my whole life and
procure me all this happiness.   I became passionately
fond of the child.

I again find these notes cast aside so long ago.
The last page bears a date four or five years old.
Often during my life I have been tempted to think
fate severe; but now that, being less proud, I can
look around me without bitterness or anger, I say to
myself: "What have I done, oh, God! to deserve the
blessings with which Thou art soothing my last moments, to deserve that my little grandson should welcome me with a smile on his first entrance upon life,
and give me his heart?   What have I done that his
little hands should smooth my white hair, his angelic
lips press my wrinkled cheeks; that the sweet angel
should nestle in my arms and love me as if I were
worthy of affection ? "

Scarcely had my daughter recovered from her
confinement when she returned to her former life with
more eagerness than ever.   Visitors came in throngs,
and she soon had not a moment to herself.   She
hastily kissed her child in the morning while opening
her letters, or getting into her carriage to attend to
her business, and so violently that the little creature
was frightened.   She overwhelmed the nurse with advice and orders, and, always in a hurry, went away
with regret.   Yet she loved her son with all her heart,
I am sure, but the requirements of her position led
her on ; she had no time, and perhaps she also knew

I was there to watch over George. My son-in-law, who was becoming more and more famous and busy, was rarely visible, and under any circumstances was not the man to spend his time upon a child. So the little fellow, seeing me always near him, grew accustomed to my caresses, to my face, and took pleasure in my attentions, which soon became indispensable to him. It was while holding out his arms to me that he said papa for the first time. And I accepted the boon—I defrauded my son-in-law, but why was he never there? It is no great crime to pick up a piece of good-fortune from which our neighbor turns away.

I soon devoted all my thoughts and time to my little grandson, and one might say that my life blended with his.

I cannot think without smiling of the continual anxieties his nurse caused me during the first months of his life. Of course it was of primary importance that this woman should give George the best quality of milk, and consequently that she herself should be in perfect health. What was my uneasiness then when, by her pallor, her increasing melancholy, I had proof that some secret sorrow was undermining her constitution? I never left her, lavished attentions upon her, and having gained her confidence learned that she was weak enough to love far too well a husband who remained in the country and gave her every reason for being jealous. The wretch was continually writing letters in which he demanded money, threatening to come to Paris at once if he did not receive a reply in accordance with his wishes. When our means of satisfying him were exhausted we were obliged to parley, find excuses, invent a thousand falsehoods, which made me blush to the roots of my hair. Oh! if my little George's milk had not been directly threatened.

"Monsieur," said the poor woman, "my husband is a dreadful man, but I love him for all that," and for

18

the hundredth time she told me the story of his court-
ship. They had seen each other for the first time at
a rural fête, mounted on wooden horses—

Thank God, my little grandson passed through
this first period of infancy without any serious accident. The nurse returned to her faithless husband,
and our old Marianne from Favras, whom my daughter had always kept as a seamstress, was installed in
her place.

She taught the little fellow the way to the attic,
grandpapa's roost, where we spend a part of our
lives. He already opens the door leading to the
back stairs himself, and I can hear the sound of his
hurrying little feet, and the toctoc he makes with his
dimpled hand. His visits are my great happiness, but
I now avoid going into his room or to my children's
apartments. I have the fears of the privileged character, who only asks to be allowed to pass unnoticed.
Therefore I was not at all troubled when the servants, from habit, continued to bring my meals to my
room. Valentine, who doubtless supposed I had requested it, and moreover often had a great many
guests at her table, made no remark. It was tacitly
settled that I should not come down without a special invitation. This was a relief to everybody—I
preferred to love my daughter at a distance, and see
her in my memory.

One would have said that in the presence of his
father and mother George shared my constraint.
Children are so keen in their estimation of the caresses we give them. I never saw him show his
feelings with perfect freedom, except up above in
our room, in my little garret. But how he makes
up for lost time! How his eyes sparkle when he
comes in! How he jumps into my arms, rummages
in every corner, inspects, examines, overwhelms me
with whys and wherefores with the freedom of a child
who knows itself to be beloved? But he is particu-

larly attentive and earnest when I open my bureau drawer. Here are all my little relics, wrapped in white paper, and carefully ticketed with signs I alone can understand. The contents of these packages have no value except to myself : Valentine's mother's hair, Valentine's picture when a child, shells she picked up in the sand on the garden walks and I afterwards found in my pockets ; ribbons, hair-pins, and a thousand things my wife had left at the time of—her departure for Italy, and which I had never had the courage to throw away.

How the joys and sorrows of a whole existence are reduced to the most trifling things. All these witnesses of my life could be held in a valise. Yet to everybody else this dusty rubbish.is only fit to be swept away with a broom. Why is it so dear to me ? From fear of curious eyes I have taken refuge with my museum in the second of my two garrets, the back one. Nobody enters here except myself and George—when we are in it together, or when I am alone, I put the key on the inside. It is not only to dream at my ease that I shut myself up—I do so that I may safely attend to a multitude of household duties, and I don't wish to be surprised by the servants with a broom or a needle in my hand lest my daughter might be wounded. Now, if I did not mend my clothes carefully, I should soon be in tatters and could no longer go to walk with George. It is very certain that they would not trust him to me if I looked like a beggar ; it is perfectly natural. In my ·daughter's position one is not very glad to have a father who wears rags. It is of the utmost importance to me always to have a suitable dress. I manage to do so, but not without difficulty : I have always been very awkward, my sight has grown much worse within the last three or four years, and then one must try one's self to know how difficult it is to put, for instance, a neat patch on the sleeve of a coat.

And then to repair linings, and darn shirt bosoms?
All this seems like nothing. The more worn the
clothes are, the harder it is to mend them. How
many times I would have thrown down my work if I
had not thought of our walk the next morning! Necessity makes one ingenious and patient. When
people are not sick they find resources in Paris
which they would never have imagined. I have
found in the Temple, which people avoid, I don't
know why, as an evil place, really magnificent opportunities : perfectly new clothes, cut with great skill,
and costing very little money. Two years ago I was
on the point of buying of the shop-keeper a coat,
warmly lined, with a large velvet collar and cuffs, and
for which he only asked thirty-six francs. It had not
been worn ten times! Unfortunately at this period
I was already destitute of means. I have regretted
that garment greatly.

If I had been able to earn a little money, as my
publisher had given me the means of doing, my life
would have been greatly simplified ; but after trying
for three or four months, I was obliged to confess
that all labor had become impossible to me. I could
no longer fix my attention ; and if I forced myself to
do so was seized in a few minutes with a sort of vertigo ; the signs and printed letters whirled before my
eyes—something was broken within me. It was a
very sorrowful time, for as I grew more miserable
the memory of my former successes foolishly returned to my mind ; I eagerly rummaged through my papers, among my books, sought out my diplomas—my
poor diplomas. I ended by nailing them to the wall.
Where will pride find a hiding-place ? I thought myself despicable, for I had never wholly lost my powers of criticism and analysis. I said to myself : " You
were of some little value once—well, what does that
prove ? your little worm-eaten stool is broken, stay in

your place." My attention was diverted by a crowd of difficulties.

About this time the sale of my dictionary ceased entirely; it had had its day, it was only just. To complete my embarrassment the little pension paid me by the ministry was stopped. True, I lived with my children, whose intention undoubtedly was that I should want for nothing; but my daughter was far too busy, poor child, to see that her orders were obeyed, and the servants forgot or neglected many things of the most absolute necessity. Perhaps they even kept a part of what was intended for me themselves. I should not allow myself to cast such a suspicion upon them, if I had not serious reason to do so. They doubtless were not aware of the trouble they caused me, and nothing in the world would have induced me to complain of it, for my daughter, who I am sure, really loved me with all her heart, would not have failed to make an example of them, perhaps might have gone beyond all bounds.

It was far better to bear these little annoyances. Besides, by searching carefully, I found several articles I could do without, and which enabled me for some time to buy a few candles, some wine, and above all coffee—I always had the weakness of liking it after dinner—and lastly chocolate. I wanted my George to find his lozenges in the green box as long as possible. These were my last days of plenty. Although I made great efforts to husband my resources, I was soon reduced to the little the servants brought me, that is, to almost nothing. Twice in succession, in the hope of obtaining something, I went down to my daughter's room at the hour I thought I should disturb her least; but there were always so many people awaiting an audience that I dared not tell her of my troubles, and I was right: I soon became accustomed to my new situation. After all, how many poorer people than I would have thought it enviable!

We attach the more value to the joys of life
the less numerous they are : those who have only
one taste every fragment, and find savors that others
would not have imagined. George has given me this
one sole joy, he has kept me alive for years.

I am like an old trunk of a deformed tree, half
worm-eaten and with but one root. Dear little fellow !
You shall be happy, God grant you may be happy,
my child !

Will he be so ? the idea that he may perhaps have
the germ of my faults in his nature sometimes haunts
me. While he is playing near me I watch him, would
fain read his heart. Moral and physical resemblances often overleap a generation. How am I to explain the strange sympathy he shows me, his affection, the pleasure he feels in being near me except
by a similarity of character, a harmony of tastes—it
is really alarming !

At certain times I would fain have him less indulgent to me, judge me more harshly, that at some future day he might say to himself, " Everything my poor
grandfather did is exactly what I must avoid." It is
something in life to have black specks on the stones
upon which we ought not to step. While waiting for
him to know me, I must not suffer him to love me
blindly, it is taking advantage of his simplicity, pre-
venting him from forming an impartial judgment
concerning me. But where could I find courage to
say : " My child, I am not the man you suppose ; the
condition in which you see me is not unjust, as you
might imagine, but the logical consequences of a life
full of culpable errors."

A man does not end his days as I am doing, by
accident ; it is not by chance that all who have known
him abandon him, and he at last dies in poverty and
loneliness. In all this there is a well-merited punishment, the trace of an immutable justice. I will
not add to my calamities the cowardice of suspecting

and accusing others. The real author of the fault is not always the one who commits it: is not the wretched man who makes it possible, still more guilty? Thou art not deceived, oh! my God, and it is for this that Thou dost punish me.

The other day, about three o'clock in the afternoon, he came to me eating his bread and preserve. I had fasted since the evening before, for the servants had not yet brought my breakfast, and was very hungry, so I smilingly asked for a piece of it. He joyfully offered me the whole. While I was eating this mouthful of bread, perhaps with too much appetite, he looked steadily at me with an expression of astonishment, then left his luncheon on the corner of the table as if no longer hungry, and began to play with a great affectation of eagerness, to give me time to eat the whole slice. Ever and anon I met his large searching eyes fixed upon me.

When about to go away, he threw his little arms around my neck and kissed me three times very affectionately.

Undoubtedly he is too well aware of my troubles, but how is it to be helped? He divines my thoughts, poor child. He loves me, that is perfectly evident. Ever since that day when he comes to lunch in my room his slice of bread is larger, and his kind heart inspires him with a thousand pretexts to make me accept half. It is useless for me to refuse, to assure him that I have just had my breakfast—he will listen to nothing, urges, entreats, pulls out of his pocket parcels of carefully packed provisions, arranges the whole upon a corner of the table, draws up a chair, pushes a little stool forward, and we dine together, while radiant with delight and proud of his triumph, he does the honors, pretending with shouts of laughter that the chocolate lozenges are roast chickens, and the bits of bread asparagus and green peas. I am so happy in yielding to him, I alone, yes, I alone know how much kindness and goodness he has in his heart.

Is it old age that draws me so near him? I do not know, but his influence over me is irresistible. When he has been in my room ten minutes, I feel that my individuality is merged in his, his ideas become mine, I see with his eyes, share his emotions, am deluded by his fancies, and this without effort, in spite of myself. With what joy we prance side by side through the fairy kingdom where the very young and very old meet and understand each other.

When he nestles up to me, puts his little legs under my dressing-gown, looks at me with his beaming eyes, and says : " Come, grandpapa, shall we talk about Cinderella ? " it seems as if a ray of sunlight enters the room.

" There never was any Cinderella, was there, grandpa ? "

" No, my dear, but that makes no difference, it's a pretty story."

" It's a pity it never happened. Peau d'Ane never happened either. Then there are no fairies. But that's not certain, I should like it better if there were some. Say, grandpa, do you dream of fairies at night ? "

" Not often, dear."

" Oh ! I do, I dream of the fairies. After all, grandpa, the ones we see when we're asleep are the real ones."

Is not the little poet right ? I dare not contradict him, his credulity seemed superior to my experience. How powerful this reality of dream life is ! How true are these falsehoods of the imagination !

Who will dare to say positively, " There is the boundary which separates the true from the false reality, the object from its image, soul from matter, feeling from sensation, what we touch from what we think we touch ? " What are hope, desire, the gift of

believing and imagining which take man by the hand,
push him forward or check him, make him sit down
by the side of the path, help him to surmount obstacles, or overwhelm him?

Are not the great, true, good moments of life those
when a man only feels the ground with the tips of his
toes, trembles at the touch of the magic ring, believes
in the good fairy, and suffers himself to be wrapped
in the godmother's cloak? Is not the joy of life the
power of coming out from it. Perhaps happiness
may be not to return to it again. He from whom the
fairies flee is a very unhappy man. Exact analysis is a
dull lantern. To count the stones in a prison and
measure its bars is not being free. Yes, darling, let
us talk about Cinderella and Peau d'Ane. You have
the true spirit of wisdom.

The want of wood is what causes me the most
suffering. The colder it grows the more the servants
steal my share to increase theirs. They do it from
habit, not out of any ill-will, but I suffer greatly.

When I had a little money I got out of the difficulty by buying peat and putting it under my arm
wrapped in a paper, and people suspected nothing.—
One can keep warm a long time with peat and ashes.
But now I no longer have this resource. I keep my
bundles of wood for my little George's visits. We
warm ourselves together, as soon as I am alone I
carefully put out the fire, and all is over.

It must be confessed that these annoyances are
more endurable to me than they would be to others.
I have breathed on my fingers to warm them so many
winters. It rejuvenates me, I am returning to the
habits I used to have when a young man—with hope
the less and memory the more.

The time seems particularly long at night. Although I stuff the windows and doors as well as I can
and pile all the clothing I have upon the bed, the
cold penetrates with frightful obstinacy. It is use-

less to say to myself : "Think of George, think of
Favras. What improvements could I make in the
house and garden? It is impossible for me to fix
my attention ; my teeth chatter, I begin to cough, and
so it goes until the next morning.

When my children receive company, which they
do more and more frequently, I amuse myself by listening to the roll of the carriages upon the pave-
ment of the courtyard, or the conversation of the
coachmen, who stamp and swear. I imagine my
daughter among her guests. Dear little thing! How
pretty she looked when she opened the stop-cock of
the rain-gauge, and I tried in vain to be angry. If I
only had a candle I could read !

The weather is growing milder. The earth and
sun are becoming reconciled, spring is approaching.
How I shall enjoy it! In a few days the trees at
Favras will be covered with a faint green hue, the
ground will become softer, and the violets will enamel
the grass and moss. To-morrow afternoon little
George and I will resume our walks. My overcoat is
the only thing that troubles me. I have ripped the
collar to turn it inside out ; but shall I succeed in my
task? Nobody must be ashamed of me to-morrow.

The weather was magnificent, a throng of pedestrians were moving towards the Champs Elysées, and
we walked on like two intimate friends who were
happy in being together. He stopped me every instant to ask questions about the different things he
saw, and I was in a very joyous mood. Two collegians passed, George looked at them an instant, and
then turning to me, said :

"Say, grandpa, when you were a professor, did
you teach little boys no larger than I ?"

"No, dear. They were not children ; some of
them had beards. Do you see the collegians walking
yonder? Well, all my scholars were older than those
young men."

" And did you have a gown ? "

" Why, of course, all the professors in the university wear gowns."

" And did you order your scholars about, grandpa ? "

" Hum—why yes, mildly. You know we ought
always to speak gently, especially to those who must
obey. We may be mistaken, you know, we are not
infallible."

" You speak gently to everybody, and yet the
servants don't obey you."

" They are your father's and mother's servants,
my dear."

" Well, then, you're not obliged to speak gently to
them, and you would have very good reason to be
cross, for they're not at all polite when they talk about
you. Louis always calls you the old man."

" There's no great harm in that, my little fellow,
everybody sees that I am no longer young. Louis
probably meant to say : the old gentleman, and forgot
to finish it ; no doubt he was in a hurry."

" Well, I thought it was very wrong for Louis to
call you the old man, but if it isn't, he'll be in a great
rage, for I said—if mamma knew what I said to him."

" What did you say ? "

" I called him a great brute. Why, gracious,
grandpa, I thought he was attacking you, so I stood
up for you. - If any one attacked me you would defend me, of course, because you say we are friends.
When people are friends, they stand up for each
other." He shook his little cane in the air. " Ah !
if anybody attacked you, you'd see, grandpa."

Not knowing how to answer this prattle, which
cheered my inmost heart, I pressed the dear child's
hand, who returned the clasp while bounding along
by my side.

" Do you think I am as strong as the collegians
who just passed by ? " he continued.

" Not quite, but you soon will be, though strength is slower to come than to go. Why are you so anxious to be strong ? "

" To defend you, of course. Then I'm not any stronger than you now."

" Not much weaker, dear, and perhaps that is the reason we are so fond of each other. When you are a man, you won't take any pleasure in walking with your grandfather."

George stopped, looked at me in astonishment, not exactly knowing whether I was in earnest or not; then raising his head drew me down to him and gave me a hearty kiss, whispering :

" I shall always love you ; when you're an old, old man, I'll love you still more, and when I get rich I'll buy you—I'll buy you a beautiful gold frame."

" What for, my dear ? "

" For your diplomas that are fastened on the wall, grandpa."

On reaching the Champs Elysées we sat down upon a bench. He was looking out of the corners of his eyes at the goat carriages which were passing up and down a neighboring walk, and I was counting the few sous in my vest pockets when I saw a carriage slowly approaching, drawn by two large lean horses. Many pedestrians paused to see it pass. It was of antique form, hung very high above the wheels, and had an indescribably stately and sombre air which could not remain unobserved. On the huge box, adorned with intricate armorial bearings, sat a coachman and footman lost amid the folds of a fawn-colored livery, excessively belaced. As the carriage approached I distinguished the coat of arms surrounded with various devices and arabesques that ornamented the doors. Two ladies, dressed in black, were talking together in this magnificent equipage. Suddenly George started, and pulling me by the sleeve, exclaimed :

" Mamma, there's mamma in that carriage."

It was indeed my daughter ; but when I had more particularly noticed the lady who accompanied her, I could not repress a cry and nearly fell senseless. I had recognized my wife, Esther Paline, my beloved wife. Yes, beloved, for I suddenly felt with strange intensity that I had never ceased to love her. She was more beautiful than ever. Her appearance now was that of a great lady with grave and dignified manners. An expression of gentleness and sovereign majesty breathed from her whole person.

The past appeared before me as if by one of those flashes of lightning which amid the darkness of night sunder the clouds and illumine the horizon. My emotion was too strong for my feeble body, and most unfortunately I fainted, as I have always done when it was my duty to be energetic.

When I recovered my senses two or three people were standing around me. George had doubtless called to them in his terror, while he, poor child, with tearful eyes and trembling hands was unfastening my cravat and kissing my forehead. I instantly remembered what had just occurred, and sought for the carriage with my eyes, but it had disappeared.

Seeing that I was better, some one wanted to call a cab, but I fortunately recollected that we had not money enough ; I thanked him, declared the walk would do me good, and rising, tottered away. Twenty times I was obliged to stop and lean against a tree. George held my hand and often said: " Won't you lean on my shoulder, dear grandpa, I think I am strong enough." He did not ask a single question about what had occurred; no doubt his quickness and tact taught him that he ought to remain in ignorance of the cause. When we reached the fountain in the Place Louis XV., I bathed my forehead and it did me good; but how long the walk seemed. George said in a low tone: " We're almost there,

grandpa, we'll soon get home." I was thinking: "How
does it happen that they are together? They know
each other—why have I heard nothing about it? I
must indeed be a wretch to have them both forget
me so utterly. I had never had so much affection
for them, never felt more beneath them, more unworthy of their tenderness."

My strength gave way as we crossed the courtyard, and my limbs bent under me. I was bewildered,
and tottered. But for George, I really believe it
would have been impossible for me to find the little
back staircase. In passing the pantry I saw the servants laughing maliciously as they looked at me, but
was too greatly agitated to pay much attention to it.
I reached my room, and sank upon my bed. I was
only half conscious of what was passing around me,
and yet saw my grandson, with infinite trouble, raise
my pillow, spread the clothes over my feet, unbutton
my vest, and getting into a chair put on my night cap.
My heart swelled with gratitude; I felt his hand gently
rub my forehead, I heard his breathing, quickened
by emotion, the beating of his heart, the fond words
his little lips murmured in my ear. What have I
done to deserve the love of this blessed child? Who
has put him in my path? Why does he love me so?
Whence comes it that logically, misfortune gives birth
to compassion, that the mere fact of being pitiable
wins a friend's caress? Whence comes it that suffering teaches you to love; that the flower which blooms
amid ruins is most fragrant and most brilliant in color?
Who has arranged this needful counterpoise, but for
which a man would be crushed by the first shock?
What is this equilibrium of moral laws, this logical re-
action of the heart, if Providence does not watch
over and sustain us?

Some one soon came for George, and the poor
child went away with tears in his eyes. Was it from
grief because he was obliged to leave me alone at a

time when I might need help, or a presentiment that the pleasant days of our companionship were over forever?

I found myself alone, and began to tremble in every limb. The idea that my wife was in Paris aroused a tempest of feelings which I had crushed down into the depths of my heart for years. The wrongs I had suffered in the past arose before me, perhaps magnified more than was reasonable, but overwhelming and terrible. I no longer remembered anything except my ambitious follies, my countless failings, my intolerable absurdities, my powerlessness, my obstinacy in seeking to be beloved by a superior person who was not suited to me, and then the sorrows and misfortunes which had resulted from it.

The meeting I had just had was a very natural punishment, and I did not think of being surprised. I had driven from me the family joys of which I was unworthy. What scorn, what disgust my daughter must feel towards me, now that being informed of the past by her mother, she knew all that I had so carefully concealed! The abyss that separated me from them had become impassable, and yet the greatness of the obstacle only awakened my eagerness and increased the tenderness I felt for them. At that moment I think I would have borne every torture if it had been possible to clasp them in my arms, obtain forgiveness for the wrong I had done them, to be for one instant a husband and father.

I was pursuing this train of thought when some one knocked at my door, and the servant told me my son-in-law wished to speak to me at once. This was so unusual an event that I was very much disturbed. My daughter's husband inspired me with a feeling of terror. Besides might not what he had to say to me have some connection with the walk we had taken that day.

He was sitting before his table when I entered

his large gloomy study, lumbered with books and strange-looking bottles.

"Be so good as to sit down," he said gravely without raising his eyes from a letter he was just finishing. When he had noisily signed his name, read it over, and folded the sheet, he looked at me steadily a moment, and then clasping his hands, said :

"You seem to be somewhat restored and consequently in a condition to listen to me, Monsieur Babolain; have the kindness to give me your attention. When I married your daughter it was arranged, was it not, that you should share our home and profit by the advantages of this cohabitation, that is, heat, light, etc. ? "

"Of course," I replied, " you intended—"

"Allow me to go on. Have I performed my agreement? Have you shelter, fire and light ? "

"Undoubtedly." Fear makes us humble and cowardly. "Undoubtedly, my dear Joseph," said I.

"I ask no more. It is admitted that I have acted honestly, and you have no cause to reproach me. Moreover, my wife and I have wished to prove our good will by trusting our son to your care almost every day. Is all this true? If you have any complaints to make against us, I beg of you to speak. You don't answer, Monsieur Babolain, I will go on: Far from being intolerant, I excuse certain peculiarities and eccentricities which entail annoying consequences; it is grief not anger that I feel at the sight of other's faults, and my instincts urge me to excuse those whom others would condemn. But there are certain failings which surpass all bounds and render indulgence impossible. The vice with which you are afflicted is one of those that deserve only the indignation of an honest man."

Having dealt me this blow, he took an envelope, slipped his letter into it, and quietly wrote the address.

I was wrong not to vehemently repel his accusation, I feel I was wrong there, but I was so terribly agitated. Besides, was I perfectly sure that I did not have the vice of which I was accused? I answered timidly:

"What do you mean, Joseph? I don't exactly understand—"

"I did not suppose I should be obliged to give you any information upon this subject, Monsieur."

"I am very poor, it is true, but of course that is not the vice to which you—"

"Certainly, you know it as well as I. I have no wish to discuss the ingenious manner in which you have squandered your fortune."

"Why you know that when my daughter married I gave her almost everything."

"I think my behavior at that time was sufficiently disinterested for me not to be accused of being a mercenary man. I wished to remain in ignorance of my future wife's property, and accepted her dowry with my eyes shut. All I know is that you were once rich and are so no longer; what is the secret cause of your ruin, granting that it is as complete as you say? How does it happen that in spite of your apparently modest mode of life, you are reduced to nothing?"

"Good Heavens, but I—"

"Let us stop there, if you please, it is repugnant to my feelings to enter into all these particulars, and besides, this is not the matter in question. I merely wished to tell you that I must beg you not to accompany George in his walks in future."

"Not go out with George any more," I cried. "What have I done to deserve such a sorrow? My poor little George; my only joy is to be with him. Joseph, my friend, you won't do this, will you? I take the very best care of him, I keep out of the way of the carriages, and if the wind blows I make

19

him put on his coat. Prevent my going out with
him! It would be too cruel."

"Cruel! I have reason to reproach myself with
only too much indulgence towards you, Monsieur.
Cruel! But you have probably not yet recovered
from your little indisposition sufficiently to understand the full meaning of your expressions."

"What indisposition do you mean? Oh! yes, I
was really somewhat ailing."

"You were drunk, Monsieur, let us speak plainly. All the people in the house saw you, and I don't
wish to have such a scandal repeated."

"It's false! Joseph, false! I swear it."

"Go and lie down, go," said he, shrugging his
shoulders. "Some one is waiting for me, good-evening."

Night had fallen. I groped my way up to my
room, I was like a man who has just been robbed of
all he possesses. "What is the use of living any
longer," I said to myself, "what is the use?"

I lighted a fragment of candle, which I still had.
It seemed as if in the darkness I should give way to
despair too easily. The room was full of the signs
George had left of his presence; there on the little
black table were the figures of peasants he had
drawn with a bit of chalk. A piece of string he had
used the evening before to play horse still hung
from the back of a chair. But all these memories
must be driven away. My poor child! my poor child!
I sat down in a corner and remained there, shivering
with cold.

It is very certain that I was not intoxicated, since
I have drunk nothing but water for so long. But
what would my innocence avail if nobody believed it!
The scandal was real, and my son-in-law had reason
to be angry. To condemn me thus he must have
held me in the most utter contempt. If I could
prove that I am a victim, my sorrow would be allevi-

ated ; but who will dare to say: " I have endured more suffering than I have caused."

We see only the scales, but never distinguish the needle that marks the weight. If, in my pride, I had not scorned the laws of my existence, I should undoubtedly have escaped all that has happened to me.

I have considered George's affection as a treasure which belonged to me, and now that I am deprived of it, am indignant, as if robbed. What right had I to enter his little heart? Is it not the wisdom of Providence that drives me from it? He might have become accustomed to my deplorable instincts, gradually accepted, and soon shared them. " Console yourself, my poor child." It seemed as if I was holding him in my arms, as if he had taken refuge in my lap as had so often happened, and was gazing at me imploringly. " Console yourself, my love; you're not going to cry because you are taken away from your old grandpa." I parted his hair, kissed his forehead, and tried to smile. " He wasn't a proper companion for you, you see ; he wouldn't have been able to follow you long with his old legs. We must always part with somebody or something in life, and it isn't so hard as you think, my darling. You'll soon smile when you recollect your old grandpa's room, our talks, our walks; you will always love me, but you'll say to yourself: ' What a funny man ! ' The memory of my absurdities will soften your regrets. It must be so. Everything the good God has done is well done, you see. Whether His justice renders our burden heavier or lighter, it is always a consolation and a support to know that this justice is infallible and immutable. I am not worth more than one tear, I know very well, but it will fall from your eyes, my darling, and I shall leave this world invoking a blessing upon you."

Such were my thoughts as the noises in the house died away one after another, and the stillness around

me grew deeper. I saw my little George, saw him
become a man ; I had been dead a long time, yet I
was always near him. I read his mind, his heart,
and was amazed at the noble, grand, and generous
feelings I saw. He let me talk to him, and we
laughed together over all the petty troubles with
which my life had been so comically enamelled. He
invited me to share his joys, confided his plans to
me, I remodelled my life in his, and felt greatly
strengthened.

Suddenly the bit of candle I had lighted went out,
and I found myself in the dark. I undressed and
went to bed.

It was not until the next morning that I realized
how much my situation was changed. My grandson
won't come to see me to-day, I thought, nor to-morrow, perhaps never, and I remained cowering under
the clothes, gazing through my tears at the vine
on the paper. From that day it seems to me as if
time stood still. My life has stopped. I know very
well that all is over for me, and yet I am waiting. So
it is true that a man cannot live a moment unless he
is drawn on by the moment that is approaching. It
is no longer hope, but a sort of anxiety, a need of escaping the present moment. I wait for the scratching he made at the door when he came to see me. I
know very well I shall not have his visit, and yet I
can't help expecting it ; if the wind makes a branch
snap near my window; if a door creaks in the distance, my very breathing stops. I say to myself:
" Who knows, perhaps it is he. If it were not he,
why should I be agitated ? " I wait as if for an event
of great importance until the ray of sunlight which
enters at a certain hour and passes around my room,
falls upon the drawing I once made of our garden and
house. The sun only shines upon a part of it, but
this little space is like a window opening upon the
country itself. I smell the fragrance of the grasses

and flowers which are growing there, I see the trees wave, hear the humming of the insects, and my feelings return to my heart with so much reality that the tears often flow from my eyes. So while listening to certain airs, heard by chance, a whole page of one's life suddenly appears, and for a few moments we see the existence of former days, forget what has taken place since, walk joyously along the well known path, and put our feet in the fresh prints of our old steps.

As our lives grow narrow, and the present grows sterner, the power of escaping from it by the imagination becomes more powerful, the poetry which was a luxury to the man of forty becomes necessary to the old man whose strength is failing. The sufferings of the close of life need the balm, the music of memory. How can one fail to see the goodness of a protecting power in this doubling of life! How can one help seeing Thy provident affection in this moral equilibrium, oh! my God! It is to the unfortunate who have no pillows on which to repose, that Thou openest Thy arms.

I wait to hear the striking of the clock in the pantry beneath me ; its sound is pleasant, affectionate, so to speak ; one would say it pays me a visit, surrounds me, covers me with caresses. I listen to its dying tones, and when it has ceased am still in an imaginary world, where life is without suffering, trouble, or chaos.

And yet I have terrible hours when the past appears to me under its evil face ; when I can no longer drive away the phantoms that torture me ; when I fall into despair, and would fain have my physical sufferings still more severe and cruel that they might keep me from thinking. Sometimes in these dark days I have rebellious feelings, I even, madman as I am, curse my wife and daughter. As if it had been possible for them to conquer the repugnance with which I inspire every one ! Who can tell the number

of griefs I have caused the two poor women whom
fate cast into my arms. The idea sets my brain on
fire. What I have done and what I might have done
mingle, blend together, and in this confusion I fancy
I behold crimes.

"Wife and child, forgive the wrong I have done
you. My strength is failing, my vital powers are becoming exhausted—has not the hour for pardon arrived? Dear ones, I hold out my arms to you. For
God's sake do not pass me by without a look, do not
repulse me. In my condition I can no longer harm
any one. When I think that at this very moment you
may perhaps both be in this house! No, I have
never loved you so much. I do not ask to be admitted to a share in your life; I should be out of
place, I do not wish to shame you. Let everything
remain as it is, but sometimes when you are getting
into your carriage, look up at my window—I will hide
behind the curtain, no one will see you. My heart
is so cold—a glance from you would do me so much
good."

About two o'clock, the hour that he goes out, I
managed to drag myself to the window and saw him
set out for his walk. He held his hoop in his hand,
and the nurse went with him. I don't think he could
have seen me, but he turned his head as he passed
through the gateway. He wore his little grey coat
and striped stockings, but was not skipping about as
he always did when we went out together.

How happy I have been in possessing his affection! I have watched him as he grew up by my side,
he was so confidential to me. Childish fancies, lov-
able conceits, charming absurdities, comical inquisi-
tiveness, profound reflections—he has concealed nothing from me. Will he ever open his heart and mind
so fully to any one else?

In the days when I had a little money I sometimes
took him to the pastry cook's; I had balanced my

accounts so that I could manage it. But the dear child, knowing very well that I was not rich, would not go in in spite of his longing to do so. He never was hungry, turned his head away, pulled me by the sleeve, avoided the temptation, and if by dint of insisting I succeeded in making him go in, whispered:

"Grandpa, a little two sous' one, that's quite enough you know."

⁻ He walked around the shop, made his choice, and asked the price while his little lips trembled. He would never take more than one, and then pulled me into a corner to offer me half of it.

One day when we were coming out of the pastry cook's he seemed very much preoccupied; I pressed his little hand and asked what he was thinking about.

"I'm thinking about the cakes, they are nice, but they cost too much, and you're not rich enough, my dear grandpa."

When we returned to the house he let me go up to my room alone and joined me a few moments after. He was flushed and eager, and held in his hands a small package which he opened immediately. It was a white pasteboard box filled with papers wrapped one about another. He began to unroll all these with his impatient little fingers, throwing box and papers on the floor as he went on with his work.

"What is it, my little fellow?" said I.

He was too busy to answer, but when he had finished showed me on his open palm a coin worth fifty centimes, and four sous.

"See, there are some sous for you," said he looking at me with his great eyes.

At first I did not know what to answer, not that I was ashamed of the alms, there was so much affection and delicacy in the somewhat blunt simplicity with which he offered me his whole fortune. I took his head between my hands, and kissing his fair curls said:

"Thank you, my dear George—keep your money, you shall buy something with it—you'll want to ride in the goat carriage, you know."

"You won't have my sous," said he with an emotion which showed he was on the point of bursting into tears.

"Keep them for yourself, my little man, keep them, dear."

He put the money back into his pocket without saying a word, walked to the window and gazed out into the courtyard, but the pane reflected like a mirror his sorrowful face, dilated nostrils, and the quivering lips he compressed with his teeth to keep from crying.

"You are not worthy of this affection," I said to myself; "by your folly and pride you are making the only creature in the world who loves you cry." I added aloud: "George—do you still want to give me your money?" He turned, his eyes beaming with delight. "Do you? Well then, give it to me, my darling. I shall be very glad to have it."

He made only one bound, threw his arms around my neck, and overwhelming me with caresses, slid the four sous and the little coin into my pocket.

"You'll take good care not to lose them, grandpa," he murmured.

I have wrapped them up in the same papers, put them back in the little white box, and they are treasured with Esther's hair and my other keepsakes.

Ah! at that time I fully believed that I should never be separated from George and my last look would meet his.

When my strength is somewhat restored and I suffer less, I shall go to the Tuileries at the time he takes his walk, remain under the trees in the shade as I used to do when I was at the normal school, and watch him while he plays. If I don't speak to him, and he doesn't see me it will doubtless satisfy them.

His father can't find fault with me for watching him at a distance—

But shall I ever dare to go out of my room, pass before the servants again and cross the courtyard? I may meet my daughter, and who knows, perhaps my wife. Besides, will my strength ever return? It seems to me that I am growing weaker and weaker, and my sufferings increase instead of diminishing.

What do they want of me? How will all this end? Why can't they let me die in peace in my corner? Thou knowest, oh! God, that I have no longer strength to make amends for anything.

Two hours ago I had just risen, not without difficulty, for I suffer a great deal, and was resting wrapped in my blankets, when some one knocked at the door, and a tall old man with a noble, dignified bearing entered the room. His grey hair fell in silken curls upon the velvet collar of his coat, which was black, cut in a peculiar style and buttoned to the chin but revealed a white cravat against which appeared the black and yellow ribbon of a foreign order. I instantly perceived by his simple and aristocratic manners that I was in the presence of some very distinguished nobleman. He advanced towards me, raised his eyes to heaven, clasped his hands, and gazed at me long and earnestly.

A shudder ran through my frame from head to foot. It seemed as if a ghost had appeared before me. Some bond united me to him; his face roused a throng of confused memories which I could not define.

" In what a state of degradation do I see you, oh, my friend, my brother!" he said, in a compassionate voice.

" Monsieur," I replied with deep emotion, "I don't exactly recognize you, and yet I have seen you, I—excuse me for receiving you in this untidy room, and be kind enough to sit down."

He pushed aside with his gold-headed cane the clothes that loaded the only available chair, seated himself with great caution, and continued:

"Twenty-five or thirty years do indeed change men, alter their situations strangely, and I am not surprised that you have some difficulty in recognizing your old friend in Chevalier Timoléon Morbegno."

"Timoléon!" I cried. "Oh God! is it you?"

And in my first impulse, almost involuntarily, I was about to clasp his hand, but there was so much pride and pity in his smile that I stopped short. I suddenly remembered the strange part he had played, his hasty departure for Italy, but this ugly vision made no definite impression upon my poor brain, my heart had no longer sufficient strength to hate any one. I felt an emotion of dislike, and trembled. This tall man frightened me.

"What do you want? Why do you come here?" I murmured, sinking back in my arm chair.

"To save you from yourself, my friend, and accomplish the mission Providence and your family have entrusted to me. Let calmness and gratitude at last enter your poor, blinded soul, have confidence in the goodness of God. Mme. la Comtesse de Monte Revilla, who was once your wife, is willing to forget the past."

"What! The Comtesse de Monte Revilla is my— Explain yourself, how can that be?"

"Don't pretend to be ignorant of what it is impossible not to know. You can't be the only person who is unaware of the titles and honors Mme. la Comtesse enjoys in Italy, titles and honors of which her virtues and talents make her eminently worthy. Your son-in-law, M. de Favras, the famous physician, your admirable daughter, Mme. la Marquise de Vé- lizy, Monseigneur de Pansol, and all the distinguished personages who frequent this house surely have not concealed from you the respectful esteem in which

they hold Mme. de Monte Revilla. I, who for
more than twenty years have been an intimate visitor
at her palace, the confidant of her thoughts, her respectful and devoted friend, have been able to appreciate the qualities of her high intelligence and great
heart. Reassure yourself, Babolain, the words I come
to bring are those of peace and pardon."

While he was speaking, I felt fascinated by the
image of this aristocratic Italian lady ; I had clasped
her in my arms ;this ideal being, this wondrous woman, whose genius was no longer doubtful, had once
been mine. Ah ! let him not relate all the particulars
of this glorious career.

The mad pride, the wild love of former days re-
kindled in my poor brain, and yet in the presence of
this aristocratic gentleman who found me degraded,
powerless, and shivering under these rags, I dared
not ask a question, and remained silent with my eyes
fixed upon the ground lest I might meet his glance.

He continued, adjusting his cuffs.

" I feel great pity for you, Babolain. Whatever
you may have done, I could not forget the ties that
united us in the past, and the situation in which I find
you moves me deeply."

I thought he was censuring my daughter's conduct
towards me, and replied :

" My children are very kind to me. I don't complain. I want for nothing."

" I know your noble daughter's heart too well to
doubt it. Mme. de Favras, whose life is a constant
succession of noble deeds and beautiful thoughts,
wept—wept I say."

" Are you speaking of my daughter ? "

" When Mme. de Favras spoke of the sad path
upon which you have entered—Alas ! my friend,
could I suspect that your skepticism when a young
man would bear such bitter fruits ? ' All family affection seems to be extinguished in my poor father's

heart,' she said despairingly;' he shuns, avoids us, and you know the deplorable consequences solitude and forgetfulness of others may bring upon a weak nature.'"

These words gave me a terrible pang: was it really possible my daughter could think so?

" Your son-in-law," continued Timoléon, "who unites to a rare intelligence the qualities of a noble heart, spoke of you with remarkable indulgence, although a certain tinge of irritation, which was certainly very excusable, appeared in his words. ' Ought not Monsieur Babolain,' he said to me in confidence, ' to have some respect for himself, if only from consideration for us? Can he forget that there is a certain joint responsibility in a family, from which we cannot escape? Can he forget that before the world and our servants we bear the responsibility of his eccentricities, and endure the consequences of his acts!'"

" This is what your son-in-law told me, my friend. It is a melancholy and guilty thing in the sight of God when the head of a family despises his own dignity, has no respect for his white hairs, forgets his authority, and thus brings reproach upon that sacred family hierarchy, the image of the social hierarchy, whose reward is the happiness of nations."

" True," I murmured; "but I have had my sorrows too, I—"

" The pious Comtesse de Monte Revilla would have a right to forget you entirely, but she will not. Yes, she who was your wife wishes to recall you to the right path, take you from this garret, draw you out of yourself, screen you from scorn and contempt; and in the first place you must understand that it is no longer possible for you to remain in this house."

" Leave the house!" I cried. " Leave my George! go away from him!"

" It is on condition of changing your place of res-

idence that Mme. de Monte Revilla would consent
to give you a pension sufficient to enable you to
maintain a style of living suitable for yourself and
your family." And as my face undoubtedly expressed
the sorrow these words excited, he added, " I didn't
suppose that such a proposal could arouse any other
emotion in your mind than that of gratitude."

" But I ask nothing. Good Heavens ! I've never
asked for anything."

" That's the very thing that troubles them. I
should rather," said Mme. la Comtesse yesterday, " I
should rather he had secretly incurred heavy debts to
maintain his position."

" My position ! What position have I to maintain ? "

" You ought to avoid giving your wife and children, who have one, reason to blush. I regret that I
am compelled to remind you of it. But I will return
to the subject of my mission. They don't wish to
impose upon you a mode of life to which you could
not become accustomed, but to give you a suitable,
agreeable place of retirement, with plenty of fresh
air—your feeble health requires special care. A
house which would suit your tastes might be found
for you in the suburbs of Paris—one man-servant
will be enough for you : they will be careful to select
a good one. Consider, Babolain, you can't always
be dependent upon your children."

" I have given all I had," I murmured, and could
not repress a sob, for I said to myself, " It is all over,
I shall never see my little George again. How am I
to resist if they want me to go ? "

" You are ill," said Timoléon. " These sufferings
ought to be a warning : see how much you need
country air, not only morally but physically."

" And when do they send me away ? "

" They are not driving you away ; don't pervert
facts. The Comtesse is above all spiteful miscon-

structions, and even your malevolence would be unable to prevent people from thinking her wish to secure your happiness and independence a most praiseworthy one."

"Yes, yes, but it's very hard for me—perhaps there might be some other way," I said hesitatingly ; " couldn't I stay here if I promised not to go out, not to show myself any more—even the servants would forget me. I could do what little work I need myself, though I'm very weak—but I should find the strength, I assure you, I should find the strength."

" Your health is more undermined than you suppose. To stay in Paris is to shorten your life : you absolutely require country air. It is for your own good that I urge the matter. Besides, the pension the Comtesse secures you isn't to be despised. Mme. de Monte Revilla acts generously in everything. If you want twelve, fifteen, twenty thousand francs, she will give them to you."

" That would be shameful," I cried, making an effort to rise ; " I would never accept it," and I thought to myself : " There are men of my age who can still work and earn their living."

" Does that mean that I'm capable of making degrading proposals to you ? " replied Chevalier Timoléon, drawing himself up proudly. " Oh ! this is your gratitude for the efforts we make to draw you out of the mire into which you have fallen. Patience and charity have their limits. Very well, Monsieur, wrap yourself in your pride, I know what remains for me to do. Good-evening."

———

During the two or three hours since he went away, I have been trembling with fear. All my ideas are confused, and I no longer know what is real. You know I am not a wretch, don't you, my little George ? Yes, I have committed great errors in the course of my life, but I take my oath, my child, that they were not premeditated. I will go away if my presence is unendurable to them, but I cannot accept this money. Poverty does not terrify me. If I could only kiss you before leaving you forever, but they will not allow it. Yet it is no crime to love the child —somebody is coming up stairs, I—

Why did I not die after Timoléon's visit? That would have ended everything, while now I will not think of what threatens me; I am afraid, and yet I wish to write all this, were it only to render it possible to wait for the misfortune that is to crush me.

Yesterday my son-in-law suddenly came into my room, but his face did not wear its habitual expression of cold indifference. He had undoubtedly been talking with Timoléon, for without the slightest preamble he paused before me and said angrily:

"So, Monsieur, it seems that you are in a conquered province. What is this the Chevalier de Morbegno tells me : that you intend to remain here by force, and refuse the benefits we expect to have you accept. But there must be an understanding, once for all ; besides, my patience has long been exhausted, and I want to have an explanation with you."

I was so exhausted, and was suffering such violent pain in my chest, that I could not answer. This doubtless irritated him, but I really could not speak.

"You are here from charity, Monsieur ; you did not suspect it, and I tell you of it," he continued, haughtily. "If, to acknowledge my favors, you had lived in a respectable and proper manner, I should always have borne the burden of having a stranger under my roof. But do you suppose I have not noticed you, that I am the dupe of your humble manners, your apparent simplicity? Do you suppose I feel no annoyance at having a stoic philosopher, a tatterdemalion who makes a scandal in the house, causes trouble among my servants, and carries his impertinence so far as not to conceal his vices, he, my wife's father, dependent upon me for everything, who owes it to my charity that he does not fall into the most abject poverty? And not satisfied with getting intoxicated in his own room, he returns to my house drunk ! "

" No, no, you are mistaken," I said, clasping my hands.

." I don't ask your opinion, I never speak as I'm doing now without being sure of what I am saying. I am ignorant of nothing you do, I know the scandalous means you employ, after the manner of faithless servants, to procure the money necessary for your , strange wants. You sell the candles that are given you, Monsieur, the oil from your lamp, your firewood—what do I know about it? A thousand other things, no doubt. The destitution I see here, and which I would not have believed, is sufficient proof."

" You are wrong, I swear you are wrong. How could I sell what was not given to me. Do not insult me—from affection for your wife, whom it would grieve."

"And then, when you are offered a way of making your escape from your present position, when from charity or shame — imagine whatever motive you please—you are assured an income and a home, you affect airs of modesty and dignity. Could it happen to be done with the object of getting more? Speak frankly."

" Leave me, leave me, I am suffering terribly," I said imploringly.

"This farce is useless. I mean to say what I think and say it at length, for I have no respect for you. You are a parasite, Monsieur, a useless creature, and what is worse, a proud, useless creature. You have taken your powerlessness as an inviolable refuge, your moral and physical weakness as a means of livelihood. You are in the category of dangerous beggars. I detest those sort of people, I give them alms, but I don't touch them with the tips of my fingers. Must I remind you of the tortures you have inflicted upon the noblest of women, who fortunately finding herself too far above you to allow herself to be overwhelmed, broke your degrading chains? Must I remind you of the absurd and wicked education you wished to inflict upon your only daughter, enveloping her in your insane egotism till she was almost stifled, and even for a long time opposing her attending to her religious duties. Do you say you have acted in this way from 'affection? You have sometimes found tears to move public feeling. Is it not by trading upon your fatherly fondness that you introduced yourself into my house, obtained food and shelter here? Confound it, be a little less affectionate, and have more courage to bear the burdens of life."

" Hush! hush! think what you please of me, but hush for your own sake, the door is wide open."

" And what do I care, whether people hear me or not? I wanted to tell you what you are—I have done. Now I have only to repeat what Monsieur de Morbegno has already told you: you will have an income and henceforth live in a private hospital in the suburbs of Paris. You pretend to be sick; I affirm it, and declare that it is necessary for you to reside in a hospital. I hope you won't compel me to make an open scandal by resorting to some act of authority, which would be very disagreeable to me, although I should not draw back from it. I must inform you that I always carry out what I have resolved. You are faint! Cease this acting, you don't touch my feelings in the least; I expect—"

He could not finish the sentence, for at that moment my little George entered the room, crying in a

20

voice choked with tears : "They are hurting you, my dear grandpa, they are hurting you—but I won't have it." He sprang toward me, and as his trembling little arms embraced me, his lips pressed my forehead, there was suddenly a strange blank in my brain and I fainted.

What has happened ? I do not know. When I recovered my senses this morning I found myself lying in my bed—"George ! George ! They cannot tear you from my heart ! And thou, my God, who readest all hearts, forgive my sins and grant me courage to bear the rest of my life !"

The notes stop here. By what cause was the poor man interrupted ? Was he removed to a private hospital ? How long did he live there ? It is impossible to answer these questions, but it is not probable that his existence was prolonged for any length of time, or he would certainly have added a few pages to his Memoirs. In the box that contained them I found a black-edged letter, fastened with a wafer, whose contents were as follows :

"Madame la Comtesse de Monte Revilla, Canoness of Saint Azème, Monsieur le Docteur Joseph de Favras, officer of the Legion of Honor and Commander of Saint-Lazare, Madame Joseph de Favras, and Monsieur George de Favras, have the honor of informing you of the sad loss they have just sustained in the person of Monsieur le Comte Babolino de Monte Revilla, Commander of Saint Grégoire, who died in his seventieth year, after receiving the sacraments of the Church."

THE END.

www.ingramcontent.com/pod-product-compliance
Lightning Source LLC
Chambersburg PA
CBHW020922120726
47905CB00008B/2345